I0110474

THE RED TSUNAMI

THE SILENT STORM KILLING YOUR FREEDOM

T. CASEY FLEMING

THE RED TSUNAMI

THE SILENT STORM KILLING YOUR FREEDOM

T. CASEY FLEMING

The Red Tsunami

The Silent Storm Killing Your Freedom

Published by Pierucci Publishing, P.O. Box 2074, Carbondale, Colorado 81623 USA

www.pieruccipublishing.com

Cover design by Stephanie Pierucci

Ebook 978-1-962578-73-8
Paperback 978-1-962578-75-2
Hardcover 978-1-962578-76-9

Library of Congress Control Number: Forthcoming

Pierucci Publishing books may be purchased in bulk at special discounts for sales promotion, corporate gifts, fundraising, or educational purposes. Special editions can be created to specifications. For details, contact the Special Sales Department, Pierucci Publishing, PO Box 2074, Carbondale, CO 81623, or Publishing@pieruccipublishing.com, or toll-free at 1.855.720.1111.

Acclaim for "The Red Tsunami"

"The Red Tsunami" is a crucial survival guide for the world we're living in right now. Casey lays out the evidence piece by piece, revealing the deliberate, whole-of-society assault being carried out against every American - and every citizen of the free world - by a technologically empowered adversary unlike anything we've faced before.

This book connects the dots with clarity and precision, giving readers the framework they need to understand and push back against the forces shaping today's geopolitical reality. Bold, unflinching, and deeply coherent, "The Red Tsunami" is more than a compelling read - it's a call to vigilance and immediate action. For anyone who wants to understand what's happening and what must be done, this book is essential."

Dr. Rob Spalding III | Brigadier General, United States Air Force (ret.) | Senior Fellow, Hudson Institute | Senior Director of Strategic Planning, U.S. National Security Council | Military Fellow, Council of Foreign Relations | CEO of Sempre | Author of "Stealth War: How China Took Over While America's Elite Slept, and War Without Rules"

"Casey Fleming's "The Red Tsunami" is an unambiguous warning of the war that the Chinese Communist Party, and their ideological allies, are waging against American citizens and those who believe in the unalienable right to life, liberty, and the pursuit of happiness that have transformed human history for the better. Casey comprehensively and systematically examines each face of the CCP's agenda, from flooding our shores with fentanyl to poisoning the minds of our youth with lies from a failed and murderous ideology.

The book is also a call to personal action from each American citizen who recognizes this threat; sitting on the sidelines is no longer an option. Read this book, share it with your family, and the new generations coming up, as time is running out. Americans can turn this around if we recognize the threat and take immediate action; this book makes a mighty contribution to that outcome.

James E. Fanell | CAPT, United States Navy (ret.) | Career U.S. Naval Intelligence Officer | Senior Intelligence Officer for China at the Office of Naval Intelligence | Chief of Intelligence for CTF-70, Seventh Fleet, and the U.S. Pacific Fleet | Co-author of "Embracing Communist China: America's Greatest Strategic Failure"

"Casey captures the full context of China's unrestricted war on America and the West, and puts it into a riveting book - "The Red Tsunami" - a book that every American and member of the free world should read. Denial or refusal to believe the evidence of China's infiltration, subversion, espionage, indoctrination, and murder of Americans only accelerates our demise.

Sadly, our leaders silo these events, enabling China to outmaneuver us across multiple fronts. Yet, Casey offers each of us options to achieve victory in this war. Read, act, as time is not on our side."

Edward Haugland | Leading expert in Cognitive War | Retired intelligence community executive | Author of "The Cognitive War"

"As a documentary filmmaker, I'm struck by how "The Red Tsunami" pulls every American into the frame. This isn't a distant geopolitical drama - it's a story we're all already in. The book gives Washington the strategic clarity it has long needed, and gives citizens the awareness they urgently deserve. Sharp, cinematic, and uncomfortably real."

Katherine Hu | Documentary Filmmaker | Executive Producer and Director of "The Final War"

"Casey Fleming has written a necessary book. It's certainly not entertainment, but it is engrossing and enthralling. It has the pace of a thriller, but is substantiated by deep research, hard facts, and an impressive Thomistic ability for insightful synthesis. *A tour de force."*

Dr. Orlando Gutierrez Boronat | Secretary General, Assembly of the Cuban Resistance

---

"Casey provides a great service to the free world by writing this book, and I believe that should be required reading in every middle school, high school, and university so that people get a clear sense of the existential threat the West and the U.S. are facing. We're in a generational struggle not just for geopolitical supremacy but for the foundational principles of liberty and democracy. This book is a crucial tool in that fight."

Ken Cao | Executive Director, Center for Asian Democratic Resilience

---

"The Red Tsunami" is not just a book - it is a wake-up siren every American desperately needs to hear. As someone who has spent years on the front lines of the fentanyl crisis - fighting the Chinese chemical networks and Mexican cartels that killed my son and over 100,000 Americans a year - I can tell you firsthand: *the threat described in these pages is real, and it's already here.*

It lays out what most people never connect: the fentanyl poisoning our children, the cyber theft crippling our businesses, the psychological warfare on our youth, the infiltration in our schools, universities, and government - none of it is random. It is part of a decades-long strategy designed by the CCP to weaken America from the inside out.

What T. Casey Fleming does brilliantly is explain the whole picture in a way every parent, teacher, policymaker, and citizen can understand. This is not fear-mongering. This is what those of us fighting fentanyl, border insecurity, and Chinese operations have been trying to warn America about for years.

The opening chapters read like a survival guide: clear, urgent, and grounded in real-world intelligence rather than speculation. If America is going to win this fight - for our children, our communities, and our future - then every single person needs to understand the enemy, the methods, and the stakes. This book gives you that understanding.

Every American should read this. Every parent should read this. And every elected official MUST read this. We are running out of time to stay asleep. This book connects all the dots - and once you see it, you can't un-see it. *I endorse it fully.*

April Babcock | Founder and President, Lost Voices of Fentanyl

---

"The Red Tsunami" is an essential and uncompromising exposé of the Chinese Communist Party's vast, multi-domain campaign to undermine and ultimately defeat the West. Fleming has produced one of the most comprehensive analyses to date of the CCP's strategy of Unrestricted Warfare - a plan I have long argued has been underway for over two decades and is far more advanced than most Western leaders dare to admit.

What makes this work so important is its focus on the totality of the threat. Fleming demonstrates, with forensic precision, how the CCP is targeting every layer of Western society: our economies, our institutions, our information ecosystems, our faith traditions, our politics, and even the mental resilience of our populations. He exposes how economic coercion, intellectual property theft, fentanyl distribution, biological manipulation, political subversion, cultural division, and technological infiltration form a single, integrated war plan designed to collapse the West from within.

Crucially, "The Red Tsunami" lays bare the "perfect storm" now engulfing America and its allies - a convergence of dependency, division, corruption, and institutional erosion that Beijing has not only exploited, but actively engineered. Fleming's revisiting of the 45 Goals of Communism is both illuminating and deeply unsettling, revealing just how far these long-standing objectives have already penetrated Western life.

This book is not merely diagnostic; it is prescriptive. Fleming offers a Whole-of-Society survival guide - a blueprint for individuals, families, communities, and nations to harden themselves against the CCP's influence. His central message is one I profoundly share: every citizen has a role in defending freedom, and collective complacency is fatal.

Above all, Fleming situates this conflict within its proper moral and spiritual context. The CCP's war is not only political or economic - it is ideological and spiritual, an assault on human dignity and the fundamental values that underpin free civilization.

"The Red Tsunami" is a wake-up call of the highest order. It is a timely, courageous, and necessary contribution to the global effort to understand and counter the most pervasive geopolitical threat of our age. Every citizen who cares about the future of the West - and the survival of liberty itself - must read this book without delay."

> **David Murrin | Global Forecaster | Author of "Breaking the Code of History"**

"The Red Tsunami" is one of the most important and urgent books of our time, documenting the alarming national security threats affecting every American. Casey Fleming brilliantly exposes the full scope of China's unrestricted war on the United States, its infiltration, espionage, economic coercion, political subversion, and the deadly chemical and information campaigns that are murdering our kids and rapidly weakening our nation.

After spending decades on the front lines of national security and the last eight years supporting families across America devastated by fentanyl, I can tell you this threat is not theoretical. It's real, it's here, and it's impacting every community in this great country.

Fleming connects all the dots with clarity, precision, and courage, revealing how the CCP's multilayered strategy targets our institutions, our security, and even the hearts and minds of our children through social media and digital influence. He provides a roadmap that every citizen, including parents, educators, law enforcement professionals, policymakers, and community leaders, must understand if we're going to protect the next generation and preserve our way of life. The gravity of the threat is enormous, and we need a sense of urgency on all fronts to confront this escalating crisis.

This book is not optional. "The Red Tsunami" should be required reading for every American citizen who cares about the future of our country and the defense of freedom itself. Thank you, Casey, for this powerful work. I'm grateful God connected us. You have done spectacular and professional work, and your dedication to exposing this threat is invaluable.

Derek Maltz | Former Director, DEA Special Operations Division | Former Acting DEA Administrator

---

"The Red Tsunami" is an essential read for anyone seeking clarity in this tenuous and turbulent moment in world affairs. With concise, highly digestible analysis, it exposes the accelerating and existential threat posed by the Chinese Communist Party (which acts in total disregard of the rights and well-being of the Chinese population). Casey's analysis is focused and demonstrates a lucidity that both informs and alarms in equal measure.

Drawing on his years of counterintelligence insight, the book connects the dots others overlook, revealing how the CCP's "unrestricted warfare" is already reshaping our economy, culture, security, and everyday lives. Fleming's work is not a political argument but a survival guide: clear, accessible, empirically grounded, and urgently necessary. We all need to understand the forces destabilizing the free world and what must be done to safeguard it.

"The Red Tsunami" fulfills that need and is an indispensable asset for those seeking to protect their family, their communities, and their nation.

Wayne Lonstein | Esq., CISSP | CEO of VFT Solutions | Member of Forbes Technology Council

---

"This book is a must-read! If you are confounded by the chaos and dysfunction unfolding across every domain of American life, this work provides the clarity you've been searching for. It powerfully exposes how the Chinese Communist Party (CCP) has infiltrated key sectors and strategically undermined America in an effort to diminish our standing as a global leader.

For far too long, hostile foreign actors have operated in the shadows. This book brings their nefarious activities into the light - clearly, boldly, and convincingly. Bravo!"

> **Dr. Kevin McGary | Project 21 Ambassador | Co-founder, Every Black Life Matters (EBLM)**

"If you're looking for one book that explains why China matters to you, you must read "The Red Tsunami." Casey Fleming lays out in disturbing, conclusive detail the decades-long war the Chinese communists are waging against America and Americans. It's not a shooting war – yet, but the PRC has killed over half a million Americans with Fentanyl, destroyed our manufacturing base, and split our society. Fleming exposes what the Chinese are doing and how they are doing it. His section on protecting ourselves and our minds is priceless advice. All Americans -- including everyone on Capitol Hill and in the White House - must read this book."

> **Grant Newsham | COL, United States Marine Corps (ret.) | Former Reserve Head of Intelligence for Marine Forces Pacific | Author of "When China Attacks: A Warning to America"**

"The Red Tsunami" is the most urgent and necessary guide for the times we're living in. As someone who studies culture, politics, and ideology for a living, very few books stop me in my tracks - this one did.

Casey Fleming has written a masterwork that finally connects the dots most Americans have sensed for years but couldn't quite articulate. From fentanyl poisoning to cultural rot, from cyber infiltration to psychological warfare, “The Red Tsunami” exposes how every one of these seemingly isolated crises is part of a coordinated global assault on freedom.

What makes this book so powerful is its clarity. Casey pulls back the curtain on the Chinese Communist Party's “unrestricted warfare” strategy and shows precisely how it touches our families, our schools, our economy, and even our faith. He explains why the world feels like it's unraveling - and he does it without hysteria, without partisanship, and without apology.

This is not fear-mongering. It is fact-based, deeply sourced, and courageously honest. It's a wake-up call written by someone who has spent years on the front lines of counterintelligence, warning leaders around the world while the rest of society remained distracted. Casey has taken that same level of intelligence briefing and placed it directly into the hands of everyday citizens.

If you have children, if you value freedom, if you feel something is deeply wrong in our country, then this book is not optional - it's essential.

“The Red Tsunami” will challenge you, empower you, and equip you to understand the war that has already reached your doorstep. This is more than a book; it's a blueprint for courage in a time of global deception.

I cannot recommend it strongly enough.”

> **April Chapman | Project 21 Ambassador | Host of “Unshakable with April Chapman” | Speaker | Founder of Standard House Media & Standard Home & Living | Author of “The Red Gospel”**

“This book will shake the soul of every American who still believes freedom is worth fighting for.

Casey Fleming has done what few men in this country dare to do - he has pulled the curtain back on the real war being waged against America. “The Red Tsunami” is not fiction; it's not speculation - it's documentation. It's the evidence of an extended, methodical plan by the Chinese Communist

Party and its willing accomplices here at home to weaken the moral, spiritual, and economic backbone of this nation.

This book reads like a counterintelligence briefing for patriots. It connects the dots between Marxist infiltration, cultural manipulation, and political betrayal - and it does it with surgical precision. Casey exposes the truth that most politicians are too scared to say out loud: America isn't falling apart by accident; she's being attacked from within.

For decades, the enemies of God and freedom have used our schools, our media, and even our churches to enslave us through lies. "The Red Tsunami" names names, follows the money, and calls this evil what it is - spiritual warfare disguised as social progress.

Every pastor, parent, and patriot should read this book. It's not just an education - it's a call to arms for the heart and mind. If you've ever wondered how America went from strength to submission, this book tells you exactly how it happened and how we can fight back.

Casey Fleming has written a masterpiece of truth. If you love your country, you need this book."

> **Vince Everett Ellison | Project 21 Ambassador | Author | Speaker | Host of The Vince Everett Ellison Show | Author of "25 Lies" and "The Iron Triangle"**

"The Red Tsunami" by Casey Fleming is the most comprehensive explanation of the demonic asymmetrical threat to America posed by China. This book should be required reading for every elected official in America; every corporate executive and member of Boards of Directors; every teacher, professor, and every elementary, high school, and college student in America and the free world.

This is a comprehensive collection of well-researched data on the methods and actions of the Chinese Communist Party to undermine America in their goal of total global domination. While chilling, the book is a wake-up call for all of us. His chapter on the steps every citizen needs to take to protect themselves, their families, and our country is compelling and a call to action that we must all heed.

Thank you, Casey, for funding the research necessary to compile this unvarnished exposé on the Chinese Communist Party's extensive program to destroy America and our American way of life.

Lynn Mattice | President, National Economic Security Alliance

---

"The Red Tsunami" is a vital call to action for every citizen in a nation under siege. Freedom endures only when patriots confront danger with clarity and courage, and Casey Fleming provides both in these pages. As someone who is a survivor of communism, who has spent decades warning America about China's strategic onslaught, and who has now lost his only son to the CCP's drug warfare through fentanyl, I can attest that this threat is not abstract. It is real, it is lethal, and already here. Fleming exposes the hidden mechanisms of Beijing's campaign against our sovereignty, our children, and our Republic. Every American who loves this country must read this extraordinary book, understand the battlefield, and stand firm. Our future depends on the courage we summon today."

Dr. Rafael Marrero | Founder and Chief Economist, Miami Strategic Intelligence Institute

---

"Casey Fleming's "The Red Tsunami" is a gripping, clearly written, and authoritative examination of the Chinese Communist Party's threat to America. Both a strategic study and a practical survival guide for every citizen, the book offers a persuasive, carefully researched blueprint for countering CCP aggression. Fleming brings rare clarity, accuracy, and urgency to the subject, establishing himself as one of the most astute CCP experts working today."

Dr. Corvin Connolly | Cyber Editor

“I have reviewed the book “The Red Tsunami - The Silent Storm Killing Your Freedom” with careful attention, both as a microbiologist trained in biodefense and outbreak response and as someone who has spent decades studying how authoritarian systems weaponize science, public health, and information.

This book is not speculative fiction, nor is it abstract geopolitical theory. It is a sober, comprehensive warning - one that aligns closely with what many of us in national security, intelligence, and biodefense communities have observed quietly and often unsuccessfully tried to communicate for years.

During my service as a U.S. Army microbiologist, I was directly involved in responses to major infectious disease threats, including MERS and Ebola. At the end of 2019, I was among the first U.S. microbiologists to publicly question the Chinese Communist Party’s handling of the COVID-19 outbreak, to identify early warning signs of suppression and data manipulation, and to raise concerns about the virus’s true origins. Those concerns were not political; they were scientific, intelligence-driven, and rooted in pattern recognition from prior biological events.

Since then, I have published extensively on the CCP’s military-civil fusion strategy specific to virology and life-science research, as a co-founder of the CCP Biothreats Initiative.

What “The Red Tsunami” accomplishes is integrating these same patterns into a unified framework that the general public can understand. The author correctly situates biological threats, narcotics warfare, cyber operations, cultural subversion, and cognitive manipulation within the doctrine of “Unrestricted Warfare.” This is precisely how modern state-level adversaries operate: not through isolated attacks, but through cumulative, deniable, and multi-domain pressure designed to erode societal resilience long before conventional conflict ever begins.

This book is particularly effective in demonstrating how abstract strategies translate into real human cost - lost lives, destroyed families, compromised institutions, and a gradual normalization of chaos. From a scientific and security standpoint, this is accurate. Biological and chemical threats do not need to be spectacular to be effective; they only need to be persistent, plausibly deniable, and poorly understood by the public. The same is true of information warfare and psychological operations.

"The Red Tsunami" should be read not as a call to panic, but as a call to literacy: strategic, civic, and moral literacy. Its value lies in connecting dots that are too often examined in isolation by siloed institutions. In doing so, it provides a clearer picture of the environment in which we are already operating.

For citizens, policymakers, educators, business leaders, and scientists who wish to understand the nature of twenty-first-century conflict - and the role that biology, technology, and information play within it - this book is a timely and necessary contribution.

History shows that free societies rarely collapse from a single blow. They collapse when warnings are ignored, when threats are compartmentalized, and when truth becomes too inconvenient to confront. "The Red Tsunami" refuses that convenience.

Xiaoxu Sean Lin, Ph.D. | Executive Director, Consilium Institute | Co-founder, CCP Biothreats Initiative | Associate Professor, Fei Tian College, Middletown, New York

---

In this time of information chaos and eroding liberties, T. Casey Fleming's "The Red Tsunami: The Silent Storm Killing Your Freedom" delivers a stark and timely revelation: the Chinese Communist Party (CCP)'s unrestricted warfare campaign isn't just aimed at distant battlefields or the U.S. government and military - it's targeting you and your family *personally." Drawing from years on the front lines of private counterintelligence, Fleming connects the fragments of the madness of daily life - from fentanyl-laced pills claiming thousands of young lives, to cyber theft shattering livelihoods, to social media algorithms sowing division and despair - to a deliberate, multi-domain assault designed to subvert our societies from within.

This isn't conventional war; it's a gray-zone campaign of cognitive, economic, cultural, and spiritual erosion, where the battlefield is your mind, your community, your very freedom. Backed by insights from top experts across the globe, the book not only exposes the CCP's totalitarian strategy but also equips you with practical steps to detect, disrupt, and resist, empowering every serious citizen to reclaim sovereignty before it's too late. If you're committed to truth, freedom, and human dignity, this guide demands your attention: understand the war being waged against you, or risk losing the fight without ever realizing you were in it.

Jan Jekielek, Senior Editor at The Epoch Times, and Host of American Thought Leaders

---

"The Red Tsunami presents a chilling reminder of the extensive international reach of the Chinese Communist Party, but it also provides guidelines on how to fight back. I wish Venezuela had a guide like this before Chavez took power. Hopefully, Americans take note before it's too late.

Andres Guilarte | VP of Opinion Research at EyesOver | The Fund for American Studies, Outreach Fellow | Venezuelan exile

---

Fleming's analysis is both sweeping and precise, exposing the war China is quietly waging - one where zero-day exploits, AI-powered disinformation, and covert influence operations converge with psychological manipulation and economic coercion.

The evidence presented paints a stark picture of the reality the West is facing: jobs lost to cyber theft, youth manipulated by algorithmic propaganda, and critical infrastructure quietly seeded with kill switches. This book is a vital warning and a call to action for every American. Ignore its message at your peril.

Michael G. McLaughlin | Former Senior Counterintelligence Advisor for United States Cyber Command | Cybersecurity Attorney | Co-Author of "Battlefield Cyber: How China and Russia are Undermining our Democracy and National Security"

Preface

Continuous chaos. Unexplained madness. You feel as if the world is falling off a cliff. This is both the explanation and the survival guide you've been demanding. It connects the dots of what's eating away at the foundations of our lives and freedoms for every citizen in the world, above partisan politics.

Right now, you're in the fight of your life - whether you realize it or not. A war has been waged against you - coordinated, ongoing, and deliberate. The chaos and division in society are all by design. You and your family have been targets of a silent, unrestricted, unconventional, and relentless war.

This war is the largest, most sinisterly orchestrated global assault on freedom in history. Governments won't talk about it. Legacy media won't touch it. But it's very real. And it's not the military that is on the front lines. You are.

Top intelligence officials - from the FBI, DNI, MI5, and allied agencies - have sounded isolated alarms about this threat for years, but they've left out the connecting threads. This guide gives you what they won't and ties it all together.

This no-nonsense exposé and survival guide cuts through the propaganda, reveals what's coming, and gives you the framework to survive - and resist - the chaos reshaping our world.

This guide wasn't written simply to inform you, but to empirically prove to doubting minds the danger that has been building while providing next steps.

Every person in every country who values truth, freedom, and basic human rights must read this guide and share it with confidence, commitment, and urgency.

If any of this seems like a conspiracy theory or makes you uneasy, ask yourself why. You may already be caught in the very system this guide exposes: a vast campaign designed to keep you confused, distracted, fearful, and compliant.

This guide explains the most important ongoing event of this century. The end point of this event is here: the world will be won or lost in the next ten years - or less. If we don't act now, we will lose our freedom to act at all.

By the time you finish the last briefing, you will never look at the world the same way again.

This war is silent. It is all around you. The threat is real. The time is now.

Stay with me. There's a path through.

Dedication

Dedicated to God, freedom, and all of humanity.

This survival guide was written for citizens of every age, of every country who desire to live free.

I would like to express my sincere appreciation to the many dedicated intelligence professionals and subject matter experts across the globe who contributed to this important work. Your expertise, collaboration, and unwavering commitment to humanity and freedom were instrumental to its success. It is a privilege to work alongside such extraordinary and devoted individuals.

My Personal Message to You

In the pages ahead, you'll access counterintelligence insights few ever see - clear facts, hard truths. You're being played, and you deserve to know how and why. I created this survival guide because no one else would, drawing on fresh briefings from trusted colleagues and top experts interviewed specifically for this work. Their insights have been distilled into sharp, easy-to-navigate briefing summaries designed to equip you to quickly master the information.

It's an honor to serve you.

Table of Contents

BRIEFING ONE
You Are The Main Character

Scenes from one day in America (and allied countries)
Location: A suburb of Boston, April 5 at 7:57AM

Sophie Ellstrom sits cross-legged at her desk in the glow of her warm yellow desk light with her SAT prep book open. Sticky notes, like a thousand petals, mark the pages she's reviewed ten times over. *You can do this. One more push. Take it through the morning and you'll ace it,* she thinks as she swallows a small tablet, something she ordered online to help her focus.

She imagines how tightly her father will hug her once the acceptance letters roll in, especially the one from the university where he met her mom. She feels a slight tightness in her chest. *Nerves*, she thinks. She imagines her new life on campus lawns in autumn - new friends, a laptop in her backpack, and, of course, looking forward to the weekends.

Numbers blur on the page in front of her eyes. Her breath grows shallow; she feels dizzy. She lowers her head onto her arms, telling herself she'll rest for just a minute before finishing the next section. Minutes slip by. Her dreams come in waves. Her father at graduation. Her mother with gifts from home to Parents' Weekend. Her younger brother, Eli, wearing her college sweatshirt to show off to his middle school friends.

Then it all melts into darkness. The pill wasn't pharmaceutical grade as advertised. It was a counterfeit pill, made on advanced Chinese pill presses just over the border in Mexico. Smuggled in. Dosed with fentanyl - just a sprinkling, a speck in the chemical powder. But enough to slowly stop her breathing, and her heart.

"Sophie?" It's Eli at her bedroom door. He's brought her an energy drink, knowing how nervous she is about the big test. He touches her arm, but it's cold. "Sophie?" His voice cracks. "Sophie!" Eli trips as he runs downstairs to the living room. All he can sputter to his parents... "She won't wake up! Sophie won't wake up!"

Location: Walnut Creek, April 5 at 9:31AM

Brody Miller had worked for sixteen years at a mid-sized electronics manufacturer, proud to be part of an American company that innovated and competed globally.

One morning, the announcement came: their core designs had been stolen in a cyber attack months ago, and now replicas were being pumped out in China at 1/4 of his company's price on the open market. Contracts evaporated because their customers were now receiving the same product at a fraction of the price. Layoffs began. By month's end, Brody was escorted out with a thin severance and the knowledge that his job - and his life as he knew it - were gone. Hundreds were fired. The building shuttered after forty years of prosperity. Nearby cafés and businesses closed down as traffic dwindled to a trickle.

Bills piled up. Nights became battles against anxiety. Now, night after night, he sits in the dark living room, staring at the photos of his kids on the wall, wondering how to tell his wife that the mortgage, the college savings, the plans, all are crumbling. Each thought spirals darker. He eyes his car. Only the thought of his children asleep down the hall keeps him from grabbing his keys and ending his pain. For now.

Location: San Antonio, July 5 at 9:22PM

On a blistering July evening in San Antonio, sixteen-year-old Natalia sits on the sagging couch in her family's small apartment, scrolling through TikTok on her cracked phone. Her father works double shifts in construction; her mother cleans offices at night. Scenes of the good life scroll past her eyes, as well as videos about how the America she thought she knew hated her. It was racist. It was sexist. It was the capitalist tool of an elite one percent. That night, a new friend who reached out to her online tells Natalia again that she is too smart, too beautiful, to stay trapped in poverty. She deserves more. She is meant for more. There are riches out there in the world and there is a way to get them.

The words feel like hope. She stays up all night texting with him. He sends photos of Luxe Life: glamorous modeling, VIP parties, huge mansions, sleek cars, night clubs, travel.

Three weeks later, Natalia vanishes. She wakes up across the border in the back seat of an old, black SUV. She remembers nothing. The sweet-talking man she had met online stands over her, telling her she is his girlfriend. She just has to prove her loyalty in his world of drugs and human trafficking.

Natalia will never see America, home, or her family again.

• • •

These stories are unfortunately true, and far more numerous than you might be able to imagine.

They are the stories of your children, your family, your neighbors, your friends, your colleagues, your fellow Americans and citizens of the world. Everyone. They involve you directly. Right now as you read, you and your family are one step away from being ensnared by a diabolical and ruthless enemy. These stories describe only a few of many tactics your enemy has perfected to weaken you, as part of their "softening" of the free world as a prelude to their well-planned complete global takeover.

I realize this may sound way over the top. But I assure you, my colleagues in counterintelligence and I have been working closely inside this battle for many years. To us, these tragedies and incursions are just another Tuesday. To you, it may seem like pure fiction at first. It did to me when I began this journey years ago. But listen closely. It will all make sense, soon. Within these pages, you will be informed, shaken, changed, confident, and ready to take action on your own behalf.

This is the beginning of your part in our whole-of-society rescue mission - for yourself, your family, your country, and the world we live in.

My job is to inform and prepare you for the war you're already in. This is a new type of war you're not familiar with. Unlike other wars, this war doesn't involve the military. It is a war on each of us. There are no bullets and no tanks.

At least, not yet.

You are about to witness documented physical, mental, and economic destruction, wrought by a dark force that, until now, you have only sensed in the shadows. Or caught only brief mentions in articles, videos, or even occasional, scattered warnings from our security agencies.

Expect to feel uneasy at first. Initially, you will seek safety in denial. After all, humans prefer to feel safe, and it's my heartfelt wish that we all could be. Then, you will become angry, because you realize you've been tricked for so long - along with everybody else.

Sadly, despite the beautiful comfort of our daily lives in the free world, under the surface, our world is no longer safe. You are about to learn a critical part of what I know, and what my colleagues and I have gleaned over many years on the front lines in strategic risk, counterintelligence, and national security.

It's exhausting to warn others of true threats and real-life monsters in their presence. Human nature makes us not want to believe these monsters are real. But heed my words: it's far more exhausting to fight monsters when they are already inside the gates - in your city, in your home attacking your children and their minds. And make no mistake: your enemies are already inside our borders, cities, companies, schools, universities, networks, government, homes, and minds.

International security expert Oriane Cohen reports that whenever she reveals urgent threats to people's lives, she is not met with readiness and a defensive response as you might expect, but with "silence, nervosity, and hostility." She says that too often, people are not afraid of the darkness, they are afraid of those who dare to name it.

I am one of the few who dare. There are others who know the full intelligence picture, but cannot speak openly due to government security requirements. Most people in government have only a partial picture due to rigid silos of bureaucracy and administration disruptions. The private intelligence network we formed years ago includes key intelligence leaders in the public and private sectors as well as dissidents, defectors, informants plus open-source information and the intelligence we collect through working with clients. This approach provides us with the most real-time, counter-checked and comprehensive overview.

For over a decade, I have been alerting, updating, and advising top government and business leaders throughout the world. I urge you to absorb this information and counterintelligence as necessary knowledge, and as your new baseline of self-education. I urge you to move forward with your families, taking decisive action as if your lives depend on it - because they do.

As you will see, I am far from alone. My colleagues in counter-intelligence, the military, and high-level strategic planning from Tokyo to London, from Vancouver to Sydney, and others throughout the free world are working day and night to both alert the public and change failed policies that embolden and fortify our enemy. The purpose of this guide, in fact, fits the definition of counterintelligence exactly: to detect, disrupt, and out-maneuver adversaries before irreversible damage is done.

In the following pages, you will understand why I say that the world has ten years or less to be won or lost. We are in a fight to the death. The enemy's forces are committed under totalitarian rule, 24/7, executing malign influence in every corner of our lives to assure that they will not lose.

This high level infiltration and subversion has occurred for years far away from your personal radar, silently while you are going about your life with family, community, deadlines, and kids' activities. But in the gaps and in silence, the enemy has been secretly advancing - locally, nationally, and internationally. You may sense it, catching seemingly disparate bits of news. Threads that have seemed disconnected, but, together, they tell a story that's admittedly, difficult to hear.

For that reason, as you begin this guide: read slowly. Take in what you read in each chapter with care. What you are about to encounter is an active battlefield of fast moving surgical strikes combined with a slow, lethal drip of cultural subversion. Take note: this is exactly how "Gray Zone Warfare" and "Unrestricted Warfare" works. Strikes are engineered to confuse and mislead, then disappear in plain sight. To stay just under the veil of plausible deniability until the next assault.

In this survival guide, you will encounter facts, sabotage, bribes, murder (and worse), infiltrations, cyber-attacks. They may seem unconnected at first. They aren't. They are, what my colleagues, Scott McGregor and Ina Mitchell call part of "The Mosaic Effect" of hybrid warfare - difficult to see close up, but when you step back far enough, you see the entire diabolical design.

Piecing it all together is what my world, the world of counter-intelligence, does every day: placing individual bits of data that appear trivial beside others, until they form an undeniable, coherent picture of a hidden strategy, or, as in this case, a comprehensive threat.

This guide will walk you through those fragments and connect them for you. You will see the calculated inflows of money, technology, propaganda, forward advanced assets that create deadly leverage points for Beijing and its "China Axis" of totalitarian aggressors. You will see how these threats often arrive with sweet smiles, friendly handshakes, and agreements that are broken as soon as they are made.

Let me be forthright: this guide asks a lot of you - to utterly shift your understanding that the CCP's China is not a mere competitor, but a totalitarian juggernaut. An enemy 100% committed to the destruction of Western society and freedoms so that Beijing can claim its title as the single hegemon of the world.

It may sound extreme to you now, in these opening pages, but, again, *stay with me.* After you have absorbed the ongoing and incontrovertible range of the CCP's self-proclaimed unrestricted warfare on us, you will not only be informed and awakened but, also, it is my hope and intention that you will be enrolled into a decisive "whole of society" response.

It is the only thing that will save our freedom.

The Deception

In classic Marxist form, the chaos of the pandemic represented chaos being stoked as a strategic tool - a golden opportunity for fostering division and increasing infiltration during orchestrated distraction.

The COVID crisis of 2019 unleashed major social shifts and triggered a planned flood of social and political activism. The operative word here is *planned.* One can only understand the CCP's financial and cultural fuel behind this social chaos within the context of the whole fabric of their unrestricted warfare against us.

For those of us in counterintelligence, multiple seemingly disjointed events revealed a deepening of China's integrated "Gray Zone Warfare" against the U.S.

Before diving into the remaining briefs, the following several pages will illustrate for you what has occurred in American society as a result of over seventy years of the CCP from Mao Zedong to Xi Jinping. Although the lists can be arduous, remind yourself that this section of lists is merely a reflection of *recent* legislation, policy, and cultural devolution. Imagine what the full mosaic of seventy years of Marxist and Communist infiltration into a free nation would look like. To be sure, it could not be contained in a single guide.

To wit...

(2010-present) Forced Hollywood Self-Censorship
CULTURE WAR

Under financial pressure and threats, Hollywood self-censors to placate the CCP by painting the U.S. as decadent and declining, beginning in 2010 under Xi Jinping's "soft power" strategy. Hollywood studios, eager for access to China's enormous and growing box office, began editing films to avoid offending Beijing, removing topics like Tibet, Taiwan, Tiananmen, or strong American patriotism. Sure enough, China surpassed the U.S. in total movie ticket sales for the first time in 2016, securing their power over Hollywood. This dependence deepened in 2017 when Chinese conglomerates like Wanda Group and Tencent Pictures co-financed blockbuster films, and U.S. studios self-censored scripts, posters, and even dialogue to avoid losing access to China's market. Films altered maps of the South China Sea, erased Taiwanese flags, or rewrote villains to avoid depicting China negatively, such as replacing "China" with "North Korea." In 2020, Beijing tightened film import quotas and Hollywood obediently doubled down on self-censorship, which several producers described as *"preemptive obedience."* Analysts from PEN America and the Congressional–Executive Commission on China highlighted this period as the peak of Chinese ideological control over U.S. entertainment output.

(2015-2025) Data Breaches
DATA WAR

In 2015, the U.S. Office of Personnel Management (OPM) confirmed that hackers linked to China had stolen sensitive personal data on 21.5 million current and former federal employees, including background checks and fingerprints. This breach was officially acknowledged by OPM and publicly reported by outlets such as The Washington Postl and Reuters that same year.

In 2017, the Equifax breach exposed the personal information of 147 million Americans after hackers exploited a software vulnerability, making it one of the largest data thefts in U.S. history and demonstrating how poorly protected critical data systems can be.

In 2025, AT&T confirmed that hackers had leaked the personal data of 73 million current and former customers, including names, Social Security numbers, and account passcodes, onto the dark web, exposing years of neglected security flaws and illustrating how major corporations continue to prioritize secrecy and profit over the protection of Americans' private information.

Based on current intelligence, large-scale breaches tied to Chinese or state-aligned actors are accelerating, with increasing focus on infrastructure, defense contractors, and biotech.

(2018-present) Supply Chain and Infrastructure Vulnerabilities
TECHNOLOGY WAR

Since around 2018, U.S. and Canadian security agencies have warned that Chinese-made electronics and network gear may contain hidden hardware or software backdoors that threaten critical infrastructure such as water, power, and pipelines throughout the U.S. and Canada. These concerns have grown through 2023–2025 as new forensic audits and cybersecurity briefings revealed continued vulnerabilities tied to Chinese manufacturing and supply-chain dependencies.

(2019-present) Politicians Compromised
POLITICAL WAR

Lucrative personal "business" dealings involving CCP or CCP-linked companies are rampant among U.S. elected politicians. One example thoroughly detailed by Brigadier General Ret. Robert Spalding is Senate Minority Leader Mitch McConnell, whose wife Elaine Chao's family shipping company, *Foremost Group*, has had extensive ties with Chinese state banks and shipping conglomerates since the late 1990s, receiving favorable financing and port contracts that U.S. Senate inquiry reports and *The New York Times* (2019) identified as potential sources of CCP leverage. Another example is Representative Eric Swalwell, who was cited in FBI briefings in 2020 and detailed by Axios (December 2020) for his connection to a suspected Chinese intelligence operative, Christine Fang, who cultivated relationships with several U.S. politicians as part of a broader CCP influence campaign.

(2019-present) Spread of Critical Race Theory (CRT) in Schools

The infiltration of Critical Race Theory (CRT) into U.S. education began to accelerate around 2010, as major private foundations *(with opaque funding sources)* and academic institutions began funding "equity" and "anti-racism" programs. By 2019–2021, these ideas were fully embedded in many public-school curricula and teacher training frameworks, a period that also saw documented CCP influence campaigns promoting ideological narratives portraying the United States as systemically racist to weaken national confidence and cohesion. One goal of CRT is to frame America as inherently racist to erode national unity and pride. Xi Van Fleet remarks on the similarities between American CRT and Mao's Cultural Revolution. Fleet, the author of "Mao's America," states:

> *I've been very alarmed by what's going on in our schools. You are now teaching, training our children to be social justice warriors and to loathe our country and our history. Growing up in Mao's China, the communist regime used the same critical theory to divide people. The only difference was they used class instead of race. During the cultural revolution, we witnessed students and teachers turn against each other, we changed the school names to be politically correct. We were taught to denounce our heritage, and Red Guards destroyed anything that is not communist...statues, books and anything else. We were also encouraged to report on each other, just like the Student Equity Ambassador program and the bias reporting system.*

Critical Race Theory is, indeed, the American version of the Chinese Cultural Revolution. CRT plainly and empirically has roots in cultural Marxism, and should have no place in our school. Together we will peel back more layers of this in this briefing's section *"They Provoked Identity Divisions"* and in "Case Study 1: Marxist Roots and the Poison of BLM."

(2020) COVID Origin Coverup
BIOWEAPONS WAR

COVID-19, called the "Wuhan flu" by early whistleblowers such as Dr. Vladimir Zelenko in his book, "How To Decapitate The Serpent," revealed suppressed warnings, delayed data sharing, and obfuscation over origins - all designed by an extremely secretive Beijing government.

(2020-present) Fentanyl
DRUG WAR

Fentanyl became the #1 killer of Americans ages 18–45. Over 125,000 Americans die from fentanyl poisoning each year. Not addicts, but kids, teens, college students, fathers, wives, and grandparents are ruthlessly targeted. Illicit Chinese fentanyl only began flooding the U.S. via mail and Mexico between 2013 and 2015. In 2019, cartels, especially Sinaloa, began mass production. **In ten years, Fentanyl went from unheard of to the #1 killer of military-aged Americans.**

(2020-present) IP Theft
ESPIONAGE WAR

Relentless Intellectual Property (IP) theft and cyber espionage indictments of CCP-linked actors accelerate. These criminals hack into U.S. companies, research facilities, and exploit government secrets. The year 2020 saw the sharpest surge with coordinated DOJ, FBI, and CISA warnings about systematic theft across biotech, aerospace, AI, and defense sectors, much of it focused on gaining leverage during the COVID-19 research race. High-profile corporate-espionage or technology theft - involving military, semiconductor, solar, EV battery technology theft, as the CCP coordinates blatant IP theft across all essential, military and military-adjacent industries.

In July 2022, the U.S. Department of Justice charged Chinese national Ji Chaoqun and his handler from the Jiangsu Province Ministry of State Security for stealing aerospace and advanced manufacturing technology from American defense contractors, confirming coordination of state-directed IP theft across military and dual-use industries, as documented in the DOJ Press Release "Chinese Intelligence Officer Convicted of Economic Espionage."

(2020-present) Chinese Military Aggression
TERRITORY WAR

In 2016, after the Permanent Court of Arbitration ruled against China's South China Sea claims, Beijing greatly accelerated military base construction on artificial islands and began intensified air and naval intimidation of Taiwan and the Philippines, actions that have continued and expanded through the 2020s. To this day, Beijing continues to build airstrips and forward military air bases on reefs throughout the South China Sea. China regularly provokes the Philippine Navy with aggressive maneuvers at sea.

(2021) R&D Theft and Scientific Espionage:
INNOVATION WAR

The U.S. Senate Permanent Subcommittee on Investigations confirmed that the CCP-originating "*Thousand Talents Program*" and its successors aimed to "transfer American research and taxpayer-funded innovation to China." These programs aimed to acquire *(steal)* foreign R&D and entice *(bribe or blackmail)* scientists. CCP-linked cyber espionage indictments reveal a deeply organized, government-linked structure dedicated to siphoning U.S. innovation and strategic data.

(2022-2025) Military Expansion
CONVENTIONAL WAR

A massive military buildup in China - ballooning to over $735 billion in military expansion by 2022, commissioned at least 20 new major warships and produced between 6-8 million drones annually between 2023 and 2025. China's industrial capacity can generate approximately 500,000 small FPV drones per month, expandable to 700,000 in wartime. Coupled with rapid technological innovation, including advanced long-range strike drones like the Scorpion and the Jiu Tian uncrewed bomber, this positions China as a superpower, aggressively closing the gap and surpassing antiquated U.S. capabilities through AI integration, swarm tactics and other *(stolen)* advanced-tech innovations.

(2023) National Security Infiltration
BORDER WAR

Chinese migrant crossings into the U.S. spiked dramatically in 2023, prompting homeland security concerns and congressional investigation into potential national security infiltration risks. During this time, an estimated 200,000 Chinese nationals of military age illegally arrived on U.S. soil during open borders. Many are thought to be PLA special forces in sleeper cells spread among safe houses to perform espionage and sabotage, while awaiting the command to attack.

(February, 2023) Surveillance
SURVEILLANCE WAR

A Chinese surveillance balloon was shot down after it traversed Alaska, Canada, and continental U.S. airspace, raising alarms about CCP aerial surveillance, CCP-linked intelligence collection, lack of U.S. response, and internal corruption.

(2023-present) Academic Takeover and IP Theft
ACADEMIC WAR

U.S. Senate investigations and DOJ "China Initiative" cases confirmed ongoing academic infiltration and intellectual property theft by China. U.S. counterintelligence officials say the problem has accelerated, but is becoming harder to detect because China hides its tracks more effectively. Hidden ties and co-research in universities and laboratories fail to disclose Chinese affiliations and recruitment programs. Valuable dual use (commercial/military) IP suddenly shows up in CCP-linked military units.

(2023) Cultural Self-Hatred and The Cognitive War (especially on children)
SOCIAL MEDIA WAR

Platforms like TikTok and other media shape narratives that encourage Americans, especially youth, to distrust, hate and reject their own history, institutions, families and core values, revealing extensive coordinated outside influence. In 2023, the U.S. Surgeon General and multiple congressional hearings highlighted how TikTok's algorithm, driven by data flows tied to ByteDance in China, disproportionately promoted content associated with depression, anti-American sentiment, and nihilistic worldviews among U.S. teens.

In 2024, a Pew Research Center report found that over 60% of Americans under 30 said they have "little or no pride" in the nation's history, a shift many analysts linked to social media conditioning. During that period, CIA cybersecurity briefings and House committee reports concluded that TikTok's data-mining and content-engineering operations functioned as tools of Chinese psychological influence targeting American youth.

By 2025, bipartisan lawmakers cited these findings while advancing legislation to limit foreign-owned social platforms that manipulate cultural narratives to erode U.S. national identity and social stability. As a national security advisor with ten thousand hours in advising our three-letter agencies, I am more than skeptical of the current U.S. commitment to hold these criminals accountable, and throughout this guide you will learn about how TikTok and other platforms are weaponized military applications.

(2024-2025) Foreign Policy and Economic Coercion
ECONOMIC WAR

Coercive diplomacy, economic pressure sanctions, trade measures, threats, bribes and high-profile detentions are deployed more brazenly to gain economic, judicial, legal and political leverage to influence foreign policy outcomes, with this only accelerating in the Trump presidency. In 2024, after several Western nations criticized Beijing's human rights record, China detained multiple foreign executives working in Shanghai and suspended rare-earth exports to Europe, moves widely seen as coercive economic retaliation intended to force diplomatic concessions and mute public criticism.

In 2025, China used economic coercion again by suspending key pharmaceutical ingredient exports to the United States after Washington expanded restrictions on advanced chip technology, triggering supply disruptions in U.S. hospitals and pressuring policymakers to ease sanctions.

(2025) Propaganda and Psychological Operations COGNITIVE WAR

State-linked influence and disinformation campaigns on social media and forums, spread through vast bot networks and propaganda farms, coordinating persistent attempts to shape public opinion and patriotic loyalty. In May 2025, the U.S. Department of Homeland Security's Cybersecurity and Infrastructure Security Agency (CISA) reported that more than 350,000 coordinated inauthentic accounts linked to Chinese state-backed operators were active across X, TikTok, and Reddit, generating tens of millions of interactions monthly to amplify pro-CCP narratives and sow division within the United States. This figure was cited in the CISA "Foreign Influence Threat Assessment 2025" and echoed in a Stanford Internet Observatory analysis confirming that these bot networks had doubled in size since 2023, indicating a sharp escalation in organized online propaganda and digital psychological operations.

As you can see, in classic Marxist form, the years succeeding the pandemic represent **chaos being stoked as a strategic tool** - a golden opportunity for fostering division and increasing infiltration during orchestrated distraction. Once the flu travelled from Wuhan across the world, the CCP and its minions wasted no time funding, organizing, and weaponizing a devils' list of movements, orchestrated to destroy the pillars that support our civil society.

In the following section, we'll continue the history lesson of this chapter with a microscope on specific identity divisions in the "cultural war" that provide a distraction for the other 100+ forms of unrestricted war against the West to advance.

They Provoked Identity Divisions

- **Wokeism and Cancel Cultural: Post-George Floyd (2020)**
  Woke ideology exploded via Marxist-funded curricula in universities, with hundreds of millions of corporate and foreign dollars being donated to "racial justice" groups promoting identity-based oppression narratives which further fracture societal unity and reconciliation.

- **Racism (2020)**
  The 2020 "anti-racism" surge, backed by $1B+ (via BLM partnerships), reframed all whites as inherent oppressors, fueling guilt and division per Marxist class-struggle tactics. Chinese diplomats and state-linked entities were revealed to be donating to organizations like BLM, Antifa, and, later, "No Kings," sowing discord.

- **Black Lives Matter (BLM) - Hijacking of the Black Community (2020)**
  BLM Global Network, with its avowedly Marxist co-founders, raised $90M in 2020, but only 33% went to charities (per 2022 audits), diverting funds to elite insiders while pitting black communities against police and economic freedom *(capitalism)*. BLM's rapid rise included partnerships with pro-CCP entities in China and others for "international solidarity" events.

- **Attack on the White Race (2020)**
  Robin DiAngelo's "*White Fragility: Why It's So Hard for White People to Talk About Racism*" (Beacon Press) sold millions post-COVID, endorsed by Marxist academics to vilify whiteness as a systemic evil, eroding national cohesion.

- **Attack on White Males (2020-2022)**
  The 2020-2022 "toxic masculinity" campaigns, amplified by NEA *(teachers' union)* resolutions, portrayed white men as patriarchal oppressors, hijacking education to dismantle male-led institutions.

- **Critical Race Theory (CRT) (2020-present)**
  Post-2020, CRT infiltrated K-12 via Biden's Education Department grants ($200M+ to "equity" programs), including teaching systemic racism as unfixable without Marxist redistribution, per Ibram X. Kendi's funded advocacy.

- **Diversity, Equity, & Inclusion (DEI) (2020-present)**
  Post-COVID corporate mandates *(e.g., a large tech company's 2021 $1B DEI pledge)* enforced Marxist equity quotas, punishing merit-based achievement to redistribute power along identity lines. Our economy grows based on meritocracy that rewards capability; DEI policies weaken our economy and safety when less capable candidates are placed into open positions.

They Amped Up Censorship and Language Control

- **Censorship - Anti Free Speech**
  During 2020 lockdowns, Big Tech censored COVID dissent at the behest of Marxist-aligned groups like Media Matters, with 500K+ posts removed by mid-2021, per internal leaks, to control narratives.

- **Political Correctness**
  The 2020 Marxist cancel culture wave, fueled by $50M+ Soros grants to activist NGOs, forced self-censorship (e.g.,

J.K. Rowling's 2020 backlash). Cancel culture used language policing to suppress dissent and Marxist ideology.

- **Hijacking of Terms**
  Democracy, Fascist, Racist, Hitler, Democratic Socialist, Conspiracy Theory, Free Speech, Hate Speech, White Christian Nationalist, Insurrectionist, etc.

  Post-2020, terms like "fascist" were weaponized (e.g., large legacy media $10M+ ad buys) to label Trump supporters, replacing debate with "hysterical diagnosing and disregarding," diluting the meaning of language per the time-tested Marxist tactic of creating the fog of semantic subversion to delegitimize opposition. Orwell called this one out a long time ago.

They Supported Violent Protests and Lawlessness

- **Violent Protests**
  The 2020 BLM/Antifa riots, organized via ActBlue ($1.5B raised) and funded in part by the Shanghai-based Singham network (detailed in "Briefing Eight") caused $2B in damages across 140 cities. These exemplified Marxist "direct action" to destabilize law and order during COVID distractions.

- **Violent Riots and Looting**
  Minneapolis, Ferguson, Seattle, NYC, and L.A., among others. While Ferguson predated COVID, the post-2020 redux in Minneapolis (2020, $500M damage) and Seattle's CHOP zone (funded by anarchist collectives) showed Marxist support and escalation, with looters excused as obtaining "reparations" by organizers.

- **George Floyd Protests**
  Kicking off in May 2020, the "mostly peaceful" George Floyd protests (per media) involved 15,000 arrests amidst Marxist chants, amplifying legitimate grief into anti-capitalist fury. During this time, videos surfaced of pallets of bricks appearing overnight near riot hotspots in cities like Minneapolis, Dallas, and Kansas City, unexplained by authorities and speculated as setups by well-heeled foreign agitators to escalate violence and chaos.

- **Defund the Police**
  Post-Floyd 2020. Marxist groups like DSA pushed resolutions in 25+ cities (e.g., Minneapolis' 2020 vote), slashing budgets by 10-20% and spiking crime 30%+, per FBI data, to erode law enforcement pillars.

- **Invalidate Laws, Law Enforcement, Eliminate or Reduce Crime Penalties**
  California's 2020 Prop 47 expansions (DA George Gascón, backed by Soros $2M+), decriminalized theft under $950, leading to a 20% shoplifting surge and Marxist "abolition" of punitive justice.

- **Pro-Hamas/Palestine Protests**
  Campus encampments surged in October of 2023 (post-COVID activism boom). Organized by Shanghai-based "Code Pink" and "SJP" (Marxist-linked, $1M+ funding), these encampments chanted the terrorist promise to "globalize the intifada" to import Middle East divisions and terrorism into U.S. civil society.

- **Anti-Semitic Protests and Rhetoric**
  2023-2024 Gaza protests (e.g., Columbia University's Hamilton Hall takeover), backed by "Students for Justice in Palestine" ($500K+ from radical donors) equated democratic Zionism as

imperialism through the dualistic Marxist oppressor/oppressed ideology, reviving dusty old Soviet-created blood libels against Jews and Israel, spiking U.S. antisemitism 400% per ADL.

They Caused Gender and Family Erosion

- **Feminism**
  Post-2020 #MeToo revival (e.g., Time's Up $25M fund), twisted fourth-wave feminism into Marxist class warfare against men, promoting "believe all women" to undermine family trust and male authority.

- **Feminize Males through Toxic Masculinity**
  American Psychological Association (APA's) 2020 guidelines, amplified by the dominant "Cultural Marxist" academics in schools, labeled traditional masculinity "toxic," pushing therapy and media (e.g., Gillette's 2019 ad) to emasculate boys amid COVID isolation.

- **Transgenderism**
  Biden's 2021 Executive Order 13988 mandated transgender protections in schools, funded by $100M+ grants to LGBTQ organizations, enforcing Marxist gender fluidity to blur biological norms and destroy family structures.

- **Hijacking of LGBTQIA+:**
  Post-COVID, groups like "GLAAD" (Soros-funded $20M+) co-opted the movement for radical causes (e.g., 2022 Drag Queen Story Hours in 100+ cities), turning "Pride" into anti-family activism.

- **Invalidating the Family**
  Marxist "family abolition" rhetoric surged in 2021 via books like *"Abolition. Feminism. Now."* (AK Press, $1M+ sales), funded networks pushing communal child-rearing to replace nuclear families with state control. This title was originally published in 2022 by Haymarket Books until AK Press reprinted the same title for activist networks.

- **Invalidating the Father as Head of the Family**
  The CDC's 2020 family policy shifts *(amid lockdowns)* and feminist grants ($50M+ to women's organizations) de-emphasized paternal roles, promoting single-motherhood as "empowering," fracturing traditional family structures.

They Funded Institutional Subversion

- **Environmental, Social, Governance (ESG)**
  One of the world's largest investment firms, 2020 ESG mandates ($10T Assets Under Management) forced companies into Marxist-based social scoring, diverting investments from merit to "equity" causes, eroding free-market pillars.

- **Climate Change**
  Post-COP26 (the 2021 United Nations Climate Change Conference), $100B+ UN funds funneled to Green New Deal activists (e.g., Sunrise Movement, Marxist ties), framing climate as a capitalist sin to justify wealth redistribution and division. Climate change also drives revenue and strength directly to the CCP through solar panels, energy windmills, and EV purchases. All of these industries are based on stolen IP from the United States.

- **Replacing Monuments**
  2020-2021 saw 100+ statues toppled (e.g., Columbus in Minneapolis), organized by Marxist BLM chapters with $20M+ grants, symbolizing erasure of Western history to delegitimize civil society's foundations.

- **Renaming Military Bases**
  The DoD commission (Biden-signed 2021) renamed nine military bases (e.g., "Fort Bragg" was renamed to "Fort Liberty"), spurred by Marxist anti-colonial pushes, to purge "racist" heritage and weaken military patriotism.

- **Attacks on Patriotism and the American Flag**
  In 2020, NFL/Kaepernick protests were revived (amid Floyd marches), with corporations like Nike funding anti-flag kneel-ins, per the Marxist tactic of shaming national symbols and fostering alienation.

- **Attacks on Religion and Christianity**
  Post-2020, the IRS relaxed rules allowing churches' tax status revocation for "hate speech" (e.g., on LGBTQ issues), backed by atheist/Marxist lobbies ($10M+), targeting faith as an "opiate of the masses."

- **Decolonization**
  2021-2024 university mandates (e.g., Harvard's $100M decolonization fund) pushed Marxist curricula to "decenter" Western knowledge, replacing curricula with indigenous/anti-colonial narratives to undermine Enlightenment pillars.

Without dedicated counterintelligence, connecting the thousands of dots that illustrate the CCP's war against the West is next to impossible. Before the FBI briefings that changed my life, which I'll describe in a moment, I hadn't connected them either. That's how the enemy wants it; distraction and confusion is literally core to their strategy. They specialize in chaos, patience, stealth infiltration, subversion, theft, and destruction.

The enemy concluded after the Gulf War in the early 90s that they could not take over the world by defeating the U.S. on the military battlefield, so they turned the world itself into a battlefield with everything short of conventional war, although Chinese military expansion over recent years predicts that tanks and bullets will inevitably follow the other forms of unrestricted war that have been detailed here, and which will be detailed in your remaining briefings. That, of course, is why this guide is critical *now*.

However, although conventional war doesn't appear evident at first glance, the CCP has stepped up an accelerating series of hostile actions that are severe but don't rise to the "kinetic" level that sets off a military response. That is strategic; it is a planned "death by a thousand cuts."

We are in "The Gray Zone Warfare," which represents an "everything but military confrontation" war; and we're decades into this war. It's an "Everywhere War." A "Peoples War." A "Whole of Society" war. A "Destroy Them From Within" war. And all of it aims to destroy our economic, political, social, and familial systems while decreasing our individual ability or will to resist. Make no mistake, while this silent war is being waged, the CCP is rapidly building up their own economy and military might in preparation for a kinetic or conventional war.

The ultimate goal is to achieve total domination and control, as the ancient Chinese military strategist Sun Tzu counseled, without the need for any military confrontation at all, or, in his words, "The supreme art of war is to subdue the enemy without fighting." Xi Jinping is on record emphasizing this concept of "winning without fighting" to the CCP's Central Military Commission.

In sum, you are learning...

You are in World War III

It does not look like earlier wars that were military-based and explosive. But what you and your family have experienced is exactly what World War III looks like. It began decades ago, not as a kinetic, conventional, "shooting war," but as one which assaults you silently, your politicians, your critical infrastructure, your kids' education, your cultural institutions, and your war readiness.

If your enemy is successful with its war on the American people and people of the free world, it will never need to move into the final phase of "hot" war. Sun Tzu's ideal of "winning without fighting" (不战而屈人之兵) as quoted by Jinping, is the supreme art of war, but it is not the only war we'll see waged if the world isn't dead serious about the warnings in this book.

To use the CCP's own terminology, this is *Unrestricted War.* That means: *No rules. No limits. No mercy. Nowhere to hide. Total victory. The Final War.*

Why Me?

Initially, I didn't want to write this survival guide. I have been waiting for others to write something decisive that speaks to and informs every citizen, including our youth. A survival guide for every citizen in the world who cherishes their freedom. Several authors have written excellent books on different elements of the CCP's unrestricted war on us, but no one has written the most important book - a comprehensive review and survival guide to inform and engage the public. The book that connects thousands of dots.

Such a comprehensive survival guide is necessary.

The biggest fear your enemy has is:

1) the public becomes informed, and;

2) they unite and take action.

I could see that we have been running out of time to awaken, engage, and win. After decades of the fog of bureaucratic fragmentation, business and government not taking action, corruption *(aka. elite capture)*, and, in fact, our elites actually facilitating a CCP takeover, it was time for me to step up.

I spent many years networking with intelligence and relevant subject matter experts, traveling the world advising and speaking to business and government organizations about the existential threat we all face.

I recently heard a senior intelligence official describe me as "the confluence of Paul Revere, Winston Churchill, and George Patton." I humbly appreciate those comparisons, as these men were all focused on protecting freedom. Revere for his forewarning of a tyrant's British troops. Churchill for his dogged "voice in the wilderness" decade in the 1930s, warning of the Nazi military buildup and quietly working to upgrade the Royal Air Force in preparation. Patton, because he led forces in World War II with mission focus and fierce intent. As the war wound down, he also warned that the fight against communist global ambition would continue, as it most certainly has.

A decade and half ago, I was invited to an intelligence briefing that changed my life forever. It took me a full ninety days to accept, digest, and confront what I learned, as well as the remaining years I spent working in counterintelligence. I have summarized that briefing and my subsequent revelations for you in this survival guide.

Get ready. Most people go through the same five stages - plus one - on the journey toward facing hard truths. First comes denial, shock, and numbness, then bargaining and disbelief, followed by depression, anger, and finally acceptance. The last stage, the "plus one," is *action, when understanding turns into empowerment.*

Today Is Your Day One

Before my "Day One" came, I languished in what I call "Day Zero." A semi-wake up call. It was April, 2001, just before 9/11. A U.S. Navy EP-3E surveillance aircraft was rammed and forced down by a Chinese J-8 aircraft seventy miles off of Hainan Island in the South China Sea. The Navy EP-3E was forced to land on Hainan where the crew of twenty-four were held captive in isolation and interrogated day and night for ten days. The Americans were eventually repatriated, but were forced to leave cutting-edge technology on the tarmac to be completely blueprinted. As expected, the CCP denied ramming the EP-3E and, instead, claimed their J-8 was rammed. This event was my initial wake up.

My Day One landed unexpectedly hard ten years later, when I was attending an FBI executive briefing at the Federal Reserve Bank. My background in management consulting and technology gave me an idea of the various growing threats to businesses and government from China. Cyber-security and theft of intellectual property (IP) was my world. But what FBI Special Agent in Charge, Steve Morris showed me that day was specific and shocking intelligence that I had never heard. I realized there had to be a master plan beyond my experience up to that point. The vulnerabilities that my clients - and all of us - faced far exceeded what I already knew to be true.

Could it be this comprehensive, this calculated, this integrated? Were my clients' threatened in ways no one was prepared for?

I didn't want to believe it at first (after all, I was a highly paid and respected expert in the field) but the evidence was undeniable. What was also undeniable was that this was only the tip of the iceberg. The CCP's campaign was much bigger than cybersecurity. It was only a piece of the puzzle. I was determined to find it. There were multiple cases of espionage, economic sabotage, and IP theft.

Our enemy was constantly perfecting that theft. They mastered the art of completely erasing the many years and vast amounts of money America and its allies spent developing a product only to immediately sell the same product to our same customers at $.40 cents on the dollar. When they target your innovation, the CCP levels the playing field in *days* by negating the cost of time and money. The cutting edge innovation which was lost from the U.S. now powers the CCP totalitarian communist regime and its ultimate war against you. At the same time the U.S. economy has lost:

- Revenue
- Profit
- Jobs
- Hospitals
- Schools
- Churches
- Additional R&D
- and National Security, *permanently.*

The FBI clearly revealed that there was more than I'd have ever imagined beneath the surface, and that the CCP's operation was more severe, complex, and wide-reaching than I'd ever imagined. I realized, for the first time, that the U.S. (and the entire free world) had *one primary enemy that was attacking us all.* And the attacks come all day, every day. Even more devastating was the realization that there existed no comprehensive, coordinated counter-force that matched the clarity, intensity and strategic planning of our enemy.

At that time, my colleagues and I in cybersecurity were focused on protecting the castle; we were stationed around the perimeter. From that stance, each year was just another groundhog day; we did the same thing with no change in tactics. But after that FBI briefing, I understood that in a war of this scale, you can't win by being reactive. You must identify the enemy and become intimate with him so you can anticipate his next move. In the cybersecurity industry, we were busy creating more software, plugging more gaps, cashing in more revenue, and telling clients they were "all good." And for a long time, I believed that. But clearly, we were not good. Not from an enemy this ruthless, committed, and sophisticated.

For thirty days following the briefing at the Federal Reserve Bank, I reeled and staggered around in disbelief; this new intelligence was a lot to absorb. In three months' time, I knew I could not accept the offer on the table to be CEO of another cybersecurity company, as I'd planned to do. In short, instead of going for the payout, I made a hard, but necessary decision. I committed to doing my part to meet this *new* threat. Or, rather, the decades-old threat that was new to me.

The decision was not simple, but it was easy.

I had to. For God. For human freedom. For country.

Honestly, I didn't know where it would take me, but I knew I could not ignore the call. I knew we needed to better understand who exactly was on the other side, who the specific bad guys were, what they wanted, and how they were coming after us.

For several years, I worked pro bono assembling a dream team and global network of top intelligence and subject matter experts, all while advising top leadership in business and government. It grew into the counterintelligence firm BlackOps Partners. Over time, the true enemy became crystal clear. It was not China. It was certainly not the oppressed Chinese people. It was the Chinese Communist Party, the CCP.

Since that time, BlackOps grew into a strategic risk company and think tank specializing in protecting intellectual property from the CCP and their axis of aggressors. I became a board member with the FBI Citizens Academy. Then, because of the devastating weapon of fentanyl and other lethal drugs produced in China, manufactured in Mexico, and smuggled over the border, I became a member of the DEA Citizens Academy. Because I am a father, this issue is personal for me. So I also helped found the DEA Leadership Academy for teens, and my own two kids were among the first through it.

There was one particular moment that put me over the top. After 9/11, the FBI hired an outside consulting firm to do a critical review of intelligence failures. They learned that if all of the United States' counterintelligence directorates reported into the same person and if private cybersecurity firms and all the "siloed" government agencies that were so bureaucratically disconnected all reported into the same executive, we could have stopped 9/11. Then in 2011, I was conclusively shown that we are facing a cascading catastrophe that far outstripped that singular event in New York City. We are facing the total loss of our way of life. Our freedom.

I never expected to be working with business, government, and political leaders to address the existential threat of our lifetime - a diabolical, insidious, tech-enabled, relentless CCP committed to eradicating freedom and Western sovereignty. I grew up as a happy, if highly determined, kid in Iowa - far from the halls of power. I was the paperboy trudging through the snow, the very picture of a hardworking Midwestern kid. I even had a golden retriever, Major, panting along by my side everywhere I went. In high school, I was the guy who got up at 4 a.m. to plow driveways and parking lots with my Chevy K5 Blazer and, of course, my co-pilot, Major.

I didn't know anything about international intrigue. Mine certainly looks like an average American childhood. But one thing that was not average was the ethic of selfless service drilled into me by my father. Dad was a WWII vet and taught me to run to the fire, not away from it. In one example, he, my brother, and I came across an overturned car smoking in the snow, wheels still spinning. We pulled a family of four out of the car and they all survived. It's events like these that molded me. Running into the fire to help is in my blood. And it was from an early age.

People often ask "Casey, why do you do this?"

And this is my answer: it's how I'm wired. If I see someone in need, I'm the first one in. I attended a military-rooted university that reinforced respect, excellence, leadership, loyalty, integrity, and selfless service (RELLIS). Early on, my family and friends nicknamed me "The Protector." It may sound strange, but I was made for this mission, this service. So when people ask me why I have dedicated my life to this cause, I add, "if not me, then who?"

Please understand, you are in a war unlike any before. There are no uniforms, and no actual front lines. This war is fought everyday, everywhere - in networks, in hospitals, in ports and in businesses and satellites. It's fought in elementary schools, farmlands and, most of all, in the hearts and minds of every American and world citizen. As such, it demands a whole-of-society response, where business, government, educators, and parents must recognize and confront this existential threat to freedom that is unlike any the world has ever faced. **Victory requires unification, clarity, discipline, and the commitment of everyone.** It is, after all, a world war - *your world war.*

Now you know why I wrote this survival guide. Not for me. For you. Your family. Your children. My children. For all of humanity and our future freedom.

I will say it over and over and you will come to see it. We have been at war. Not a war we're familiar with. A war unlike any other. The United States and the freedom we represent and defend has been the CCP's arch enemy since their rise to power in 1949. And under the iron grip of Chairman Xi, they have amplified their claim that we must be completely destroyed so that they may achieve their "Chinese Dream" and goal of total global domination by 2049. And they are well ahead of that goal.

Kelley Currie, the Former Ambassador to the UN Economic and Social Council, said it as well as it can be said: "We have to recognize that these are real threats that we face as a nation and this is not about going abroad looking for monsters. The monsters are coming whether we want them to or not."

There is no running away. No covering our eyes or ears. There is nowhere to hide. This is your war.

It requires the collective effort of all of us: every American and citizen of the free world. This war requires mobilizing the entire information economy, white collar expertise, counterintelligence coordination, and effective countermeasures. It requires citizens to make the commitment to serve strongly in school boards, communities, and universities. We must achieve representation in the local, state, and federal government. It requires parents enforcing digital diets. It requires universities to clean ranks, and parents and government to stop financing our enemy and its destruction of our society. It requires that we must be on the same page in understanding this existential threat to our freedom. And, it requires eternal vigilance, which, founder Thomas Jefferson famously said, is "the price of liberty."

A great leader in this fight is John Moolinaar, Chairman of The Select Committee on the CCP. On October 21, 2025, he said:

> *The United States and the Chinese Communist Party are locked in a contest that will shape the century ahead. Not simply for markets or for influence, but for the rules and values that govern the modern world. The CCP has made the expanse of its ambitions unmistakably clear. Xi Jinping's government has fused economic, technological, and military power into a single system of control. One that uses innovation to crush individuals and entrench the party's authority. They're building a surveillance state as they export repression abroad while consolidating control at home. And they are doing so with the help of Western technology. Semiconductors, software, and tools originally designed for progress that are now being used in turn towards repression. That's the challenge we face. Ensuring that America's openness, ingenuity and free enterprise are never again weaponized to strengthen an authoritarian rival. We cannot afford complacency or nostalgia. Engagement has not moderated the CCP. It has emboldened it. And while economic ties have grown, so too has Beijing's willingness to threaten our allies, steal our technology, and undermine international norms.*

The fight is on.

BRIEFING TWO

The Battle for You and Your Freedom

"Make no mistake: this is China versus the world. We and our allies will neither be commanded nor controlled."
~ U.S. Secretary of the Treasury Scott Bessent

You and your family have been on the front lines of a war you didn't know you're in. You feel it. It's been building. The incidents you read about in the previous chapter suddenly do not feel isolated at all. You are beginning to understand what I began to understand years ago during that FBI intelligence briefing. This war is here.

"We will weaponize everything against the West."
~ Xi Jinping, Chairman, Chinese Communist Party

When the Chairman of the Chinese Communist Party (CCP) in China says he will weaponize everything, he literally means everything. You will see in the following chapters that *the modern battlefield is everywhere.*

It's CCP doctrine, and it's been unfolding for decades. The war is about the air your children breathe, the apps on their phone, the thoughts in their head, the pills in their schools, parties, and streets, the money in your wallet, the water in your faucet, the light switch on your wall, your brain, your soul, and your right to speak your truth without fear of being silenced or imprisoned.

The Chinese Communist Party (CCP) is a radical, dark, and diabolical mafia-type criminal gang - the most strategic, lethal, committed, and capable in history. They are not preparing for war "someday." They are waging a deadly war against every institution and value that has anchored our civil society.

But the terrifying part is that most Americans, Brits, Europeans, Canadians, Aussies, Kiwi's, Latins, Africans - all free people - don't know the big picture and that they're in the fight. And we have less than 10 years to win. It's either that, or we lose the world and all freedom so many before us fought to preserve.

Unrestricted Warfare and Disintegration Warfare

The origins of unrestricted war is something that every American and Western citizen must understand.

In 1999, two senior colonels in China's People's Liberation Air Force, Qiao Liang and Wang Xiangsui, wrote the now infamous manual called "Unrestricted Warfare." They knew then what is true now: America is devoted to firepower and we're damned good at it. Aircraft carriers. Bombers. Missiles. Artillery. What is called conventional or kinetic warfare. The authors knew that China would not be able to beat the U.S. for many decades, so they redefined war itself. They changed the game.

As they write in the opening of the book:

This kind of war means that all means will be in readiness, that information will be omnipresent, and the battlefield will be everywhere. It means that all weapons and technology can be superimposed at will, it means that all the boundaries lying between the two worlds of war and non-war, of military and non-military, will be totally destroyed.

In other words, it's an everywhere and everything war. As illustrated in the previous chapter, the CCP grounded their thinking in the ancient military wisdom of Sun Tzu. And then, they used "The Art of War" to engineer a playbook of how the CCP could defeat America and the West. They laid out a plan to dominate the world without firing a single shot. If the playbook worked, it would cripple America's ability and its resolve to fight. And if it ever did come to a shooting war, America would be so hobbled from the start that it would not be able to recover.

"The supreme art of war is to subdue the enemy without fighting.
The greatest victory is that which requires no battle."
~ Sun Tzu, The Art of War

"Unrestricted Warfare" determined that the U.S. was vulnerable because we view war too narrowly. To win today, they argued, modern war needed to be redefined as "using all means, including non-armed force, armed force, non-military, military, and non-lethal or lethal methods" to compel an enemy to capitulate and accept their goals.

Colonel Qiao was quoted as stating that: "The first rule of unrestricted warfare is that there are no rules, with nothing forbidden."

Unrestricted war follows a continuum from the least noticeable tactics to increasingly noticeable assaults with conventional war being optional, only used at the end. We are nearing that end.

Meanwhile, there are no rules, no borders, and no limits. Everything is weaponized and there is only one goal: total victory. There is no sportsmanship, no obedience nor respect for international law nor treaty, and certainly no moral compass.

The book "Unrestricted Warfare" outlines twenty specific methods of waging war, including economic war, cyberattacks, financial and market manipulation, drug trafficking, bio-attacks, cognitive war, cultural destruction, fomenting social unrest, media propaganda, the manipulation of public opinion, and lawfare, to name a few. Today, there are over 100 methods. To add insult to injury, unrestricted warfare tactics exploit the openness and legal protections of democratic societies. They use our own laws and virtues against us to force their objectives (aka “lawfare”).

Unrestricted warfare is known by other names, such as hybrid warfare, asymmetric warfare, irregular warfare, and others. No matter what you call it, Colonels Qiao and Wang illustrate clearly that non-military methods can be far more destructive than bombs. An economic collapse, a viral outbreak, or a coordinated cyber blackout could paralyze a superpower effectively. Combined, they would be devastating.

As thoroughly illustrated in Briefing One and as you will see further ironed out in the coming chapters, the blueprint has been tested and implemented in increments, and it’s working well.

“Unrestricted Warfare” was the ideological groundwork for the CCP’s playbook. Where “Unrestricted Warfare” said “everything is a weapon,” what is termed “Disintegration Warfare” or “Collapse Warfare” (2010) by military theorist Li Er Bing and published by the People’s Liberation Army’s publishing arm, instructs on how to weave all those methods and weapons into a single net and pull the enemy apart from the inside. It details how to combine finance, propaganda, and legal warfare systematically to fracture alliances, paralyze governments, sow mistrust, and leave an adversary rotting from within before the first shot is fired - or so no shot ever has to be fired.

“Unrestricted Warfare” is broad and almost theoretical. Disintegration or Collapse Warfare is operational. It identifies precise levers - political capture, economic seduction, lawfare, psychological manipulation, media control - and explains how to synchronize them so an enemy disintegrates without realizing what’s happening.

“Unrestricted Warfare” threw open the arsenal; Disintegration Warfare taught the CCP how to aim that arsenal’s weapons directly at countries and coalitions (i.e. NATO, ASEAN).

We can see the application of both military strategy works today: TikTok hollowing and reprogramming minds. The Belt and Road Initiative hollowing economies and installing authoritarians. Lawfare hollowing sovereignty and protecting State criminal networks. A population that no longer trusts its leadership or itself. Disintegration Warfare is doing its job.

"All war is based on deception"
~ Sun Tzu

Another way of describing unrestricted warfare is a term we first used in Briefing One: "Gray Zone Warfare, which identifies war that is executed without declaring war, in the "gray zone" between peace and war.

The CCP hacks our companies, government data, and powergrids. They buy our politicians, flood our streets with fentanyl, rewrite our history books in our schools, sabotage our alliances, and hijack our kids' minds, values, and attention on social media. No troops, tanks, or bombs. No headlines. A constant drip of silent sabotage until we wake up on our knees, weakened, confused, helpless - ready to submit.

The term, "death by a thousand cuts?" It originated in China.

This is its modern incarnation.

The dark genius of Gray Zone Warfare is that it looks like normal life. A constant stream of seemingly unrelated events, none big enough to trigger a national response. Trade deals to promote co-prosperity with our partner, the big friendly Panda, while they steal our trade secrets and our strength. Student visas give access to our most advanced university research in the name of friendly cooperation to Chinese students. But those students have been forced to swear allegiance to the CCP before they were permitted to travel here. Apps are designed by the CCP to infiltrate our kids' minds and track them, while our apps and cultural information are blocked by the Great Firewall of China. Cultural exchanges become smuggling routes for communism via seemingly innocuous presentations, performances, and lectures. Our cultural production is intimidated. Our industrial infrastructure is flooded with cheap products, destroying our economy.

It feels random, but every move is coordinated, directed, and weaponized by the CCP.

Why have we let this - some would call it "slow suicide" - happen? The answer has a few parts.

First, we've desperately wanted to believe that cooperation would soften up the CCP and it would lose its iron grip on their populace. That they would have a "peaceful rise" while moving towards democracy. They dangled the possibility before us. We were played.

Second, China's a huge market, "the world's factory." Our business leaders don't want to risk losing billions of shareholder value as well as personal wealth. The truth: China's population is much less than their reported 1.4 billion.

Third, many of our political leaders are compromised with CCP campaign contributions ("elite capture"), family investments in Chinese companies, massive Chinese investment in their family businesses, and lobbying money.

Fourth, we flatly refuse to believe that China has their gunsites pointed at our entire way of life because we are busy living our good lives, and naturally assume the same of others. We were not raised as communist ideologues bent on world domination and the crushing of civil society and the individual soul. Their whole mindset feels so alien to us that we suffer from cognitive dissonance. We find it hard to believe it's real. But it is.

Fifth, frankly, being targeted is not only alien to us, but it's so genuinely scary that people remain in denial for as long as they can, at their own expense. Our aversion to digesting these facts is another form of a survival instinct: fear is corrosive. But denial, much more so.

Sixth, no one has connected the dots - until now.

Until these pages.

The West's potentially fatal error has been that our institutions think and operate in silos. Additionally, we have rotating leadership and shifting partisan objectives.

TikTok? It's just a harmless teen app. We promote free speech, right?

Fentanyl? It's just another drug crisis caused by junkies and Mexican smugglers.

Spy balloons? Just a stunt. How much damage can a balloon do after all?

IP theft at U.S., UK, EU, AUS, and Canadian companies? Just a few bad eggs trying to make a few extra bucks.

Confucius Institutes at universities and middle school classrooms? Just innocent cultural outreach.

But these are not isolated annoyances. They are weapons deployed in a single, coordinated war. And the damage compounds daily while we stay distracted with work and sleep.

It can be and has been argued that unrestricted warfare begins with cognitive warfare, which is the battlefield for your mind. Cognitive warfare is a constant, invisible, corrosive effort, not merely to tell you what to think, *but how to think.* Day-by-day, it erodes your ability to rationalize clearly and to question narratives.

Is a man a man? A woman a woman? Who is my friend? Who is my enemy? How can I really tell? What's real? What's the truth? What's good? Is my country good? What's an American, anyway? Who should I trust? Who should I not? What should I believe? What do I believe? Cognitive warfare raises doubt about everything we might otherwise believe is true. It permanently destroys your critical thinking ability to determine what is real and renders one totally complacent and accepting of poisonous narratives.

When you can't trust any institution, value or authority, what's left? Isolation and suspicion. And an isolated individual is the easiest prey for propaganda. That's where cultural warfare swoops in, designed to subvert our shared values and trust in our institutions (e.g. anything that can resist totalitarian communist rule).

Government? Corrupt. Religion? Mocked and spat upon.

Police? Laws? Demonized and defunded.

Family? Fractured. Despised. Through social media and bot farms, the CCP poisons the cultural bloodstream with Marxist ideology camouflaged as "equity," "social justice," and "democratic socialism." The language is designed to sound compassionate, but it's a linguistic Trojan horse for the dissolution of social order in preparation for absolute control by a centralized authority. Social media is deployed as cultural debilitation. TikTok, WeChat, "study apps," online games all are data-harvesting, behavior-shaping, mind-altering, propaganda-pumping machines. Algorithms are perfected to drive dopamine addiction, instill rage, divide us from each other, foment violence and despair. Even, as you will see, teenage suicide. Now add to that AI and algorithmic amplification, and the CCP gains brain capture at massive scale.

The CCP weakens our social and mental environment, as well as our actual bodies. They quietly mainline fentanyl, nitazenes, and seemingly harmless synthetic drugs and vapes into the bloodstream of our nation. These deadly chemicals are shipped en masse to the West under CCP cover, moved by cartels, laundered by CCP/crime syndicate networks, and sold in our streets. They don't only kill over 125,000 military-aged young Americans a year, they destroy families and communities. Combine that with toxic-chemical-drenched weed grown in thousands of secretive CCP grow houses here in the U.S. and the damage multiplies beyond measure.

The end result? A traumatized, dumbed down, dulled, doubt-ridden, hateful, destabilized generation and country. Think about it: a grieving, drugged-up, dopamine-addicted population doesn't fight back. It scrolls...and submits.

In these ways, the CCP is relentlessly weakening and programming our minds and bodies. Public fronts amplify the destruction. Legacy media looks away like clockwork, timid to offend.

During COVID, dissent wasn't debated openly, as it should be in an open society. It was censored, fed by CCP propaganda and intentionally falsified information. Dissenting doctors were deplatformed, whistleblowers silenced, alternative narratives shamed and buried.

With COVID, you had censorship warfare, narrative warfare and lawfare deployed all at once. And it all happened in a free and sovereign nation.

Similarly, our leaders are self-shackled, though for different reasons. Business leaders caution against offending the Chinese state for fear of losing markets and cheap supplies. Many of our political leaders are compromised, not only nationally known figures but also countless congresspeople with significant financial interests in China or cloaked campaign contributions. This is also true at the state and local government levels.

We see the damage the CCP does one dagger at a time; but they are executing them all as part of a complex web.

"Intelligence has evolved past secrets. It's about analyzing many types of data and making fast decisions in an increasingly complex geopolitical environment."

~ T. Casey Fleming

These remaining pages may scare you. And you know something, they should. Because, likely for the first time, you will see clearly how the CCP is waging war against every aspect of your life. What is about to come into focus for you are the spokes of a single nefarious wheel. Together, they form a seamless and nonstop campaign where the weapons are anything that can weaken, divide, control, or destroy.

Between the late 1970s and the early 2000s, Deng Xiaoping relentlessly pushed the principle, "hide your strength, bide your time, achieve things," emphasizing patience, a submissive posture, low-profile diplomacy, and long-term strategic planning.

But things have changed. Beijing accrued power and wealth by opening to the world of free markets and stealing the West's technology. Thus, they developed an aggressive, integrated war that is now being waged on us. On all fronts, all at once. It is a careful choreography of entrapment. A noose, every strand of which - drugs, data, dollars, ideology, technology, resources, and infrastructure - is being pulled tighter. It is designed to strangle us, and it will, unless we act.

What must be done? I won't leave you hanging. I will set forth a series of strategies to assure that the CCP's plan, so far successful, is thwarted. But this requires your full-on commitment.

As colleague Mike Studeman, Rear Admiral USN (ret.) and former Commander of the Office of Naval Intelligence, said to Congress:

> *The China problem is not "over there" but inside our very lifelines. We have been lulled into a false sense of security by co-opted entertainment, corporate and news industries exacerbated by equivocation from multiple government administrations on the true nature of the threat. The path forward will not be easy, he warns. It will be an ongoing struggle, because the tentacles of the CCP are already planted deep within our systems. We must not drift into complacency...we must know the beast which lives within and among us. And that beast is the CCP.*

The CCP Totalitarian Communist State is not a Competitor - it is a Diabolical Enemy

Here's the hard truth: despite their decades-old publicity campaign, the CCP is not engaged in a "peaceful rise" as "a tough but friendly competitor." It is a one-party, rigorously atheistic, autocracy that openly claims total control over every breath of life on planet Earth. The Party's own slogan spells it out: "Party, government, military, civilian, and academic, north, south, east, west, and center, the Party leads everything." Written into the CCP Constitution in 2017, it is the ideological spine of Xi's China and the absolute negation of individual conscience, pluralism, freedom, and faith.

China is rated severely "Not Free," scoring 9 out of 100 on Freedom House's global index. It also identifies China as among the very worst on the planet for internet freedom. This is the predictable outcome when the State sets itself up as God and polices thought, speech, and worship of anything other than the State, all of which are prosecuted as serious crimes.

The CCP's sales pitch in the West has been delivered in sweet talk: "equity," "win-win," and "social harmony;" but their inhumane operating system fundamentally cannot adapt to democracy and freedom. In fact, freedom is a direct threat to communism that must be completely eliminated.

"We owe the success of our Party...to the fact that Marxism works," Xi said in his report to the 20th Party Congress. The model he calls "Marxism" is actually a one-party totalitarian dictatorship preserved through a brutally controlled state-led capitalist influx: a vast market micro-managed to support the Party's goals. If you step out of line, you get "disappeared," or worse. Ask Jack Ma.

The CCP is not strictly "a party," as we commonly use the term. Political economist Chenggang Xu grew up amid the horrors of China's Cultural Revolution and was beaten, tortured, imprisoned, and subjected to years of forced labor by the (CCP). Today, he is a senior research scholar at the Stanford Center on China's Economy and Institutions and author of the book, "Institutional Genes: Origins of China's Institutions and Totalitarianism." He lays it out:

> *The so-called communist party is not a political party in the common sense...by definition, a political party is a party within political competition [where] multiple political parties compete to gain the votes for power. But a communist party violates all of these definitions. A communist party does not allow other organizations to exist. It controls all organizations. It's not within; it's above. All*

the organizations have to be controlled by the communist party, entering and exiting the party are not voluntary.

Xu goes on to detail how the party organization is Leninist in origin, exported from Moscow, and built on a pre-revolution terrorist organization called "People's Will." In other words, it is a criminal syndicate.

Furthermore, its military was built on top of an older secretive society called the Brotherhood Society. The CCP, therefore, from its very origin, is not a political party. Rather, by nature, it is a structure and culture. It is a secretive, violent, terrorist, top-down mafia. You may soon think of the word, "diabolical," as I do, when you hear the term "CCP."

The CCP does not allow and will not allow anyone to organize anything outside the party, including religious groups. For example, says Xu, "a Catholic must obey the communists; the Buddhists and the temples must obey the communists. Anyone trying to have an independent organization or their own ideas is going to be eliminated."

This is especially true with the Falun Gong, a peaceful organization combining meditation, exercises, and moral teachings rooted in Buddhist and Taoist traditions, as you will learn in horrific detail in Briefing Nine. Falun Gong is the parent organization of Shen Yun dance troupe which has the tagline "China before communism."

The West has blinded itself, wanting to see China's growth as capitalist modernization arcing toward freedom. But that is an illusion that has long faded by anyone who studies China carefully. As Xu says, "Under this kind of regime, it's impossible to transform peacefully into democracy because democracy has to have a civil society. Civil society means independent organizations; only when citizens organize themselves do they have power. So when no one can organize anything, no one can have power. This is the key to understanding totalitarianism."

China's economic growth is strictly chained to communist control. Despite the glitz of gleaming skyscrapers, drone shows, and fast trains, every human being in China must submit to total surveillance, dependence, obedience, and CCP control.

The reality grows darker. To really know the - and I use the term advisedly - "satanic" nature of the CCP, you have to know the scale and depth of brutality, misery, and murder the Chinese communists have imposed on their own people.

Indeed, Mao Zedong's utopian experiments erased human life at a scale that has outpaced Hitler and Stalin combined. Mao's "Great Leap Forward," with its forced collectivization and impossible quotas, triggered the deadliest engineered famine in recorded history. Historian Frank Dikötter estimates at least 45 million deaths from 1958 to 1962 alone *(over 30,000 deaths per day)*. Let that sink in.

Then, partly to distract from the catastrophic economic failure of the "Great Leap Forward," Mao instituted a Cultural Revolution which weaponized children against parents and students against teachers. Mass persecutions, public humiliations, and murderous purges killed another 1-2 million people. For over one brutal decade, it wrecked a proud civilization's memory, even incinerating books, art, and other relics of an ancient and remarkable history.

The Cultural Revolution was nothing less than a war on China's soul. Mao targeted what he branded the "Four Olds:" old ideas, old culture, old customs, and old habits - the four pillars of an ancient, dignified civilization stretching back millennia. These values were now targets. Under this slogan, anything that carried memory, tradition, or meaning became fair game for annihilation or incineration (including people.)

How did Mao do it? He unleashed a generation of indoctrinated youth, the Red Guards, against their own families, teachers, and neighbors. Armed with Mao's "Little Red Book," they rampaged through cities and villages, smashed temples, burned ancestral tablets, destroyed priceless works of art, ransacked libraries, and tore down monuments. "Destroy the Four Olds, Establish the Four News" was their rallying cry, a license to erase history, destroy at will and remake society in Mao's twisted image.

How awful was it? Wearing glasses could get you beaten or killed, because spectacles meant you might read "old books." A small family heirloom was enough to identify you as a class enemy, marking you for torture or death. Students dragged professors through the streets, forced them into humiliating "struggle sessions," or beat them to death with their own hands.

Even Confucius, the sage who had guided Chinese thought for 2,500 years, was branded a villain; his hometown was ravaged. The Red Guards stormed cemeteries, dug up corpses, and desecrated the dead. Any continuity with the pre-communist past was treason.

The CCP instituted broad, state-sanctioned barbarism. Mao understood that to rule absolutely, he had to hack off the roots of Chinese civilization itself. The "Four Olds" campaign, the systematic demolition of history, memory, and morality, represented an act of cultural genocide.

Historians estimate that two million souls were murdered outright, with tens of millions more persecuted, imprisoned, or driven into exile during this frenzy.

FACT: Since their founding in 1925, the CCP is responsible for more than double the murders of all other communist regimes in history *combined.*

They severed a civilization from its past, murdered the storytellers and historians, incinerated their books and doctrines, and taught an entire nation to kneel before the communist Party as its only god. Mao demanded that China forget who it was, so it could worship only him and his despotic apparatus.

Today's CCP continues that logic, only with new and far more advanced tools:

- **Total Surveillance and the Social Credit System:** In Xi's China, every move is recorded. American technology was weaponized for Digital ID, facial-recognition software, cameras that blanket the landscape, and AI that scrapes faces, actions, online speech, and data - all at speed. The infamous social credit system rewards obedience while punishing any hint of dissent. It blocks "untrustworthy" citizens from their money; they are prevented from buying train tickets, traveling, enrolling kids in schools, or even accessing the internet. Dissent is algorithmically erased until there is total compliance and submission.
- **Violent Repression in Xinjiang:** The UN High Commissioner for Human Rights found "serious human rights violations" that "may constitute...crimes against humanity," including arbitrary mass detention, forced indoctrination, and the crushing of religion and culture. Millions of Uyghurs (Chinese Muslims), Tibetans, Falun Gong, and Kazakhs live under permanent suspicion, with reports of sterilization campaigns, mosque demolitions, children separated from their parents, and "re-education" (torture).
- **Forced Labor Supplying the West:** A state-run pipeline has moved hundreds of thousands of Uyghurs into factories across China. CCP members move into incarcerated Uyghur homes to replace the father of those families, furthering total indoctrination and submission. Workers live under slave-like poor conditions, 24/7 surveillance, are forced into political study sessions after long shifts of the 9-9-6 work week (9 a.m. - 9 p.m., 6 days per week with 15 minute lunch breaks), and are denied freedom of movement. These factories produce goods for global supply chains - meaning Western consumers unknowingly buy products tainted by coercion and extensive human suffering. Suicide is rampant.

- **Repression Without Borders:** Freedom House calls China the global leader in "transnational repression," documenting 272 incidents of stalking, intimidation, threats, and even physical assaults against critics living abroad. Families back in China are harassed, detained, and beaten to silence those who dare to speak out overseas. Beijing's control is not bounded by its borders - it follows dissidents everywhere. Even recently, there were, at last count, 40 CCP police stations throughout the U.S., on sovereign U.S. soil, to facilitate communist espionage, infiltration, and targeted persecution of anyone, including U.S. citizens who hinder the CCP's aggressive progress of total takeover.
- **The 'Live" Human Organ Harvesting (Murder) Industry:** An independent tribunal in London concluded in 2019 that "forced organ harvesting has been committed for years throughout China on a significant scale," targeting Falun Gong practitioners, Uyghurs, and "infant farms" where babies are farmed with the DNA of the future donor recipient. Another word for "live" or "forced" in this case is "murder." Medical researchers have found troves of published papers indicating that donors were killed by the extraction itself. Estimates suggest well over 100,000 transplants annually, far above official figures. To date, the total estimate of forced organ harvesting deaths far exceeds three million. This is state-run murder-for-profit - organs for order, disguised as healthcare. In the book, "Killed to Order: China's Organ Harvesting Industry and the True Nature of America's Biggest Adversary," Senior Editor of the Epoch Times, Jan Jekielek reports on the CCP's organ harvesting industry.

My esteemed colleague, a governmental advisor, hedge-fund manager, and leading strategic global forecaster David Murrin recently summarized the CCP's strategic assault on the West to me in one quick, clear blurt:

The CCP plans to dominate the world. It considers independence, individual thought, and democracy to be a virus - freedom and decision-making as a threat. And they have constructed a system of social engineering to ensure that the system obeys them. It ensures the people at the top control everyone else. If you dissent, you are removed. In China, their software picks up the few individuals, like ourselves, who would speak out against them. It removes them and their 'genes,' so that the gene pool will obey them. We can already see how effective their system is, because they applied it to the Uyghurs. They tortured them, conditioned them, sterilized them, things which, honestly, everyone should be jumping up and down about in woke camp; but no one seems to take any notice. They subdued a population of 12 million people - that's equivalent to the entire population of Greece or Sweden.

That, Murrin, correctly points out was just a test run:

Then they took that technology and went to Hong Kong. Six generations of democracy and capitalism crushed in three months! Bang: leaders arrested. Peaceful gatherings unpeacefully wrecked. Newspapers, journalists, and media: crushed. The history of Hong Kong was gone with a whimper. The system works. Now the CCP has the proven engineering to go to any country in the world and subjugate it. No one's ever had this ability. Yes, Germany and the Soviet Union did it – crudely. But this is precision, clinical subjugation of a population by removing individuals. As many as they want. The only thing that's held them back from this expansionary process has been American power.

Which, Murrin, confirms, is exactly why they developed their Unrestricted Warfare doctrine:

The only way they could break through the American imposed glass ceiling was to covertly induce us to invest in them to get cheap manufacturing and keep our inflation down. They then nicked everything we had, whether it was IP, the manufacturing bases, or, through their extraction process with 200,000 hackers with IQs over 150, stripped everything of ours that moved. Then they used their new manufacturing base and stolen tech to create an arms race. And just when the arms race really accelerated, they released a pandemic to destroy our debt dynamics.

Murrin is as impressed as he is alarmed by the CCP's long term strategy. He adds:

At the same time, they developed, dominated, and kept in reserve rare earths and rare earth processing. And now, just when we are learning that the CCP is not a competitor but a mortal adversary, and want to rearm, just as we are waking up, the very things we needed to rearm - rare earths -were taken from us. That is a strategic plan of depth and complexity that no one in the world has ever created. That's 30 years of precision planning.

Stanford's Professor Xu writes in a telling article entitled, "The CCP Dupes the West and We Keep Falling for It:"

The Cold War has not ended. When people thought that there was a final victory in the Cold War or even said that was the end of history, that was a misunderstanding because the Chinese communist Party is still there. Now it (the cold war), is a continuation, just in a different format.

Our opponent represents a true moral abyss. Communism isn't just another ideology. It is a spiritual war against the human soul. True to form, the CCP is anti-faith, anti-family, and anti-individual. Religion is outlawed or co-opted. Betrayal is rewarded. Neighbors denounce neighbors. Surveillance is everywhere. Freedom is destroyed. Trust vanishes. One's humanity is erased. All for a better social credit score.

That's your enemy. And it has had you in its sights. Xi Jinping calls the current moment a "once-in-a-century transformation of global order." What he means is that his plan and commitment is to globally end freedom, forever.

Global Puppetmaster

It's important to recognize that Beijing is not fighting this war to the death on its own. Senator John Barrasso has stripped away the polite fictions:

> *I view China as the puppetmaster...pulling the strings with Russia, Iran, North Korea, Pakistan, Venezuela, and the cartels. Iran manages the terrorist organizations. Beijing has architectured an axis of evil totalitarian aggressors, with itself at the center.*

China experts are unanimous in sounding the alarm. Michael Pillsbury, a senior Defense Department veteran who has served in Presidential administrations from Nixon to Obama, states flatly, "China is propping up Russia and Iran."

Retired Rear Admiral Mike Studeman says, "The CCP's political warfare efforts are a highly orchestrated, interconnected, and multi-tiered set of activities" carried out globally, every day.

Indeed, Beijing, in recent years, has increasingly positioned itself as the arsenal and protector of America's enemies, supporting proxy wars to weaken and distract the U.S. and allies in Ukraine and the Middle East.

It's clear who is now #1 out there. General Xu Qiliang boasted that Sino-Russian military ties have "reached new heights."

U.S. Secretary of State Antony Blinken confirms that "when it comes to Russia's defense industrial base, the primary contributor is China," citing Beijing's provision of "machine tools, microelectronics, [and] nitrocellulose" powering Moscow's war machine.

China is the top supplier of dual-use goods that Russia needs to reconstitute its arms industry, from electronics to propellants. "Moscow would struggle to sustain its assault...without China's support," says Blinken.

Iran's regime, too, survives because China writes the checks. In February 2024, 89% of Iranian oil exports went to China. That lifeline bypasses sanctions and pours billions into the coffers of the IRGC and its terror networks.

U.S. Treasury sanctions reveal the mechanics: millions of barrels of Iranian crude are shipped to China and the CCP. Reuters has documented the "shadow fleet" that enables this trade, dark tankers, spoofed transponders, ship-to-ship transfers. Without China's demand, Tehran would be strangled. With it, the Mullahs can keep funding missiles, militias, and murder.

Even more dependent is North Korea. In 2024, China accounted for 98% of North Korea's foreign trade. UN reports and U.S. sanctions expose ships moving banned North Korean coal and iron ore to Chinese ports, and investigative journalists caught Chinese fishing vessels illegally hiring North Korean crews. Every artillery round Kim Jong Un fires across the DMZ and every missile test into the Pacific is financed and enabled by China's protective umbrella. An umbrella America paid for through blind commerce.

Put the evidence together: to challenge, weaken, harass, and destroy the West, Beijing:

(a) fuels Russia's war industry;

(b) bankrolls terrorist Iran with oil purchases;

(c) sustains North Korea's nightmare regime through trade and sanctions evasion, while funding the Taliban and Latin American drug cartels.

This "China axis" represents a global authoritarian bloc designed to shore up America's adversaries while appearing to maintain "clean hands. "The CCP believes itself to be a master of the art of "plausible deniability."

For too long, the CCP has kept its intentions muted, leveraging the good will behind Washington's desire for "constructive engagement." Following Sun Tzu's dictum, "deceive the heavens to cross the ocean," they cloaked their "Hundred Year Marathon" in humble talk of sharing global power.

Ken Cao, an ex-pat Chinese fund manager and Executive Director of the Center for Asian Democracy & Resilience, states that you don't have to look far to see through the lies:

CCP propaganda is very effective, not just at brainwashing its domestic citizens, the Chinese, but it's also very effective in deceiving Western policy makers. You need to look past what they say and look at their deeds, their actions, to tell their true intentions. For instance, when the Chinese President Xi or other Chinese diplomats meet with U.S. diplomats, they'll say, 'The China-U.S. relationship is the most important bilateral relationship. We want a win-win relationship. If we have a great relationship, it's going to benefit the people of both countries. And we have no intention to change the world order.' Western policymakers hear that, those words, and they believe it. 'Oh, China doesn't have any bad intentions against us, they want a win-win relationship.' But you must look at their actual deeds. They're selling dangerous weapons or helping countries like North Korea develop nukes. They are propping up regimes in Iran. They're selling fentanyl to the U.S., they're gutting U.S. manufacturing, they're stealing intellectual property, they're slapping tariffs of various kinds on U.S. goods. Their deeds tell a completely different story than what their propaganda is telling us.

According to Michael Pillsbury, their admission of a desire for a multi-polar world has always been a lie. "The Communist Party is realizing its long-term goal of restoring China to its 'proper' place in the world. The CCP is now much more open about their desire to become the single power ruling the world, perhaps because they realize it may already be too late for America to keep pace."

More and more, American national security officials are telling the truth.

"The greatest long-term threat to our nation's information and intellectual property, and to our economic vitality, is the counterintelligence and economic espionage threat from China. It's a threat to our economic security-and by extension, to our national security."
~ FBI Director Christopher Wray, 07.07.2020

Throughout this guide, note that I do not refer to the enemy as the "PRC" (People's Republic of China) or even "China," but rather the CCP. That's because the true adversary, the true criminal, is the CCP regime, not the Chinese people, who are suffering more than we are in the West and whose lives have been stripped of humanity, dignity, trust, and soul by the CCP. In fact, many Chinese citizens have refused to pledge loyalty to the CCP and dream of being free of its totalitarian control.

In this distinction, I am joined by former FBI Director Christopher Wray in his Opening Statement to the House Select Committee on the Strategic Competition Between the United States and the Chinese Communist Party (now the Select Committee on the CCP) on January 31, 2024.

I want to make very clear that my comments today are not about the Chinese people. And they're certainly not about Chinese Americans, who contribute much to our country and are often the victims of Chinese Communist Party aggression themselves. Rather, when I talk about the threat posed by China, I mean the government of China, led by the CCP. The CCP's dangerous actions - [its] multi-pronged assault on our national and economic security - make it the defining threat of our generation.

As you are learning…

- **Your body is targeted:** The CCP funnels fentanyl, poisoned food, counterfeit drugs, synthetics, viruses, dopamine into our bloodstream.
- **Your mind is targeted:** Social media (TikTok), apps, games, censorship, propaganda debilitate our critical faculties.
- **Your survival lifelines are targeted:** Kill switches already are embedded in our water and electricity grid, internet, cyber.
- **Your faith is targeted:** Mocked, outlawed, subverted and to be replaced by Party worship.
- **Your family is targeted:** Fractured, depressed, rebellious, dumbed-down and destabilized.
- **Your economic future is targeted:** Mortgaged to an authoritarian regime that believes it must destroy America to regain its supposedly rightful global power position.

Chairman Xi isn't hiding the CCP's ambitions any longer. He's been decoupling from the U.S. by stockpiling grain, buying up land near our military bases, mobilizing civilians, buying off foreign leaders, purging military officers who are too soft on the West, pushing his borders outward in the South China Sea, building the largest military arsenal in the world to rival ours, and openly declaring a "People's War against America."

The war is total. It is personal. And it is rolling out at full speed.

My only question is this: will you take action?

BRIEFING THREE

The Battle For Your Body
Biological War

"Biology will become the new strategic commanding heights of national defense."
~ General He Fuchu
PLA Academy of Military Sciences

The Chinese Communist Party (CCP) has declared war on every human body - every man, woman, and child in the world, including what the ruling Han Chinese consider "inferior" races inside China and throughout the world. *If you're not Han Chinese, you are the enemy.*

I'm not sharing this as a metaphor or tin-foil "conspiracy theory." As you will see. It is actual CCP doctrine.

They don't need bombs to achieve global supremacy when they can poison your bloodstream, rot your lungs, and destroy you, your community, and even your ethnicity with deadly viruses. They can hijack your brain, kill your food supply, lock down your economy, harm your elections, and addict and murder your children with monstrously potent illicit drugs.

Under the doctrine of Unrestricted Warfare, the everything and everywhere battlefield includes your physical body itself. Across China, virology labs, genetic engineering, and synthetic biology have been weaponized against you, the citizen.

Colleague and former U.S. Army microbiologist Dr. Sean Lin says, "The CCP's greatest weapon is that Americans still believe biology is about medicine. For Beijing, biology is about power."

That power resides, as all power does, in China, and in one place: the CCP. No commercial lab is strictly civilian. Under the Party's system of military-civil fusion, every company, every lab, every hospital, every doctor, and every biotech company - not to mention every Chinese national working in hospitals, labs, or pharma companies abroad - is a CCP soldier for the cause.

Anything that weakens the adversary is fair game.

COVID-19 Test Run

The Chinese Communist Party no longer hides its malicious intent around biowarfare. Frankly, after COVID, it couldn't even if it tried.

As China's economy and bravado ballooned on the back of stolen Western technology, the CCP declared in 2017 in "The Science of Military Strategy" that biology had officially become a battlefield. It brazenly envisioned the potential of "genetic specific effects," meaning weapons tailored to strike ethnic or demographic groups with precision.

General He Fuchu of the PLA Academy of Military Sciences spoke of "brain control" weapons as the future of war. General Zhang Shibo, president of the PLA's National Defense University, was even more explicit. New genetic weapons would be, to use his words, "unprecedentedly terrifying."

And back in 2015, eighteen Chinese military scientists outlined how coronaviruses could be engineered into new human pathogens and unleashed to collapse an enemy's healthcare system. That paper is entitled: "The Unnatural Origin of SARS and New Species of Man-Made Viruses as Genetic Bioweapons."

Paying attention yet?

These are not fringe voices. These are their generals and leading military scientists inscribing doctrine into policy.

Dr. Lin sums up the communist mindset in stark terms: "The CCP sees biology as a battlefield and pandemics as opportunities for dominance."

COVID-19 gave them their chance to see how to master that battlefield. Within weeks of its spread, COVID became a field test in unrestricted warfare, a live-fire experiment to measure just how far Beijing could push us, how quickly the West would fold, and how effectively the CCP could weaponize materials such as the flow of information, fear, confusion, and control to permanently tilt the global balance of power.

Let's review the facts as they rolled out:

- **Fall 2019:** The CCP leadership knows COVID-19 is human-to-human transmissible. But they delay disclosure to the outside world.
- **December 2019:** Chinese labs are ordered to stop testing, destroy viral samples, and suppress the news to every extent possible. As word starts leaking out, Beijing locks down and destroys information, refuses repeated WHO requests for access to Wuhan Institute of Virology logs, and aggressively silences anyone who speaks openly.
- **January 1, 2020:** Eight people, including medical doctors, are investigated by police for "spreading rumors" about the severity of COVID-19. In the first week of January alone, 254 Chinese nationals are charged with the same crime. Doctors who warn of transmissibility get silenced. Beijing strenuously denies human-to-human spread while international travel continues.
- **January 2020:** While denying the danger internationally, Beijing hoards PPE. Imports surge: surgical masks +278%, gowns +72%, gloves +32%. At the same time, exports collapse: surgical gloves −48%, masks −48%, gowns −71%, ventilators −45%, thermometers −53%, and swabs and cotton

balls curtailed. DHS intelligence later assesses that China intentionally concealed severity while cornering crucial supplies.

- **January 14–20, 2020:** China reaffirms the lie that there is no human-to-human transmission. The WHO, obediently, tweets the same.
- **January 19, 2020:** The first U.S. case appears in Snohomish County, Washington. A 35-year-old man recently returned from Wuhan tests positive.
- **January 22, 2020:** WHO attempts to declare a Public Health Emergency of International Concern (PHEIC). China blocks it.
- **January 23, 2020:** Wuhan goes into lockdown. But by then, Wuhan's mayor admits that five million people had already exited the city, scattering across China and onto flights bound for cities worldwide. The virus is now in motion.
- **Late January 2020:** Domestic flights from Wuhan to the rest of China are finally halted. But international flights from Wuhan continue for weeks, exporting the virus abroad.
- **January 30, 2020:** WHO votes again to issue an international warning. The CCP again tries to block it, but fails.
- **January–March 2020:** Inside Wuhan, police-enforced lockdowns are imposed. Police forcibly lock people into their homes with iron bars. Violators are publicly chained to posts. Human Rights Watch reports widespread abuses.
- **February 9, 2020:** Fang Bin, a Wuhan businessman who films corpses piling up at hospitals, is disappeared.
- **Early 2020:** Chinese "expert consensus" claims ventilators are the first choice for moderate and severe cases. Panic spreads in the West. Governor Andrew Cuomo demands ventilators. Jared Kushner pushes to buy 100,000 in 100 days. China "donates" 1,000 units to New York City. Doctors soon realize the disaster: ventilated patients - especially older ones - die at rates exceeding **97.2%.

- **Mid-March 2020:** Western reporters from the New York Times, Wall Street Journal, and Washington Post are expelled from China.
- **May 2020:** The New York Times reports 3,600 U.S. first responders dead from lack of protective gear which has been hoarded by the CCP in China.
- **September 2020:** 42% of U.S. nurses still report shortages of basic equipment like masks and gowns. WHO admits the shortages endangered health workers worldwide.
- **Throughout 2020:** Chinese state media mocks U.S. shortages as "a farce" and delights in images of U.S. government agencies fighting over dwindling supplies.

And so the global nightmare unfolded.

The CCP's method - conceal, delay, exploit, weaponize and hide behind plausible deniability - directly causes millions of deaths.

Whether the genetically altered COVID-19 pathogen was released intentionally or by accident, the CCP took advantage of the outbreak, turning it into a weapon release: the CCP planned and orchestrated chaos by seeding the world with the virus.

To review:

- It silenced its own doctors and punished its citizens for speaking.
- It expelled foreign reporters to ensure only the Party's narrative would spread.
- It hoarded masks and gloves while telling the world there was no danger.
- It pushed other countries to keep borders open, helping local outbreak become a global crisis.
- It vetoed WHO warnings until the virus had spread globally.
- It promoted treatments that killed patients and destabilized hospitals.
- It exported authoritarian lockdowns as a model to be admired, then mocked America for adopting them.

And through it all, the West complied. U.S. media outlets cravenly echoed China's false claims that Beijing had "conquered COVID" by Spring 2020. Imperial College of London - long a CCP partner institution - published dire projections of millions of U.S. deaths, based on intentionally faulty Chinese data, driving people onto lethal ventilators and turning everyone else's home into prisons. Those lie-driven projections drove the most severe shutdowns, with all its resultant economic and psychological destruction, in modern Western history.

Meanwhile, the CCP donated surveillance drones to U.S. police departments, carrying loudspeakers to enforce lockdown orders. "Authoritative" CCP voices claimed that only authoritarian methods worked, chiding America openly as chaotic, divided, and weak.

CCP leaders were quite clear that they saw the pandemic as a prime opportunity to test unrestricted warfare tactics. Li Shenming, a deputy director of the Twelfth National People's Congress, wrote in the summer of 2020 about the pandemic: "international struggles are entering an age of unrestricted warfare waged in all fields, directions and dimensions."

He saw China's role during the outbreak as being the one voice in charge, stating "It is China, in the final analysis, that is in control of this important period of strategic opportunity for development."

The virus was, as he wrote, "deeply revealing of the decadent and declining nature of the capitalist system and values in the U.S.... The key lies in which country can outlast the other.'"

COVID-19 quickly became a test run to experiment how China could "outlast" the West. Once the virus was released, the CCP took actions that amounted to pouring gasoline on the world while everybody else was fighting the fire.

And they have never been held accountable.

Where did the virus begin? No lost bats or pangolins or "wet market" street conditions birthed this scourge.

The Wuhan Institute of Virology synthesized it. The lab's history reveals multiple layers of CCP perfidy. The lab itself was originally pitched as a French-Chinese cooperative project, but quickly morphed into a CCP/PLA-controlled fortress. French scientists were promised access, but once the facility opened, the CCP locked the French out.

Alain Mérieux, the French billionaire who was fooled into investing in the project, resigned, announcing that it had become a thoroughly Chinese tool.

The virus itself, whose spike protein bound most strongly to human ACE-2 receptors, not their original animal host, which is how all zoonotic viruses behave in nature, was suspicious from the start. This altered virus binds to humans ten times more efficiently than SARS in 2002 or MERS in 2012, and so it spreads exponentially faster.

Make no mistake: COVID-19 is a SARS-based virus crafted to attack humans.

When Western scientists began to sound this alarm - echoing their now jailed or murdered Chinese counterparts - the CCP-propaganda chainsaw descended, and hard. Robert Redfield, former CDC Director, testified that after voicing his belief in a lab leak he received death threats, not from the CCP directly, but from colleagues. So totalizing was the CCP spy-ops campaign that one colleague of his wrote that he should "wither and die." Others branded him "racially insensitive." His words remain haunting: "I expected it from politicians. I didn't expect it from science."

Meanwhile, the cyberwar arm of the CCP was slashing its way through attempts by the West to slow or stop the march of death. The FBI and DHS both disclosed that Chinese actors were targeting U.S. COVID research, with the DOJ later charging PLA-linked hackers of vaccine-related intrusions, including getting inside vaccine-producing companies including Moderna.

Dr. Lin summarizes the integrated attacks of the CCP's Unrestricted Warfare in action, stating, "COVID was a live-fire study of how a novel pathogen degrades Western readiness, logistics, and civil order."

The lab that had once been pitched as a cooperative project had become a CCP/PLA weapons launch pad.

The CCP Military Moves Fast

While the CCP turned the pandemic into supply-chain, medicinal, informational, cognitive, and cultural warfare, it also took advantage of the chaos as a military test run for future armed conflict.

With the outbreak, the CCP's military moved quickly. By mid-2020, the United States had lost over 100,000 citizens. Whole cities were under lockdown.

And, to Beijing's great interest, our Navy was forced to withdraw from the Indo-Pacific. The U.S.S. Theodore Roosevelt retreated after an onboard outbreak, followed by the U.S.S. Ronald Reagan. For the first time in decades, U.S. carriers ceded presence in a contested theater, not to missiles or submarines, but to a virus. A bioweapon.

The CCP saw a window. Almost immediately after U.S. carriers left the region, China deployed its own Liaoning aircraft carrier battle group through the Miyako Strait off Taiwan, a show of force in waters the CCP had long wanted to dominate. At the same time, Chinese naval and air units staged deliberate incursions into international and territorial waters claimed by Japan, the Philippines, and Vietnam. In the South China Sea, the PLA accelerated its aggressive maneuvers, testing how far it could push while the world was preoccupied with fear, lockdowns (that the CCP itself engineered), and surging death counts.

Thus, COVID quickly became a stress test of Chinese military readiness. Rather than working to contain the devastation, Beijing used the cover of global chaos to probe America's vulnerabilities, measure the speed of our withdrawals and reactions, and watch how quickly our assets went dark.

To the CCP, the virus became a dress rehearsal for how to fight and win a shooting war while America is distracted and divided at home, which is something they continue to fund nonstop today. (See Briefing Eight: Cultural War)

Biowarfare Beyond Covid: The Nightmare Intensifies

COVID-19 was a warm up. A dress rehearsal.

In August 2023, researchers in Wuhan bragged in the Journal of Virology that they had engineered a new bat coronavirus strain, SMA1901, making it more lethal through nineteen rounds of "passaging" in mice. The results were chilling: 85 percent of mature mice died within a week.

The original virus already bound tightly to human cells, which made it jump with such ease into and among people. But Shi Zheng-Li's team at the Wuhan labs identified mutations in spike proteins and other genes that ramp up inflammation and also suppress immune defenses. In other words, while the world was still counting the dead from COVID-19, CCP labs were busy brewing even more deadly strands of the virus with clear potential to infect humans.

But they were not stopping there.

The CCP continues to race forward building new invisible arsenals: bio-weapons that cross borders without passports, slip through airports without alarms, and hide inside "dual use" research (it looks innocent and commercial, but can be turned into military mechanisms of death).

These bio-weapons move fast, blend into commerce and medical science, and stay below thresholds that would trigger a traditional military response from our leadership.

CCP military labs are currently experimenting with new pathogens far deadlier than COVID, viruses like Nipah. Nipah belongs to the henipavirus family, carried by fruit bats, and is terrifying because it causes rapid, severe multi-organ damage, including brain swelling and respiratory failure, with fatality rates reaching up to 80%. Its lethality is amplified because its incubation is deceptive. Symptoms begin like a flu, but then spiral into suffocation from the inside out, violent fevers, and catastrophic swelling of the brain. Patients slip into confusion, delirium, and seizures. Many fall into a coma within days. For survivors, permanent brain damage is common. There exists no vaccine. No cure. No proven treatment.

The CCP claims they are "researching cures" for Nipah but here's where their dual-use (military-civil fusion) engineering becomes a threat to our whole way of life. Next time, they probably won't wait for these deadly pathogens to spread "slowly" like COVID. Dr. Lin and other experts report that the CCP has developed nanotechnology delivery platforms to turn the next plague into an engulfing, airborne tsunami of death.

How does this nanotech work? Picture a rush-hour street. A drone hums overhead, no different from a thousand others, say, delivering packages. But this one releases an invisible cloud of tiny particles, structures so small that a speck of dust is gigantic by comparison.

Medicine uses these particles to sneak drugs into hard-to-reach places in the body. But in the wrong hands, the same trick can deliver a virus like Nipah into the human body in multiple ways. Nanobots can slip past the immune system, carrying biological warheads that shut down organs with pinpoint precision. The drones can release millions of these viral invaders. Crowds inhale them on the streets and in their cars, unaware. Hours and days later, fevers, seizures, and lung collapse spread through the city, while the delivery particles dissolve, leaving zero trace.

That's only one scenario. Now imagine an office tower or the Pentagon. CCP sponsored actors pump nanoparticles into the ventilation system and they ride the airflow into every cubicle, every conference room, every hallway in the building. Imagine this scenario in airports, malls, theatres, and stadiums.

Western hospitals dream of using nanotech to deliver chemotherapy with perfect accuracy to cure the sick. But this weaponized payload could easily leave the entire population of the building wheezing, convulsing, comatose, or dead. Security cameras would reveal nothing.

Similarly, nano delivery could be dropped into our water supply. Deadly Nipah particles could be programmed to cling to cells inside the gut and only once they are imbibed, release the virus to devastating effect. There would be no taste, no smell, nothing unusual in the glass. Parents would hand the water to their children, believing it to be clean. Days later, emergency rooms would fill with patients gasping for air, their brains swelling, their bodies dying.

And no one would know the water was the weapon.

The CCP may not even need drones. They have engineered a more familiar weapon. CCP vast mosquito engineering projects already provide a ready means for release. Mosquitoes are being bred as delivery drones. Imagine a world where every mosquito bite becomes a potentially lethal infection point, a carrier of a whole host of pathogens and neurotoxins (they are currently deriving them from snake venom). And the picture darkens further. With CRISPR tools now being used at the level of chromosomes, entirely new pathogens can be designed with "programmable" traits: who they infect, how fast they kill, how long they remain dormant. According to Dr. Lin:

The COVID-19 pandemic generated massive social upheaval inside the United States, destabilized the Presidency of Donald Trump, and left enduring political fragmentation inside the American political system and broader society. It is a reasonable assumption that the CCP closely observed, analyzed, and has fully assessed the 'whole of system degradation effects' that a novel pathogen can have on American society. The impact of a weaponized Nipah virus inside of the United States...would completely eclipse that of COVID-19.

COVID was the rehearsal. Nipah would be the headline act.

They are coming after our bodies, yes, but they are also coming after our foods, our eco-systems, and the very life-systems that sustain us. In a recent post on CCP bio-sabotage, retired CIA Officer Rick de la Torre writes correctly:

> *For three decades, we've been under attack - and most Americans still don't know it. While Washington argues over tariffs and spy balloons, China has been quietly waging biological sabotage, flooding our forests, waterways and farms with invasive species that cripple industries, degrade ecosystems, and drain billions from our economy. What began as ecological nuisance has evolved into strategic sabotage. And we're still treating it like a paperwork problem.*

As de la Torre details, the emerald ash borer and spotted lanternfly are tiny, but they are mighty and precise China-imported economic weapons. Causing over $60 billion in nationwide losses, the ash borer has systematically decimated American urban forests and agricultural regions. Denver alone faces over $1 billion in removal and lost canopy value. The lanternfly has caused agricultural losses in Pennsylvania surpassing $550 million annually, hitting New York grape growers with $8.8 million in potential devastation, and sending Georgia's $3.5 billion fruit markets teetering on collapse.

Federal prosecutors have definitively exposed the deliberate nature of these bio-attacks. In a shocking Michigan case, a Chinese national was caught smuggling fusarium graminearum - a vomitoxic-laced fungus into the states. This strain endangers both farms and national security by contaminating feed, spiking grain costs by $1 billion yearly, and unraveling supply chains. The Department of Justice didn't mince words: this strain represents a "potential agro-terrorism weapon."

Former diplomat John R. Mills stated in *Newsweek* that these pathogen smuggling attempts reveal nothing less than "a Chinese campaign to bring down American agriculture and food supply."

Every year, biosecurity becomes an increasingly concerning battlefield. These aren't accidents; they're precision strikes on our agriculture and timber backbone, driving up food prices, crippling rural economies, and leaving us exposed. The evidence piles up. The USDA confirms over 400 invasive species from Asia now cost us $120 billion annually in environmental devastation alone.

It goes beyond bugs: Chinese shore crabs now swarm our coasts, Asian carp devour inland lakes and fisheries, and golden mussels, freshly detected in California, threaten to choke dams, irrigation, and hydropower, ballooning infrastructure losses into the tens of billions. With aquatic invasive species contributing $120 billion annually in nationwide losses, this is deliberate, calculated economic warfare. China expert Gordon Chang says the cost of these kinds of biowarfare may end up being far worse economically than the fentanyl and COVID-19 campaigns and their follow ups. The softest underbelly of the United States turns out not to be politics or even IP theft, but biosecurity. Our food and timber industries are also now part of our battlefield, whether we like it or not.

Biotech Weaponization: What's Coming Next

Mirror, Mirror in Our Blood

U.S. Army microbiologist Dr. Sean Lin is a tireless warrior for truth, He warns that Chinese scientists are well into whole new biological frontiers. One of the most terrifying, he says, is engineering "mirror life."

In the state of nature, life obeys "a rule of handedness." Amino acids, the building blocks of protein, are on the left hand side of the DNA strand. Nucleotides, the letters of DNA, are on the right hand.

Our immune systems have been trained over millions of years to recognize these familiar shapes and patterns. But synthetic biology has now made it possible to flip them. By engineering D-amino acids and L-nucleotide constructs - the "mirror images" of what nature provides

- CCP scientists can create microbes, enzymes, and even whole chromosomes that appear utterly alien to the human body.

To our immune systems, though they are simply reversed, they are ghosts. Utterly invisible and unrecognizable. Thus, white blood cells don't attack, antibodies slide on by, and vaccines can offer no counterforce. A mirror-life pathogen could spread invisibly, 100% unchecked, leaving doctors to stare while bodies collapse before them, leaving zero diagnostic trail.

Even more insidious, Beijing has prepared for years to target specific ethnic groups with genetically altered pathogens. They have been harvesting DNA from multiple foreign populations through hospital "friendly partnerships," siphoning the genetic blueprints of millions of Americans and Europeans. Chinese hackers (2014) stole data from 80 million Americans through Anthem Insurance. The Office of Personnel Management (2015) breach exposed biometric and health records of 21 million federal employees. MyHeritage (2018) over 92 million user accounts were exposed in a breach. The 23andMe (2018) data leak exposed genetic information of approximately 1 million users. At Ancestry.com (2020) a security incident led to unauthorized access to user data, affecting millions of accounts. Several DNA testing companies have reported multiple breaches.

With all this data, mirror-life pathogens as well as other genetic killers could be tailored to attack and eradicate specific populations. They could be engineered to exploit genetic vulnerabilities of a specific ethnicity or race.

Dr. Lin confirms that Caucasians are their top target, stating, "The top enemy and the core long term strategy have never changed - no matter how friendly they act and how they embrace open markets - the CCP's aim is to destroy Western Civilization."

I'm certain that all this sounds like Hollywood science fiction, or a horror film, and frankly, it feels like both. But it's as real as it gets.

Bio-weapons are the ultimate "assassin's mace" tools, designed to strike fast, quietly, and without attribution, maximizing both damage and strategic shock.

Nanotech, gene-editing, and the synthesizing of deadly viruses are all banned in the West. However, they thrive in Wuhan, as well as other Chinese locations and axis aggressor countries. These are not defensive experiments. They are offensive asymmetric weapons designed to cripple societies, sow chaos, hold entire populations hostage and kill at scale.

In short, the CCP is building weapon systems outside the boundaries of the laws of nature, and indeed, one might say, the Laws of God. These are weapons designed to exploit blind spots within human biology. Applications of mirror life and nanotech warfare are literally demonic and potentially apocalyptic, representing the possibility of an extinction-level bioweapon, one that no immune system, no vaccine, and no existing medicine could ever stop.

The CCP is waging a whole-of-society war right down to the microscopic level of your cellular tissue. **Every American must understand: the CCP is at war with you, your children, and your body itself.** (Fentanyl murders are significantly less in other countries.)

BRIEFING THREE | PART II

The Battle For Your Body

Drug War

"If you wanted to design a chemical weapon to destabilize a country, it would look a lot like fentanyl."
~ Derek S. Maltz Sr.
Former Chief, DEA, Special Operations Division

"This is not just drug trafficking. This is chemical warfare that the PRC is waging on us."
~ Anne Milgram
DEA Administrator

"My Son Became a Casualty of a War Most Americans Never Choose
I have spent decades warning policymakers about China's strategies - from supply-chain dominance to gray-zone warfare. Yet nothing prepares a father for the moment a medical examiner looks you in the eye and tells you that your son, your pride, your blood, is now a statistic in a silent war our nation refuses to name.
The fentanyl catastrophe is not merely a public-health crisis. It is a geopolitical weapon - engineered, trafficked, and unleashed through networks linked to the Chinese Communist Party.
I am not asking for sympathy. I am asking for courage.
Courage to confront the CCP's responsibility without euphemism.
Courage to hold accountable those who enable this chemical assault.

Courage to protect our children with the urgency we would summon in the face of any foreign attack - because that is precisely what this is. The CCP will not stop on its own. And our children deserve more than silence, denial, or ceremonial condolences.
Stand firm. Speak boldly. Prepare early. Protect fiercely.
For them. For us. For love of country.
For me, the war against fentanyl - and against the CCP's malign influence - is now painfully personal. I have lost my only son to this war."
~ Dr. Rafael Marrero, Founder and Senior Fellow, Miami Strategic Intelligence Institute, Advancing Geopolitical Analysis and Policy Research

Fentanyl is a weapon of mass destruction. *A weapon of war.* It is the single deadliest drug threat our nation has ever encountered and, I regret having to add this, *"so far."* That's because the drugs the CCP is now filtering into the West are even stronger, and more deadly.

Sure, you've heard about the celebrities who have died from fentanyl - Prince, Mac Miller, Tom Petty, Lil Peep, Michael K. Williams (actor, "The Wire"), Angus Cloud (actor, "Euphoria"), Coolio (rapper), Adam Rich (actor, "Eight is Enough"), Luke Bell (country musician), Bobby Brown Jr. (musician, son of Bobby Brown), Justin Townes Earle (singer-songwriter). But this scourge spares no one, old or young, including babies. And it notoriously preys on the innocent.

According to the official U.S. government statistics, over 70,000 Americans are officially recorded as dying from fentanyl overdoses annually, but intelligence experts say the true figure is closer to 125,000-150,000 *murders* from fentanyl each year. That's more American lives lost *annually* than:

- The total of ten-year wars in Vietnam, Iraq, and Afghanistan *combined.*

- The equivalent of two loaded Boeing 737-800/900 or Airbus 321 aircraft crashing - *every. single. day.*
- Losing an entire city: Eg. Charleston, Akron, Stamford, Jackson, College Station, Palm Bay, Pomona - *every. single. year.*
- The number of deaths the U.S. had each year in World War II. *It's as if WWII never ended.*

Feel this: *350+ families attending funerals - every. single. day.* Why does our media avoid reporting this? *Ask yourself why.* It's past time to change your media sources.

Let's start with the facts:

- Fentanyl is not only a medicinal pain drug. In slightly higher doses, *it is a weapon.* It's a synthetic opioid 50 to 100 times stronger than morphine. Only 2 milligrams, the equivalent of ten *grains* of table salt, can kill.
- It is the *leading cause of death* for Americans ages 18 to 49. It's a highly efficient *weapon of war* designed to eradicate military aged men and women with minimal collateral damage. Let that sink in. In their prime of life our next generation: *wiped out.*
- In 2022 alone, fentanyl was linked to 71,000 deaths out of 100,000 total "accidental" deaths. Compare that to the Vietnam War - 56,000 killed over a decade. (Again, the actual figure is estimated to be *125K-150K murders each year).*
- The CDC confirms the scale: 2021 poisoning deaths were six times higher than in 1999. And the fentanyl curve is even steeper: *23 times more fentanyl deaths in 2022 than in 2013.* This is an *exponential* increase in destruction, *not an accident.*
- Fentanyl kills at the rate of *one American every 5 minutes.* There is no "safe dose." Fentanyl is now mixed into *nearly every street drug:* counterfeit Xanax, Adderall, Percoset, cocaine, meth, heroin, among others.
- Fentanyl deaths are becoming exponentially stronger and *more difficult to treat.* I spoke with Harry Fisher, former Army medic

and paramedic on the front lines in Oklahoma. Paramedics were usually able to revive patients with .4MG of Narcan. Now, *even 6.0MG (15X the intended dose) fails to awaken many recent cases.*

- A report issued by the American Society of Anesthesiologists, analyzing federal health data, found that over the past eight years, U.S. adults aged 65 and older have experienced a *9,000 percent increase* in poisoning deaths (murders) involving fentanyl mixed with stimulants such as methamphetamine and cocaine.
- The grief touches nearly every household. *One in three Americans* - about 100 million people - personally know someone harmed or killed by fentanyl. Fentanyl is a major factor in America's historic decline in life expectancy - courtesy of the CCP.
- The financial damage rivals the human carnage. In 2020, the opioid epidemic cost the U.S. $1.5 trillion. By 2024, that ballooned to *$2.7 trillion, nearly 10% of our GDP.* Some analyses now put the figure at $4 trillion. That's an *economic warhead detonated inside the American body politic.*

And the danger is escalating. A new synthetic opioid, nitazine, is:

- 40 to 500 times deadlier than fentanyl;
- Narcan resistant
- 250 times stronger than heroin;
- Has already killed hundreds in the U.K....

... and is now spreading into the U.S. homefront battlefield.

The thing is, you can't really *feel* the devastation by the numbers, horrific as they are. Fentanyl has slashed a vicious wound across America that bleeds into every corner of life; families are shattered, futures have been stolen, and entire communities are left lost and weeping. Parents bury children who were not reckless addicts in alleyways, but young adults who made a single mistake in just one fatal moment of trust or experimentation.

A kid who wants to score some Adderall to make it through finals or Xanax to help quell their anxiety can simply hop onto Snapchat or another social media platform and order what looks like perfectly pharma-grade pills. Then they receive silent killers in the mail or through "friends." These pills are so professionally engineered that you can no longer tell them from legal pharmaceuticals. The precursor chemicals and up-to-date industrial-scale professional pill press machines are manufactured in China and shipped to the southwestern Mexican port of Michoacán. Criminal cartels in turn, provide processing, distribution, and money laundering back to the CCP. In 2025 alone, the Mexican Marina (Navy) seized 800 tons (1.6 million pounds) of precursor chemicals originating in China. *The real question is how much actually got through.*

The threat is so overwhelming that the DEA has a program on their Home Page called "One Pill Can Kill." A slight sprinkle of fentanyl can silence a heartbeat forever. Mothers describe the shock of finding their child lifeless on the bedroom floor. Fathers hold photos at countless community and church meetings instead of the warm hands of their beloved sons. Entire towns, especially those already struggling, are losing young workers, students, and leaders before they ever have a chance to contribute to society. School counselors face classrooms full of teenagers who know someone who has been poisoned - a friend, a cousin, or a neighbor. They speak in whispers about "laced pills" and carry the quiet dread that any party, during any experiment, any mistaken pill could be their last.

Communities pour resources into treatment and prevention programs, but the sheer potency of fentanyl makes it nearly impossible to keep up. Emergency responders are drained, running from one tragic call to the next, often reviving someone only to see them collapse again later.

The economic toll compounds the emotional one. Billions are lost in productivity, healthcare, and law enforcement, but these numbers pale compared to the despair at the unseen cost: *a generation robbed of its potential.* Parents who work two jobs to cover rehab costs or funerals instead of saving for college. Grandparents raising children after losing their own sons and daughters to weaponized fentanyl. Classmates and sports teams endure more empty seats. Entire neighborhoods lose their vibrancy, replaced by fear and an aching sense of absence that never goes away. Fentanyl, and now Nitazene, hollow out the core of what makes communities thrive, leaving behind a landscape of grief and desolation.

The DEA doesn't call them "overdoses" anymore, because they're not. They call them "Accidental Poisoning Deaths." The questions you need to ask are: who is doing the poisoning, why are they doing it, *and these are murders, plain and simple.*

Chain of Custody

As mentioned, Wuhan, China remains the primary source of precursor chemicals for illicit fentanyl production in Mexico. The Sinaloa Cartel and CJNG convert Chinese precursors into powders and counterfeit pills in clandestine super-labs in Sinaloa, Jalisco, and Michoacán. Over 90 percent of fentanyl seized at the Southwest border is interdicted at legal ports of entry in vehicles and freight. FBI Director Christopher Wray testified that seizures over two years equated to lethality enough to kill 207 million Americans. *Yes, 207 million - 63% of the U.S. population.*

Former Treasury Special Agent John Cassara describes the state–criminal complex as "CCP Inc." - the world's largest producer and launderer of synthetic drug value. In 2025, Treasury and FinCEN mapped Chinese chemical sellers to hundreds of factories across China, Mexican intermediaries, and then U.S. distribution to specific banks, and trading firms.

DOJ indictments have identified PRC companies selling fentanyl precursors, nitazenes and xylazine (we'll get to these in a moment) into U.S. and Mexican networks as well as direct-to-consumer stealth shipping on Chinese social and shopping platforms. Entities include Hebei Shenghao Import & Export Co., Lihe Pharmaceutical Technology (Wuhan), Henan Ruijiu Biotechnology (Zhengzhou), Xiamen Wonderful Biotechnology, and Anhui Ruihan Technology. DOJ and Treasury materials have also named Hanhong Pharmaceutical Technology executives in xylazine, nitazene, and meth networks.

The source and supply of these drug-weapons are common knowledge. According to the U.S. House Select Committee's investigation, (Source: U.S. House Select Committee on the CCP – Fentanyl Findings) the People's Republic of China, under total CCP control, has been directly complicit in fueling America's fentanyl crisis.

Despite their protests of innocence, the CCP's pervasive surveillance and airtight financial controls make large-scale fentanyl precursor production and distribution impossible without state knowledge and/or tacit approval. Nothing happens in China without the CCP approving it. It's a hard communist regime with airtight command and control. To add insult to injury, as if spitting in our faces…

- **Subsidies:** The CCP *subsidizes* the manufacturing and exporting of illicit fentanyl materials through *tax rebates.* Many of these chemicals are illegal under PRC law. *This secret program incentivizes global narcotics sales.*
- **Rewards for traffickers:** Beijing hands out *monetary grants and awards* to companies openly trafficking fentanyl precursors. Provincial officials even tour these facilities, praising their "economic contributions."
- **Government-owned traffickers:** The CCP openly holds ownership stakes in companies tied to narcotics, including a *prison enterprise linked to human rights abuses* that owns a chemical trafficking firm, and a publicly traded company hosting thousands of illegal drug sales.

- **Shielding criminals:** Instead of prosecuting fentanyl manufacturers, CCP security services have tipped them off when U.S. investigators came asking for help.
- **Open online market:** On China's tightly-censored internet, fentanyl precursors are openly sold. A review of seven e-commerce sites found *over 31,000 listings.* Undercover probes showed sellers eager to ship to the U.S. (Remember, each must be approved by the totalitarian CCP.)
- **Only for Export:** The CCP censors keywords about domestic drug sales, but leaves export-focused content untouched. This ensures the lethal poison flows outbound.
- **Strategic gain:** The crisis enriches the CCP's chemical industry, empowers CCP-linked organized crime groups as premier global money launderers, and devastates American communities. Because of all this, U.S. Attorney Roger B. Handberg claims: "The protection of our country from the deadly scourge of fentanyl is a key priority of the Department of Justice and my office."
- And yet, and yet…

WHY ARE WE NOT FIGHTING BACK?

If the U.S. government knows exactly where the deadly flow of poison comes from, then *why does it keep pouring in?* Pay attention here, because this is where the integrated net of the CCP's Unrestricted Warfare reveals itself. You can't understand the drug war on our bodies without understanding the economic and political levers the CCP has over corporate and political leaders.

Author Peter Schweizer tied a PRC triad (mafia) facilitator of Sinaloa's fentanyl entry directly to a $5 million interest-free, forgivable loan to the Biden family. This crook is literally the business partner of the Chinese gang leader known as "the White Wolf," who has been instrumental in setting up the fentanyl trade across the U.S. Then there's Mitch McConnell, whose father in-law, through his wife Elaine Chao, owns a massive shipping business that is wholly dependent upon the good graces of the Chinese government. If McConnell says or does anything to offend the Chinese government, they could destroy the family business overnight. Hence, according to Schweizer, "he will occasionally say something kind of tough, but he will never support any action to actually deal with it." Additionally, Gavin Newsom has long associations with leaders in Chinese organized crime. The list goes on.

These politicians are not alone. CCP money has filtered into political coffers on the federal, state, and local levels across the U.S. and the West. In Schweizer's words, this kind of leverage directly "dampens political will to confront Beijing."

The United States is not bearing the brunt of this one-sided war alone. Canada reported 3,787 opioid toxicity deaths in the first half of 2024, many involving fentanyl. In Britain, nitazenes, synthetics up to 500 times stronger than heroin, are already deeply embedded in the drug supply, hidden in everything from vapes to cocaine. In one London weekend, a single clinic logged 32 related deaths. Experts warn that as many as 20,000 Britons could die within five years if nothing changes. Australia, too, has seen illicit CCP-originated drugs surface in wastewater, proof that the chemical war is spreading. *What began as an American nightmare is now a global war.*

I want to give credit to my colleagues in the DEA and thousands of patriotic Americans who are doing their best to raise awareness and fight back. But without the political will, we are shackled by financial and political imperatives from higher up.

Another challenge to forcing effective political action is that fentanyl deaths do not occur all at once like Pearl Harbor or 9/11. They arrive quietly, one body at a time. And because the carnage is spread out across towns, small cities, and isolated households, it remains "invisible." An honor student in Ohio, a baby girl in New Mexico, a young parent in West Virginia. The scourge is atomized, fragmented, ignored by the media, and denied the centralized spectacle that normally stirs national outrage.

Another challenge is narrative control and denial. Families often hide overdose deaths, fearing judgment. Politicians hesitate to hammer China's role in exporting precursor chemicals when Wall Street remains tied to Beijing's markets. Meanwhile, cartels serve as the convenient villain. Yet DEA Administrator Anne Milgram told Congress bluntly: "The Sinaloa Cartel and Jalisco Cartel, fed precursor chemicals from China, are responsible for virtually all of the fentanyl flooding into the United States."

What should be seen as chemical warfare is reframed as either "Mexican crime" or "drug abuse." The focus gets shifted. The source gets shielded. The dead bodies pile up..

A final challenge is that the American public is exhausted and distracted. The pandemic, cultural polarization, economic instability, and nonstop political crises (many stoked by the CCP - see Chapter 8) have dulled public senses. Amid the noise, fentanyl deaths are treated as background statistics, not front-page warfare. Local headlines fade. Local sheriffs sound passing alarms. Parents grieve alone.

The CCP's "Assassin's Mace" genius lies here: killing quietly, denying fingerprints, letting Americans believe the collapse is self-inflicted. Anger has no single target, so it dissipates. That is how an enemy wages war on the body and on the will to resist.

It's important to note that the dopamine addiction of social media and smartphones is commonly referred to as "digital fentanyl."

What's Even More Deadly Than Fentanyl?

The war on our bodies and the bodies of our children has recently intensified beyond Fentanyl to a surge of hyper-lethal synthetic drugs whose origins can be traced directly back to the same shadowy networks operated, subsidized, and shielded by the Chinese communist Party.

- **Carfentanil (Weapon #2) -** A compound invented as an elephant tranquilizer, Carfentanil, is so potent that one kilo could snuff out *50 million lives* in an instant. Supply chains of this poison track back to Chinese chemical factories and Triad-run networks whose exports routinely find their way onto U.S. streets.

- **Nitazenes (Weapon #3) -** A new synthetic horror, up to 40 - 500 times more powerful than fentanyl, are being actively marketed to American dealers by China-based companies, with federal indictments identifying explicit shipments and the CCP's subsidies for exporters.
- **Xylazine (Weapon #4) -** The so-called "Zombie Drug," is a veterinary tranquilizer never approved for human use. On the street it is known as "tranq," "tranq dope," or simply "zombie drug." It is not an opioid, but when mixed with fentanyl, it acts like one, slowing breath, dropping blood pressure, and shutting down the heart. The White House admits: *"There is no antidote to rapidly reverse a xylazine overdose."*

The human toll of China's drug war on the West is catastrophic. In 2024, thirty-six percent of fentanyl powder samples and nearly 6 percent of fentanyl pills seized by federal authorities were adulterated with xylazine. In Maryland alone, more than 20 percent of fentanyl deaths between 2020 and 2023 involved xylazine. The drug literally rots living flesh, producing necrosis that often ends in amputations. Tranq dismantles human beings limb-by-limb. Hospitals are unprepared; they are unable to recognize withdrawal symptoms or treat the gangrenous injuries.

Like fentanyl, the supply chain and money laundering all point straight to Beijing. U.S. Customs and Border Protection reports xylazine arriving "primarily in powder form within the air cargo and express consignment environments originating almost exclusively from companies based in the PRC."

The DEA and Department of Justice have indicted multiple China-based chemical companies for exporting xylazine alongside fentanyl precursors and nitazenes. These are not rogue actors-they are part of a broader, strategic CCP-enabled narcotics export infrastructure. *This is state-enabled chemical warfare disguised as commerce.*

American and international agencies have repeatedly tied all of these deadly drugs, and the global syndicates that peddle them, directly to Chinese criminal organizations operating with impunity and support from the CCP. Camouflaged in legitimate business fronts, hidden in stacks of fraudulent invoices, powered by virtual currency, and shielded by state policies that reward profit over life, *they are murdering our population. This act of war is a highly profitable business model fed by the blood of American lives.*

Weaponizing Weed

People generally don't think of weed as a weapon of war. But anything that is ingested, smoked, drunk, sniffed, or injected can be weaponized.

Chinese criminal networks, working with the blessing of Beijing, are flooding our country with neurotoxic weed. This is not your father's feel-good marijuana. These are strains over 10X stronger than the weed from the 70's and 80's, designed to dumb down and slow-kill Americans. Far worse, they are soaked in Chinese-manufactured toxic chemical fertilizers and herbicides so poisonous that, in many cases, law enforcement officers in California reported burning skin, nosebleeds, and neurological symptoms such as twitching eyes or neurological numbness after simply walking into secret Chinese-run grow sites.

The neurotoxins used to grow weed in these sites were so bad California's "National Guard Weapons of Mass Destruction" team had to be called in to identify the substances. Why? Because they're illegal worldwide, almost never tested for, and so deadly they don't even appear on U.S. lab panels.

Investigators traced these toxins back to intentionally mislabeled Chinese packaging, sold openly through WeChat QR codes, and shipped in bulk from China to California, then on to states like Oregon,

Oklahoma, New York, Massachusetts, and Maine where thousands of secretive CCP grow houses operate.

In Maine, cops reported the same thing when raiding Chinese-controlled grows. These cops have walked straight into clouds of toxins that have been shown to linger for years inside ordinary homes. Where these criminal grow teams have moved on, unsuspecting families have since moved in. One California police commander warned: "My teams will not go in if the garden is hot... We are not equipped for it."

They will not allow any law enforcement to enter without full hazmat suits.

These aren't minor pesticides. The list includes killers like chlorthiophos, fenobucarb, isoprocarb, procymidone, and tridemorph-agents tied to cancer, reproductive damage, and central nervous system failure. Lab tests showed marijuana sprayed with these toxins was not only sold on the black market but also slipped into the legal supply chain. And because American testing labs aren't looking for these chemicals, they can, and do, stamp poisoned products as "safe."

This stuff is being sold to your kids.

Chinese mafias coordinated with the CCP have hijacked the U.S. cannabis trade. Meanwhile, the Chinese triads running these grow farms are armed with AK-47 assault rifles, responsible for shootings in Los Angeles, Riverside, and Monterey counties. They operate on an industrial scale with vast "hoop house cities" where tens of thousands of plants are sprayed with these chemical weapons.

In Oklahoma, over 3,000 illegal farms were set up by Chinese syndicates, often using straw-man owners. Workers lived in slavery conditions: locked inside greenhouses and forced into prostitution. These grow houses are run by Chinese mafias, or triads like The 14K Triad syndicate overseas operations. *The poison gets funneled directly into American communities and homes, and the money gets funneled back to China.*

This is classic unrestricted warfare: poison the land, poison the lungs, poison the future. As one veteran national security official said, organized crime is now "doing services for the Chinese government."

The deal is simple: Beijing looks away - or quietly profits - while triads move product, launder billions of dollars, and spread toxins abroad that are not tolerated in China itself.

Americans are literally *smoking chemical weapons* designed overseas and imported through a CCP-protected logistics pipeline. Weed has become a weapon as real as a missile, only quieter, cheaper, addictive, and aimed straight at our children.

Weed is a weapon in another way: it destroys the brains, ambition, and capabilities of our youth. It's bad enough that it's a gateway to harder, more dangerous drugs, but legalization, intensification of THC, the active chemical (now up to 95% intensity in common "wax" or "butter" extracts) make what used to be an old-fashioned, seemingly harmless joint, debilitating and even deadly in ways that we've been trained to deny.

Top neuroscientist and "America's #1 Brain Doctor," Dr. Daniel Amen, has scanned over 300,000 brains. His research is clear. Marijuana does not "chill" the teenage brain, it wounds it - permanently. The human brain is not fully mature until age 25. Every puff before then is exponential in damage since the brain is in high-growth mode. It permanently chips away at the area of executive function - the very circuits of memory, focus, and motivation that a young person needs to succeed. Amen's scans show permanently diminished blood flow and activity in the prefrontal cortex, the command center for judgment, planning, and impulse control. He states: "Up to age 25, while the brain is still in high development mode, parents must protect their child's brain. After 25, the brain can protect the child." Several recent studies now show the brain continues to develop up to age 32.

This means a teenager who thinks he's only getting high is in fact numbing the very part of his brain that prevents him from becoming addicted, failing in school, or sliding into depression. What begins as "relaxation" can hardwire into lower IQ, poorer grades, slower reaction time, and higher risk of depression, psychosis, and death. In fact, a May 2024 study in the journal Psychological Medicine discovered an 11 times higher risk of developing psychosis and psychotic disorders, including schizophrenia, for marijuana users.

Some of the CCP's massive land purchases in the United States, used to grow and push high-potency, toxic weed - often laced with fentanyl - is all part of what the CCP themselves call "cognitive warfare" against the U.S.; the goal of which, as Schweizer says, is "to dumb us down, to weaken and undermine American society."

Think about it: a drugged-out populace is easy to conquer. It's a lesson the Chinese learned the hard way when Great Britain flooded China with opium in the 19th century, hooking an estimated 25% of the population and destroying their centuries-strong power and economy in a matter of years. This humiliating memory of "The Opium Wars" of the mid-1800's still stings deeply in Chinese consciousness.

The CCP has decided that it's time to turn those tables.

New Wave of "Natural" Synthetic Drug Abuse

Addiction professionals worldwide are seeing an additional troubling trend: more people are becoming dependent on synthetic and herbal drugs marketed as "safe," "natural" or "legal" from the corner store. Products like K2, delta-8, kratom, "bath salts," and kava are often sold in corner stores and even wellness stores or online under the promise of relief, calm, or energy. But behind the packaging lies a growing serious public health concern that flies under the radar with regulators.

Vapes

Another front in the war on our bodies is vapes. Yes, those sleek little gadgets sold at gas stations, malls, and online to our children. Vaping, marketed as cool, convenient and harmless, is in fact yet another precision-engineered weapon. More than 90 percent of the devices come from China and inside these pens of poison, cadmium heating coils - a heavy metal carcinogen - release toxic particles with every puff. The liquid inside, when heated, decomposes into formaldehyde and acetaldehyde, chemicals that scar lung tissue and cause the irreversible, horrific condition known as "popcorn lung." What's more, the nicotine salts within are not the old organic tobacco leaf; they are weaponized synthetic chemistry, engineered to deliver a harder, faster hit to the brain's reward system. Vapes represent addiction on overdrive, designed to hook and enslave a new generation of Americans. The addictive qualities are supercharged with nicotine and THC additives. Vapes act similar to marijuana as a "gateway" drug, driving addiction to even more dangerous drugs like Fentanyl and synthetic opiates.

But the vape assault does not stop with the lungs. The electronic device itself is a Trojan horse, charged through malicious USB connections, a perfect gateway for hidden malware. Investigators have found Chinese-made chargers, peripherals, even charging cables capable of exfiltrating data, *turning a teenager's habit into a silent surveillance channel.* So what looks like a nicotine or fruit-flavored delivery system is also a backdoor into personal devices, privacy, and even national security. Remember the CCP dictum: "we will weaponize everything against the West."

Vapes, therefore, represent a double strike: highly toxic chemical dependency wrapped inside digital infiltration. It's both a health crisis and a cybersecurity crisis. The CCP has found a way to invade our homes, our children's brains, and our nation's very bloodstream all at once. *Every puff is a programmed surrender.*

All this evidences the CCP's slow, steady war against the lifeblood of the West: a concerted effort, systematic and deliberate, to poison, corrode, and weaken from within.

We must forge a shield of vigilance - personal, legal, regulatory, and scientific - against the CCP's toxic campaigns. We must educate ourselves and our children, galvanize our politicians, or elect new leaders who are not compromised by CCP money. We must defend ourselves with every tool and every truth we can.

BRIEFING FOUR

The Battle For Your Mind
Cognitive War

"The cognitive domain is the primary battle ground between freedom, independence, opportunity, and tyranny."
~ Edward Haugland
Retired Intelligence Community Executive
Author of "The Cognitive War"

The CCP's Cognitive War may be the most insidious of all unrestricted warfare campaigns... Because this one has been launched in silence.

It operates invisibly, *inside the gray matter of your brain.* But the deterioration and destruction happens little-by-little, until you are rendered *functionally helpless.* A colleague and Senior U.S. Naval Counterintelligence Officer recently made the distinction, saying, "Propaganda wants you to believe a certain thing. Cognitive warfare doesn't care what you believe; *it cares about disrupting how you think."*

This makes it far more difficult to counter than "information warfare." Information warfare throws lies at you. Cognitive warfare destroys your critical thinking ability, rewiring the very pathways of your mind. It erodes your ability to distinguish what is true and what is propaganda, literally damaging the internal machinery that makes conviction, devotion to your values, decisive judgment, basic willpower, and even shared reality, *possible*.

A senior U.S. military specialist recently described it to me as the difference between hacking a computer with bad data, or *rewriting the operating system itself.* Your neurons become the casualties. "Cognitive warfare rewrites your ability to rationalize-your ability to make decisions," he says.

"It works at the *biological* level."

PsyOp

This is the ultimate invasion of your privacy and freedom: your brain tissue. The Jamestown Foundation calls this the "next-generation evolution of psychological warfare." It changes *everything.*

My colleague Ed Haugland says, "The Cognitive Domain encompasses all other domains - the umbrella under which mankind operates, functions, learns, advances or regresses. All other domains - Cyber, Air, Land, Sea, Subterranean, Space, Sub-surface - are all one operating domain, not separate."

Destroy the brain and you destroy a country's ability to defend itself. The stakes here, Haugland warns, are as high as they get. The CCP's cognitive war on us underpins "an ideological war between tyranny and freedom, control and independence, subjugation, and democracy."

The tools the CCP is deploying may sound like science fiction, but they are real, they are built, and the CCP invests its growing billions to weaponize them as both "hard" and "soft" diabolical weapons of war... *every day.*

The "hard" arsenal can be broken down into three categories of weaponry: "bugs, drugs, and toxins," according to Professor James Giordano, former Senior Science Advisory Fellow of the Strategic Multilayer Assessment Branch of the Joint Staff of the Pentagon.

Bugs: Engineered viruses and bacteria that sicken the body and destabilize societies through panic and paranoia.

Drugs: Compounds introduced to alter judgment, sap willpower, and dissolve focus. Widespread opioid abuse in America, engineered, encouraged, and exploited, is creating a fog of addiction that kills, demoralizes, and makes entire communities easier to control.

Toxins: Subtle poisons that disable citizens across age and economic strata. Toxins cloud memory and sow distrust in food and water supplies. As a U.S. Counterintelligence report warns, their true power lies in weaponizing uncertainty. "You never know if the next sip of water or breath of air carries the threat."

Together, these form a three-headed monster. Bugs spread fear. Drugs dissolve clarity. Toxins deliver paranoia, disease, and death. Together, they collectively corrode trust, disable reason, and leave nations floundering from the inside out.

The destructive power of these hard weapons is matched by the "soft" cognitive weapons which you unknowingly encounter every day. While the old Soviet Union experimented with primitive attempts at cognitive warfare, a Senior U.S. Navy Cyber Operations Officer with whom I consult regularly said in a recent conversation, "they didn't have neuroscience, big tech, or the internet of things. Now citizens are plugged into everything - your car, your TV, your house, your phone, even your watch, Fitbit, and your pet. All that constant feedback becomes a weaponized stream of data. *Your brain is a whole new battlefield."*

This Officer identified three current converging forces that make the CCP an existential cognitive threat:

1. **Advanced brain science**

   The CCP's focus is on how to hack perception and destroy decision-making itself.

2. **Dual-use technology**

   Turning civilian tools like social media into *24/7 weapons of war.*

3. **New algorithmic business models**
   Where systems designed to sell ads are hijacked to sell communist ideology.

This combination of tech innovations, now hyper-accelerated by AI, have made cognitive warfare an unstoppable force. Left unaddressed, cognitive warfare leaves behind social confusion, demoralized militaries and citizens, degraded political judgment, pervasive nihilism, and ultimately the shattering of the fundamental civic "shared agreement" that holds a free society together.

"If the enemy can disrupt and destroy that agreement," the Officer warns, "then they've created a permanently dysfunctional society. That's their goal. Lock us into chaos so we can't respond to threats, to attacks, or to total war."

Colleague Xi Van Fleet, author of "Mao's America," who grew up in the horrific carnage of the CCP's cultural revolution and is now a keen critic of the CCP astutely states, "Chaos is a vehicle for disempowerment and it makes it easier to impose control. Once you are in power, once you have power, then you shut down the chaos. You want total control."

A recent Senate Armed Services Committee finding revealed that the Pentagon lacks the cohesion of "strategic clarity" to contest these methods even as China accelerates research into neurocognitive tools, such as AI deepfakes and voice-synthesis for mass deception.

It's like a thousand-headed monster. An omni-assault ranging from endless simple memes to *sophisticated brain-disrupting audio weaponry.* And is it fed by the juggernaut of CCP sponsored labs, platforms, and propaganda farms, all converging on a single objective: destroying our decision capabilities at scale.

This chapter will document the doctrines, the devices, and the cognitive damage currently being wreaked. As you read, the results should sound eerily familiar to you. It is a steady creep punctuated by sudden attacks. And if we do not name the methods, study the instruments, and inoculate our institutions and minds, losing the cognitive war will decimate us. And here's the ghoulish thing: it won't even feel like defeat. It will simply feel like an incremental continuation of normal life. Only that "normal" life we are living will no longer be ours. It will no longer be free. It will thoroughly belong to the Chinese Communist Party.

The Devil's Toolbox

The Chinese Communist Party did not invent the strategy of debilitating minds. It industrialized it. It massively funded it. It built the platforms and the labs and found the guinea pig-humans to test it and make it effective.

When Unrestricted Warfare was first fully articulated in 1999, declaring that "weapons may include television, newspapers, computers, and the media of the enemy country," little did they realize just what advanced, nefarious, and effective tools they'd have in their hands the coming decades. Now, we are confronting a highly networked war aimed at something no civilization has ever had the tech, funds, manpower, and evil to wage before. *It's war on the internal human operating system itself.*

Let me bring you inside the CCP's growing, advanced online weapons...

- **Microcognitive microtargeting**
  Algorithms build a psychological profile of *YOU.* They then feed you tiny, personalized messages designed to alter what you believe, how you feel, and what you decide.

- **Deepfakes (realistic AI video and audio)**
  Fake, but perfect-looking video clips replace what people think happened, trigger outrage, and/or amplify doubts and fear.

- **Addictive app and game engineering**
  Adapting game technology, variable rewards, attention-grabbing notifications, sound cues, and design tricks. These hijack dopamine so that you keep coming back... and your habits shift without you even noticing.

- **Biometric-driven persuasion**
  Data from Fitbits, face scans, microphones, and even EEGs are used to tailor messages or subliminal cues to your body's signals, subconsciously influencing choices at the moments you are most vulnerable.

- **Filter bubbles and algorithmic bias**
  Platforms intentionally isolate you inside echo chambers that confirm what you already think and hide contrary facts, making persuasion easy, beliefs reinforced, and correction difficult.

- **Neurotech and brain-interface manipulation**
  Neurofeedback and brain-computer interfaces can directly alter mood, attention, and cognition through stimulation or data-driven feedback.

- **Subliminal and sensory engineering**
  Tiny sound tones, image framings, and timing tricks work below conscious awareness to prime emotions and behavior.

- **Data fusion and cross-platform orchestration**
  Combining ad data, social signals, wearable biometrics, and research leaks to create a hyper-detailed profile that can be pushed across apps, newsfeeds, emails, and games for relentless influence.

All of these online weapons have been *exponentially accelerated* by the emerging technologies of AI and quantum computing. And still, this is only a sampling of the CCP's "devil's toolbox." Each method of cognitive war is stronger than it appears because these weapons don't exist in isolation. The CCP integrates them, compounding their destructive power.

Here's how they attack your brain, making you easier to control:

1. First, neuroscience *rewires your brain chemistry* so that panic, suspicion, numbness, and lethargy become automated, unconscious habits.
2. Then, big-data tracking stitches every search, swipe, location, purchase, and heartbeat of yours into a *personalized blueprint of your weak spots* and tell-tale moments.
3. Next, they flood every entry point to your brain. These include Television, TikTok, YouTube, Facebook, memes, classroom videos, altered curricula, and the speeches and policies of compromised leaders. You are, summarily, pelted from all sides until the signal drowns in CCP noise. *You don't know what to believe or what to think, thus you give up trying.*
4. The attack intensifies. Algorithms amplify, with pinpoint precision, whatever enrages or mesmerizes you at the specific moment at which you are either enraged or mesmerized; *because it's reading you.* Simultaneously it learns what are the exact stimuli that keep you *hooked, agitated, anxious, paranoid, and off-balance.*

And all those feeds lock you into self-magnifying echo chambers. In these echo chambers:

- Outrage multiplies;
- Lies grow louder with every share;
- Neighbors turn on neighbors;
- Young men pick up guns and fire on schools and leaders;
- People riot;
- Blood is shed;

– ... And the puppeteer never needs to show its hand because you've been primed to believe you are making your own decisions.

It grows more diabolical. China's inter-connected assault on the Western mind moves beyond the screen, physically attacking brain tissue itself. Beijing has developed both "neurotype" and "organotype" weapons. These are infrasound waves too low for the ear to hear but powerful enough for the body to suffer. Hit the right resonant frequencies and you can destabilize the brain, upset heart rhythms, and shake vital organs loose from equilibrium. With phased-array tech, the CCP doesn't need explosions on the battlefield. No flash. No bang. No shrapnel. No concussions. One moment a soldier stands steady; the next he's staggering. A pilot is flying fine; seconds later he's mysteriously nauseous, panicked, and blacking out. Or, in the homeland, an entire targeted neighborhood lies awake night-after-night, wired, anxious, and incapacitated. And nobody knows why.

These weapons scramble the mind and the very ability to think. The arsenal includes noise bombs and long-range acoustic missiles to rattle whole populations from miles away. They slow cognition, wreck reaction time, and crush the will to fight. These are weapons built for deniability. No bleeding wound to photograph. No crater to inspect. Only the aftermath: a soldier collapsed, a population that is angry or can't make a clear decision, an enemy that loses its grip on reality and never sees the weapon that hit it.

This vast toolbox is being put to work 24/7 on you and no prey makes for easier hunting than our youth, including (especially) our young people in the military services. That's where the CCP focuses its targeting: where minds are most pliable.

Dr. Daniel Amen, the renowned psychiatrist, has long emphasized that the brain is still under construction well into a person's mid-twenties, noting, "The prefrontal cortex - the part responsible for judgment, insight, and impulse control - isn't fully developed until about age 25."

This leaves young people with less ability to filter out manipulation or make sound decisions. They are supremely vulnerable when their habits and worldviews are being shaped. Our younger generations are having their brains permanently marred and fractured while their brains are still in their developmental stage. Drug use, most widely, marijuana, also permanently harms the brain during this stage of final growth.

Jonathan Haidt, in his book "The Anxious Generation," highlights the vulnerability that arises from this neural unfinishedness. "Smartphones and social media poured jet fuel on the anxiety and fragility that already existed," he writes, pointing out how these tools "take advantage of the developing social brains of kids and teens."

Both Amen and Haidt warn that if we fail to recognize how impressionable and emotionally reactive those under 25 truly are, we risk letting technology hijack our next generation's thinking, and their fundamental ability to think.

The CCP is explicitly building programs and communications to influence global youth. One *Newsweek* piece titled "China's New Propaganda Strategy Aims at American Youth" (11.29.2023) reports that high school influencers are recruited to present China as peaceful, progressive, and the inevitable "ruler of the world."

Small cost. High strategic payoff.

The tactics? These young people are provided everything from pre-crafted influencer content to free student exchange spots. China has offered 50,000 of these all-expense paid trips over the past five years to American teenagers for the purpose of shaping a generation and modeling how they view China, its leadership, and the alleged benefits of their (*communist)* societal model.

Working across all fronts, the CCP is corralling Western hearts and minds into Beijing's narrative. And it's working. According to field studies reported even in left-leaning periodical "The Guardian," pro-

China narratives grow and public opinion shifts whenever exposure is sustained. That's operational success. And it must be stopped immediately.

Rise of Artificial Intelligence

By far, the greatest danger of artificial intelligence is that people conclude too early that they understand it."
~ Eliezer Yudkowsky

I reached out to my colleague, Wayne Lonstein, Esq, CISSP; a CEO at VFT Solutions and member of Forbes Technology Council, for a crisp summary of the risks of AI. He outlined how AI's biggest dangers aren't even "data hacks" but, rather, the malicious manipulation of human thought and behavior that distort judgment. As people innocently feed sensitive information and emotional vulnerabilities into AI tools, these systems can now exploit trust, mimic empathy, invent false emergencies, gaslight users, and destabilize decision-making. Such harms are already appearing in lawsuits alleging that chatbots are both addictive and psychologically dangerous.

For businesses, Lonstein continued, manipulated AI outputs pose untold financial risk, especially if AI vendors gain Section 230-style immunity that leaves companies free of liability for bad decisions made from faulty AI guidance. Even more concerning, national security is at stake as governments rapidly adopt AI, creating a dependent "AI - industrial complex" with little transparency or chain of responsibility. Increasing the danger, AI is expected to rapidly defeat cybersecurity protections. The race is on.

Bottom line: A great cognitive threat is our misplaced trust in AI, because it can be weaponized for control on every electronic platform. Protecting human agency is the strongest defense and we lay out steps to take in the final chapter of this (survival guide) book.

Social Media - Permanent Adolescent Damage

Just an hour of additional social media use each day is enough to drag down adolescents' reading and memory scores, in a new study that tracked more than 6,500 children.

Based on data from the "Adolescent Brain Cognitive Development Study," researchers measured cognitive skills in children ages 9 to 13 using standardized tests of reading, memory, and vocabulary. The findings revealed that even low levels of increased social media use were associated with measurably poorer performance. Which makes them sitting ducks for incremental cognitive assaults.

Cognitive Casualties

The CCP doesn't always hide their malign intent. According to the leading CCP/PLA theorist Zeng Huafeng of China's National University of Defense Technology (NUDT), the cognitive battlefield is, "The area in which feelings, perception, understanding, beliefs, and values exist; the field of decision-making through reasoning."

He signals in the PLA Daily (10.17.2017) that the goal is to disrupt "intangible factors" such as "leadership, morale, cohesion, training level and experience; situational awareness and public opinion."

In his foundational paper, Zeng specified four tactics to win "mind superiority" in the cognitive space:

1. "Perception manipulation" through propaganda narratives
2. "Cutting off historical memory" so targets (*we, the People*) are open to new (communist) values
3. "Changing the paradigm of thinking" by targeting elites to change their ideology
4. "Deconstructing symbols" to challenge national identity.

Here's my layman's translation of these goals. The CCP simply wants to...

1. Make Us **Dumb**
2. Make Us **Hopeless** (and Helpless)
3. Make Us **Hate Ourselves**
4. **Confuse** Us
5. Promote Communism (**Destroy Freedom**)

1: Make Us Dumb

The Australian Strategic Policy Institute (ASPI) warns that the CCP has built one of the world's most sophisticated "digital influence ecosystems" to "exploit social divisions, alter perceptions of reality, and erode trust in institutions." Over time, this creates a public more likely to accept simplistic slogans, amplify falsehoods, and disengage from critical debate-the exact conditions where autocracy thrives.

And that starts with trying to simply make us dumber. They want us less capable of independent thought, less able to reason, and less able to resist manipulation. How? Through a coordinated mix of digital manipulation, psychological operations, and potential biological and neurological interference.

One method that has made news for years, without the urgent response it has required from the U.S. Government, is TikTok. President of the Government Accountability Institute, Peter Schweizer, identifies TikTok as a leading edge of Beijing's cognitive warfare arsenal. He sums up the first problem: "Our kids are getting cotton candy from ByteDance; children in China are getting spinach."

The Chinese version of TikTok (Douyin), restricts children's use to forty minutes a day. Feeds are filled with science experiments, patriotic history clips, and educational content. The Western version streams endless meaningless entertainment, outrage porn, harmful stunts, and an infinite stampede of addictive, mind-numbing trends. One app company, two opposite missions. While Chinese youth are shown educational, scientific, and patriotic content, Western children are drowning in an insatiable destructive dopamine fog. It's no wonder many officials are now calling social media, and especially TikTok, "digital fentanyl."

The U.S. Intelligence Community's 2024 general threat assessment explicitly identified TikTok and similar platforms as "cognitive disruption technologies."

The damage is steady, and huge. Research published in the Journal of Computer-Mediated Communication in 2023 showed that exposure to fragmented, emotionally charged social media content reduces attention spans by an average of 47% and decreases analytical reasoning scores by 23%. As Dr. Michael Rich of Harvard Medical School's Digital Wellness Institute warned, "We're seeing measurable cognitive decline in populations heavily exposed to algorithmically-driven content designed to maximize engagement rather than understanding."

In other words, we're dumber.

Seeing that it's working, the CCP continues to invest heavily in the neuroscience processes of emotion and reward, then crafting content to bypass critical thinking and stoke rage, fear, confusion, and gratification. By flooding social and digital spaces with conflicting or emotionally charged content, ("narrative flooding") CCP-aligned operations fracture attention spans and erode patience for complex reasoning. Citizens conditioned to react instantly rather than think critically are easier to influence, more likely to repeat falsehoods, and more prone to mistake rumors for truth.

Chinese research labs are taking this debilitation many steps deeper, exploring neurotechnologies that can alter perception, disrupt memory, and impair executive function-the brain's core ability to plan and decide. Remember, the cognitive war against us is an assault with both hard and soft weaponry.

A 2019 RAND Corporation study on China's military science literature warned of the PLA's increased interest in "brain control weapons." The same study cites Chinese research into "penetrating human brain tissue with microwaves, electromagnetic pulses, and nano-technology to influence mood, memory, and cognitive performance."

Imagine this nightmare scenario: an aerosolized "nano-swarm" so microscopic that it leaves no trace, yet diminishes or wipes out cognitive performance for an entire population. Science fiction? *No.* Chinese military-affiliated researchers openly discuss such techniques in academic journals. *The very mental capacities - focus, skepticism, and problem-solving - that our democratic societies rely on are being targeted and endangered.*

China's "Military Brain Science" program, explicitly announced in 2018, aims to "enhance, degrade, or control brain functions." In 2021, The U.S. Department of Commerce sanctioned China's Academy of Military Medical Sciences and eleven related institutes for developing "brain-control weaponry" capable of influencing human cognition and behavior. Congressional testimonies by counterintelligence officials have warned that these efforts could lead to targeted neurological attacks ranging from short-term confusion to long-term cognitive damage.

Dr. Robert Epstein, Senior Research Psychologist, warns: "We're witnessing a systematic psychological dismantling" of the West.

"The goal isn't to convince, but to confuse and paralyze."

The endgame? To create a mentally softened adversary, incapable of mounting an effective defense economically, culturally, and when it comes to it, militarily.

Make the U.S. Hopeless, and, Therefore, *Helpless*

"War is fundamentally about attrition and political will," a Senior U.S. Navy Counterintelligence Officer recently said to me and the team at Freedom Forever.

"In the 1960's," he illustrated, "for North Vietnam, the theory of victory wasn't that they would march down Pennsylvania Avenue. Their goal was to sap our political will until we decided that we don't want to participate."

The Chinese Communist Party has weaponized this principle with surgical precision, targeting our collective motivation, hope, and willingness to resist.

Lieutenant General Robert Ashley, former Director of The Defense Intelligence Agency, described this strategy bluntly in a 2022 classified briefing: "The goal isn't to defeat us militarily, but to convince us that defeat is inevitable before the first shot is fired."

They are working to make our youth hopeless, powerless, and nihilistic, which will induce what Dr. Michael Nagata, former Strategic Multilayer Assessment director at U.S. Special Operations Command, calls *"a pervasive sense of helplessness."*

How are they doing it? They flood our brains 24/7 with emotionally triggering content heralding the downfall of America and the West. This content wildly exaggerates social problems, cultural or political conflicts, and America's moral decline. By contrast, the glory, order, cleanliness, and foresight of China are celebrated in our own American media as part of a psychological weapon against our own people.

The goal? To get our youth to give up and switch sides. Our enemy understands that belief in one's self, in the free individual, and in a free country that thrives precisely because of that free individual's contribution must be attacked. When you attack the individual and their worth, you attack the very backbone of Western society, a government of the people, for the people, and by the people. Take away faith in oneself and one's future, and you are left with disconnection and nihilism.

Dr. Anna Lembke from Stanford points out that these techniques are deliberately designed to "create dopamine-driven feedback loops that amplify anxiety, depression, and a sense of powerlessness."

Sure enough, a 2023 RAND study confirmed that repeated exposure to these narratives can reduce civic engagement by up to 37% within 18 months. And The Oxford Internet Institute documented that users exposed to this kind of persistent negative algorithmic content showed a 42% increase in feelings of hopelessness about societal change.

In other words, they are stripping us not only of our will to fight the communist red tsunami, but *our will to live together as a people, or to live at all.* Recent studies show:

- 68% of American young adults report feeling "consistently hopeless about the future"
- Depression rates among 18-24 year olds have increased 89% since 2010
- Civic engagement among millennials has dropped 55% compared to previous generations

Dr. James Giordano, a leading expert on cognitive warfare, describes this as "neurological pacification," a deliberate strategy to reduce populations' capacity for collective resistance.

"By systematically overwhelming cognitive resources," Giordano explains, "you create a population more interested in individual survival than collective action. The brain becomes trained to perceive resistance as futile."

As my colleague in the U.S. Navy Intelligence reminds us, since "all of warfare is about the attrition of will to fight," if you can shape the war within that one domain, you can affect all the other domains.

Dr. Elsa Kania, a leading expert on Chinese military innovation, describes their strategy as "whole-of-society cognitive engineering."

General Michael Hayden, former CIA and NSA Director, succinctly conveys that, "The most effective war is the one where your enemy surrenders before understanding they're under attack."

The silent war.

The silent storm.

They aim to win without ever firing a shot.

They aim to cook us before we realize we're even in hot water.

And indeed, no one surrenders more easily than a hopeless, helpless population.

Make Us Hate Ourselves

"To achieve world government, it is necessary to remove the minds of men, their individualism, loyalty to family traditions, national patriotism and religious dogmas."

~ Brock Chisholm

The first Director-General of the World Health Organization (WHO)

"The most effective way to destroy a society is to delegitimize its fundamental values," warns Dr. Michael Pillsbury, director of The Center on Chinese Strategy at the Hudson Institute.

"China understands that physical conquest is unnecessary if you can hollow out a civilization's core beliefs from within."

Therefore, a key component of the CCP's efforts to destroy our will to stand for ourselves, our culture and our country is to undermine the beliefs that hold us together.

Their messaging is clear and comes from the top. These are a few of the calculated "us vs. them" messages being translated, repurposed and streamed into the eyes, ears, and minds of our population in a million subtle and unsubtle ways:

1. *Xi Jinping at the 19th Party Congress (2017)*
   "The West is experiencing an unprecedented crisis of values. Their so-called democracy has become a tool for the wealthy elite, while their people **lose faith in their institutions and moral foundations."**

2. *Central Party School Speech (2021)*
   "Western liberalism has led to moral relativism, family breakdown, and social decay. This is the inevitable result of prioritizing individual desires over collective responsibility."

3. *Wang Yi (Foreign Minister) Munich Security Conference Response (2022)*
   "American society is plagued by gun violence, drug addiction, and racial conflict. This is what happens when a civilization abandons its moral compass in pursuit of absolute individualism."

4. *Zhao Lijian (Former Foreign Ministry Spokesperson) Press Conference (2021)*
   "The United States lectures others about human rights while its own society crumbles from within. Mass shootings, homelessness, and social division reveal the bankruptcy of Western values."[4]

5. *General Wei Fenghe (Former Defense Minister) Shangri-La Dialogue (2019)*
   "Western military decline reflects deeper civilizational exhaustion. When a society loses its moral foundation, its capacity for sacrifice and discipline inevitably weakens."[5]

6. *Jin Canrong (Renmin University, prominent strategist) Beijing Foreign Policy Forum (2022)*
   "America's strength was built on Protestant work ethic and social cohesion. Now they embrace hedonism and fragmentation. This is China's strategic opportunity."[6]

7. *Global Times Editorial (2023)*
   "Western societies have become laboratories of social experiment-gender confusion, family dissolution, and moral chaos. China offers stability while the West descends into ideological madness."[7]

8. *Yan Xuetong (Tsinghua University) Foreign Affairs Analysis (2020)*
   "American decline is fundamentally a moral decline. A society that cannot distinguish between right and wrong, male and female, citizen and non-citizen, cannot maintain global leadership."[9]

9. *Zhang Weiwei (Fudan University) "The China Wave" (2012, updated lectures 2022)*
   "Western civilization is exhausted. Their young people have no purpose, no children, no hope. China's youth build the future while theirs retreat into virtual reality and drugs."[10]

10. *PLA Strategic Assessment (2021)*
    "Western military recruitment faces a crisis due to declining physical fitness, mental health issues, and lack of patriotic motivation among youth. This represents strategic vulnerability."[12]

11. *Li Keqiang (Former Premier) World Economic Forum (2021)*
    "While Western societies debate pronouns and historical guilt, China focuses on development and progress. This difference in priorities explains our different trajectories."

12. *Wang Huning (Politburo Standing Committee) Party Theory Journal (2019)*
    "Western culture has become a culture of death-abortion, euthanasia, declining births, and spiritual emptiness. Socialist culture promotes life, family, and collective purpose."[14]

The CCP injects this messaging into both our social and legacy media, accelerating the already plummeting trust across the board in our institutions. Studies show their work is succeeding in the U.S.

Trust in the "U.S. Government" is 20%, down from 54% in 2002.
Media credibility is lowest in recorded history at 29%.
Political institution trust is 17% among the aged 18-34 demographic.

Confuse Us

The Chinese Communist Party (CCP) aims to destroy our ability to perceive reality. At the core of this strategy is a deliberate methodology of "cognitive disorientation." By flooding information channels with deliberately contradictory narratives, AI-generated content, and hyper-targeted psychological triggers, the CCP creates an eco-system of perpetual uncertainty, ruining our ability to form coherent thoughts.

The weaponization of artificial intelligence has dramatically amplified these cognitive warfare tactics. Machine learning algorithms can now generate millions of seemingly authentic social media personas, each crafted to exploit specific psychological vulnerabilities. As Dr. Eliot Higgins, founder of the noted investigative collective, Bellingcat, observes, "The sophistication of these AI-driven influence operations is unprecedented-we're witnessing a new form of psychological warfare that operates at the speed of light and the depth of human vulnerability."

What makes this threat so insidious is its multi-layered approach. These influence campaigns don't push a single narrative; they simultaneously promote contradictory perspectives, creating a deliberate stew of confusion. Colleague Robert Spalding, PhD, BGEN U.S.AF (ret.) describes this as "a strategy of cognitive paralysis, where the goal is not to win an argument, but to make argument itself seem futile." By overwhelming cognitive processing capabilities, individuals become less capable of performing critical analysis.

Additionally, by systematically undermining institutional trust, whether in media, government, or academic sources, the CCP creates an environment where individuals feel increasingly isolated and uncertain. Michael Pillsbury notes critically, "This is a form of unrestricted warfare where the most powerful weapon is doubt itself. When citizens can no longer trust their own judgment, democratic societies become fundamentally compromised."

Most alarming is the real-time adaptability of these cognitive warfare techniques. AI-powered systems can instantaneously adjust messaging based on audience responses or events, creating a non-stop, dynamic psychological battlefield where traditional defensive strategies become obsolete. As Claire Wardle, an international expert on disinformation, warns, "We're not just fighting against false information, but against an adaptive system designed to exploit our cognitive weaknesses in real-time."

The ultimate objective is clear: to destabilize our "cognitive immune systems." Retired Admiral James Stavridis captures the existential nature of this threat: "This is a war fought with algorithms and narratives, where the casualties are trust, critical thinking, and social cohesion." By making truth itself feel unreliable, the CCP seeks to create populations that are more easily controlled, less capable of unified resistance, and increasingly vulnerable to external manipulation.

Indeed, Paul Buvarp, a senior researcher at the Norwegian Defence Research Establishment, warns us that the danger is that many of us have started to let our guard down, learning to ignore the signals that used to help us separate facts from lies. Paul's research shows that instead of being skeptical or rational, people get swept up by the flood of flashy (many times fake) stories or viral memes, locking into sides and getting emotionally invested before they even realize what's happening. As he says, "the real danger here isn't just bad information: it's that people will turn on each other, get lost in their own realities, and leave our society wide open for outside forces who want to take advantage of our confusion."

Promote Communism & Destroy Freedom

And who is that "outside force" stealthily stepping into this fog of doubt and confusion? The CCP.

While you've gotten a taste of "the West is a moral failure, plummeting into decline" messaging above, you have also subtly been fed a steady stream of pro-CCP propaganda messages.

As my colleague, Colonel Grant Newsham, wisely points out in his book "When China Attacks: A Warning To America," if you've ever said or thought any of the following, you've been influenced by Chinese psyops:

- *COVID-19 couldn't possibly have come from a Chinese laboratory.*
- *China intends to "reunify" with Taiwan.*
- *The United States must have China's help on climate change.*
- *We simply have to be invested in the China market.*
- *China won't like it - to make China an enemy, treat it like one.*
- *How can I criticize China, given what the West has done?*
- *China is no longer communist. It is capitalist.*
- *Criticizing the CCP is racist. China's rise is "peaceful" and "inevitable." Chinese culture isn't compatible with democracy.*
- *China is militarizing/aggressive/expansionist because of the trauma of a century of humiliation.*
- *Fentanyl is just payback for the opium wars.*
- *China is not expansionist. It has never attacked its neighbors.*
- *China is just doing what all great powers do.*
- *We welcome a strong China. The only thing worse is a weak China with nuclear weapons.*
- *You can't say that about China! You will offend Chinese people.*

In sum, if you believe or have repeated that China is safe, friendly, orderly, and has solved the problems faced by the West, you have swallowed a carefully manufactured mythology. The CCP is organ harvesting en masse, committing mass cultural genocide against the Uyghurs, Tibetans, Falun Gong, and non-Han Chinese, terrorizing their neighbors on land and sea, and terrorizing their own civilians at home.

And yet, they put *equal effort* into maximizing confusion, overwhelm, and cultural demoralization abroad.

Legacy Media to The Rescue?

Legacy Media, meaning the established national newspapers and TV news organizations, are just about entirely compromised. They rely on CCP-scrubbed sources, quoted without skepticism or fact-checking. These "sources" are guided their way by their local-hire "researchers" who themselves are supplied by the Chinese Ministry of State Security–controlled Foreign Enterprise Service Corp. These sources are all thoroughly trained in CPD (Central Propaganda Department) journalism or foreign language schools and have overseas Xinhua or China News Service tours under their belts.

As Colonel Newsham reports, "they are all instructed directly by the MSS on what intelligence to collect, and by the CPD in Beijing on what stories to cover, what angles to play-up, what statistics to use."

Here's a quick reality check: how much of what you have read so far in this guide has been discussed in mainstream or legacy media?

Mainstream media are also the first to "cry wolf" or, more accurately, to cry "anti-Asian racism!" Shaming citizens about being racist (when they're asking legitimate questions) causes Westerners to doubt their intuition (or common sense) about obvious CCP political, economic, and military moves. This facile, woke-inspired name-calling or "diagnoses" replace real, hard-nosed investigative journalism. The result: *truth dies in darkness.*

For clarity and factual reporting, it is my expert opinion that you would do well to believe nothing you hear from legacy media about China and its intentions, reduce your exposure to the algorithm-manipulation of social media scrolls, institute the protocols in the Citizen's Action Guide at the end of this guide and educate yourself by accessing the factual resources you will find in this guide's appendix.

Your mind and your ability to think clearly and make rational, informed decisions in defense of your life, your family's life and the hard-won freedoms of the West literally depend on you taking these actions.

BRIEFING FIVE
The Battle For Your Data
Cyber War

"Every time you hear of a data breach anywhere in the world, a chunk of your freedom is gone forever."
~ T. Casey Fleming

The CCP's cyber attacks began when their students were learning coding and "internet security" alongside our own students in universities across the globe. Universities cheeringly gave the CCP/PLA this knowledge and intellectual property. Then, it was all about espionage and theft of intellectual property (IP); the lifeblood of the free world's economy.

As the CCP/PLA grew in sophistication and capability, their unrestricted warfare execution expanded including their malicious and nefarious intent.

Marooned by Typhoons

The first sign of trouble was the sudden silence…

A field engineer at an Illinois power utility bolts upright at his console and freezes: screens dark with an ominous message. He thinks, at first, that it's routine maintenance somewhere.

Far to the south, in a Texas water treatment plant, a supervisor notices valves cycling open and shut without input commands.

On the Eastern seaboard, data packets shoot through telecom backbones at midnight - traffic that looks ordinary, yet carries the fingerprints of something nefarious.

In a hospital in Denver, an ICU nurse taps a touchscreen to adjust a patient's ventilator settings, only to watch the numbers slide back on their own.

At a grain terminal in the Dakotas, loading conveyors grind to a halt mid-operation, while diagnostics report "no fault detected."

And in a quiet suburb outside Seattle, a city traffic grid begins cycling lights out of sync, twisting rush-hour into chaos.

This is Volt Typhoon - a vast CCP Cyberattack - in full bloom. For three full years, the intruders have been crawling through America's lifelines: the grids that power our homes and hospitals, the pipelines that keep our trucks moving, the treatment plants that keep our water safe. These intruders have come to penetrate... and wait.

They bury themselves inside routers and firewalls, invisible, indistinguishable from routine traffic. By the time investigators uncover them, the kill switches are already implanted. At the moment of Beijing's choosing, the lights go dark, the water pumps stop, the internet, and all communications go dead.

The battlefield is being prepared throughout America's electronic body.

That was a CCP cyberstrike on our national sovereignty and security.

Then comes the Salt Typhoon. Salt strikes in a swarm. Entire botnets, made of hijacked machines across continents, turn their firepower on the arteries of global communication. AT&T, Verizon, T-Mobile, Lumen - giants of telecom - suddenly find their backdoors pried open. Rootkits with names like Demodex dig into the operating systems of routers.

Backdoors like GhostSpider whisper commands that cannot be traced. Conversations - real voices, real texts, even encrypted law-enforcement wiretaps - get siphoned into the shadows. An entire U.S. Army National Guard network gets compromised. Leaders of nations, candidates in elections, CEOs and everyday citizens.

"I can't imagine any American was spared, given the breadth of the campaign," said Cynthia Kaiser, a former top official in the FBI's cyber division, who oversaw investigations into the hacking.

And indeed, in September, 2025, the NYT ran a major article on Salt Typhoon, saying that it:

> *...may have stolen information about nearly every American and targeted several other countries. Some countries hit by Salt Typhoon warned in an unusual statement that the data stolen could provide Chinese intelligence services with the capability to 'identify and track their targets' communications and movements around the world.*

Despite Washington's warnings, the ravenous hunger of the CCP's cyberthievery of your and our private data continues unabated. The U.S. Government's Cybersecurity and Infrastructure Agency (CISA) described the scope of their operations:

> *Malicious cyber activities attributed to the Chinese government targeted, and continue to target, a variety of industries and organizations in the United States, including healthcare, financial services, defense industrial base, energy, government facilities, chemical, critical manufacturing (including automotive and aerospace), communications, IT (including managed service providers), international trade, education, video gaming, faith-based organizations, and law firms.*

By August 2025, the FBI confirmed that at least *200 companies across 80 countries* had been hacked. This number represents only the FBI's caseload of active investigations. Many more hacks (breaches) were not reported in the past because companies never knew it occurred or didn't want a hit to their stock price.

The dark genius of Salt Typhoon is its camouflage. The attacks look like noise, maintenance pings, routine background traffic - the kinds of things technicians ignore. But behind the curtain, every American life gets reduced to data points flowing eastward to a dark regime. Every packet of private information could be used now and forever to disrupt, blackmail, destabilize every individual American, one at a time.

Think of Volt and Salt as a network of millions of land mines, planted and ready to explode and knock out all our vital systems. If Beijing chooses to move on Taiwan, or anywhere else, the first strike will not be heard as an explosion, but as something worse...

Silence.

Phones do not ring. Power grids do not hum. Water taps run dry. Life support systems power off. Panic spreads. Hunger and thirst become immediate threats to staying alive. Chaos reigns. The economy collapses. Government is offline and consumed.

A once mighty nation is brought to its knees.

This is only one face of the CCP cyber war on the U.S., one that we know. Salt and Volt Typhoon exposed a sobering truth: our critical systems are wide open. Hackers could live inside power and water networks for years without detection. Our communications have been pried open and all our secrets could be pulled out at will.

"Because cyberspace has no borders," writes Anne Neuberger, Former Deputy National Security Advisor of the United States, "the U.S. homeland is always in the fight. Every hospital, power grid, pipeline, water treatment plant, and telecommunications system is on the frontlines, and most of the United States' critical infrastructure is unready for battle."

The next move will be about more than theft and sabotage: it will be about paralysis. It will be about using what they've already built, silent kill switches, to turn daily American life into chaos.

Volt and Salt taught us that the enemy is not at the gates. They are inside the village.

And are armed to kill.

States are expected to spy on each other. The CCP had been long known to steal IP and surveil civilians at scale and beyond the acceptable range of statecraft. But Salt and Volt Typhoon represented something else.

An act of war.

"When we woke up and realized what we were looking at," colleague and former U.S. Cyber Command, Senior Counterintelligence Advisor, Mike McLaughlin stated,

> *...we saw they represented a significant pivot in TTP. This was different. You don't break into an electric grid and slip back doors and kill-switches in. This wasn't robbery. This was prepositioning weapons in case of a war. We saw concentrated infiltration on the West coast, Guam and infiltration in force concentration centers should China invade Taiwan. They were turning their new capability to gain unauthorized access to our critical infrastructure into preparation for military operations. This was a cyber attack with a military intention.*

McLaughlin bristles, "this was a red line that the United States should never have allowed to be crossed. They breached our sovereignty."

It was the cyber equivalent of sending saboteurs into every American town. Volt Typhoon targeted civilian life support systems, a violation of every supposed "rule of war." It's proof the CCP is preparing to hold ordinary Americans hostage in the next conflict by cutting power, wrecking supply chains, silencing communications, and plunging cities into panic.

On January 31, 2024, FBI Director Wray said in his Opening Statement to the "House Select Committee on the Strategic Competition Between the United States and the Chinese Communist Party:" *(Renamed "Select Committee on the CCP")*

> *The CCP's dangerous actions-China's multi-pronged assault on our national and economic security-make it the defining threat of our generation... PRC [People's Republic of China] hackers are targeting our critical infrastructure-our water treatment plants, our electrical grid, our oil and natural gas pipelines, our transportation systems. China's hackers are positioning on American infrastructure in preparation to wreak havoc and cause real-world harm to American citizens and communities. If or when China decides the time has come to strike, they're not focused solely on political or military targets. We can see from where they position themselves, across civilian infrastructure, that low blows aren't only a possibility in the event of a conflict. Low blows against civilians are part of China's plan.*

This pre-positioned sabotage could easily wreck the United States' ability to organize a military response to any provocation or attack. As Anne Neuberger writes:

> *By threatening these systems, China could impede U.S. military mobilization without directly attacking military targets-avoiding the clear escalation that bombing American bases would represent. Similarly, disrupting seaports and airports could delay reinforcement deployments to the Pacific while appearing to target civilian infrastructure with nonlethal tactics. Chinese military theorists explicitly embrace this logic, describing offensive cyber-operations as a form of "strategic deterrence." More than most conventional forms of deterrence, cyber-operations offer plausible deniability.*

The U.S. Government knows the danger, and yet, we did nothing. We should have struck back "hard and clear," right after Volt Typhoon, McLaughlin suggests. That would have changed everything that has happened since.

"If we hit Mischief Reef - China's illegitimate, militarized outpost built on coral reefs in the waters toward the Philippines, it would have reset the balance of power for years," McLaughlin says.

"A decisive strike. No civilians. No moral ambiguity. Just a hard, clean message: you attack us, we attack you. Your expansion stops here. And yet, no one in Congress had the courage to demand this kind of response."

They are each too economically enmeshed with China, each too intimated to rock the boat - or more accurately, "the gravy train."

Theodore Roosevelt told us: "Speak softly and carry a big stick." That's all well and good, but you have to know when to use the stick! By failing to act, America taught the Chinese Communist Party (and Russia, Iran, and North Korea) the most dangerous lesson of all: our red lines are illusions, our sovereignty negotiable, and our leaders unwilling to defend the very Republic they swore to protect.

America's great political failing is that we draw red lines and then quietly erase them the moment they are tested. Every time we blink, every time we hesitate, Beijing learns the same lesson: America will not act on its own behalf.

How bad were the Salt and Volt Typhoon attacks? FBI Director Christopher Wray and Jen Eastman reportedly had to call America's political and corporate leaders and tell them: Stop using SMS. Stop using Email, Use Signal. It's the only secure line left. Think about that: the heads of our own law enforcement and intelligence agencies begging CEOs not to use basic text messages because they are already compromised by foreign adversaries. That is how deep the penetration went.

OPM Hack: Injury Before Insult

In fact, Salt and Volt Typhoon never should have happened. Here's why they did...

In 2015, hackers linked to the CCP infiltrated the Office of Personnel Management (OPM), the federal agency that holds the background investigation files for millions of government employees and contractors. What did they take? Everything. Social Security numbers, addresses, financial records, fingerprints, even detailed SF-86 security clearance forms - the intimate questionnaires that map out an individual's family, foreign contacts, health history, debts, and vulnerabilities.

The scale was staggering: more than *21 million Americans* had their most sensitive personal data stolen. Not only employees, but their spouses, children, friends, references as well. Anyone connected to them. They stole 5.6 million fingerprints, biometric identifiers that never change, along with detailed SF-86 security clearance forms, foreign contacts, past travels, Social Security numbers, addresses, and employment histories - a full dossier on every target - *including their families.*

The damage? It was a counterintelligence treasure trove. With this data, the CCP could now identify U.S. officials, track intelligence operatives, pressure vulnerable family members, blackmail individuals with debt, addiction, or personal secrets and with vulnerabilities in hand, they could more easily flip Americans into assets.

But Washington barely responded. Greg Gonzalez, former DOJ National Security division attorney, describes it as "A handshake and a smile." As a result of a diplomatic protest, Xi Jinping promised President Obama that China would scale back cyberattacks, and there was, indeed, a very brief lull. Then in 2024, "Salt Typhoon" emerged. Beijing flaunted the fact that they can get whatever they want, whenever they want it, with zero consequences.

A New Kind of Enemy

During the Cold War, everyone knew the Soviets were the enemy. It was taught in schools, preached in churches, and broadcast on every channel. The danger from China isn't discussed openly, and the reason is as chilling as it is obvious. With the U.S.S.R., America had zero commercial dependency. But with China, he says, "our economies are interwoven, which complicates responses.

During the Cold War, Americans knew what was at stake: a free world threatened by a dark communist force bristling with tanks and nuclear bombs. But today, most don't realize a war is already being waged against us - in cyberspace, in infrastructure, in our personal data, in our very DNA.

The CCP's daily war on us goes beyond traditional espionage. It is mass surveillance. It is personal, private, corporate, government, and military data harvesting on an unimaginable scale. The attacks pile up...

And OPM wasn't the last.

It was only the beginning of thousands of targets, naming *only a few:*

- **Equifax (2017)**
  147.9 million Americans compromised. Social Security numbers, addresses, birth dates - stolen by PLA hackers.

  The weapon: A map of America's identity grid, primed for targeting, impersonation, and blackmail.

- **Marriott / Starwood (2014–2018)**
  500 million guest records stolen, including 25 million passport numbers.

  The weapon: A global travel surveillance machine. Beijing can track diplomats, soldiers, and CEOs wherever they go.

- **DOJ Records (2020, SolarWinds)**
  27 U.S. Attorneys' Offices breached, 3% of DOJ mailboxes rifled through.

  The weapon: Advance access to America's own legal strategies, investigations, and informants.

Each breach is a strike in the same war. Each haul of stolen data feeds Beijing's ability to profile, pressure, penetrate, leverage and blackmail. Their weaponry for turning Americans or "visa-guests" into assets. *They want all of your data:* Your gambling debts. Your DNA. Your child's medical records. Your facial recognition. Everything is targeted. Nothing is off limits.

"The ultimate fear," says Gonzalez, "is social credit type analyses of Americans."

Imagine Beijing compiling these databases not only to monitor, but to control; deciding who can travel, who can be intimidated, and who can be silenced. Gonzalez warns it could one day extend into DNA-specific targeting, even the design of bioweapons for particular vulnerabilities *(see Briefing Three).*

"Is this Sci-Fi?" he asks. "That's what most people thought on September 10, 2001, when the idea of flying planes into skyscrapers seemed impossible."

We Built Our Enemy: Cyber Theft

One of the most lethal of the ancient Chinese Thirty-Six Stratagems in the "Art of War" is the maxim "Kill with a Borrowed Sword." This means you can destroy an enemy not with your own blade, but with his own weapons, his own allies, or the hands of another. In the cyber domain, the CCP has perfected this nefarious art, making every Western server farm, software update, bug, network - even your child's TikTok feed - their borrowed sword. They invade without uniforms, exfiltrate without gunfire, and let Americans pay for the privilege of hosting our own demise.

China's spectacular rise from communist-induced plague, famine, desperation, and poverty has been driven, to an extreme extent, by IP stolen from the West. Here's a very brief overview of very few of what we know:

The Winnti Group

An umbrella of MSS-controlled hackers, Winnti plundered defense, aerospace, pharma, biotech, and energy firms across three continents. They stole hundreds of gigabytes of blueprints, diagrams, formulas, and proprietary know-how. Translation: the crown jewels of Western innovation, carted off to Beijing.

Westinghouse

Hackers stole technical designs and internal emails while Westinghouse was negotiating with a Chinese state-owned partner. China literally sat at both sides of the bargaining table-one side in suits, the other in servers.

Boeing C-17

In 2009, Chinese agents working with Su Bin in Canada stole 65 gigabytes of schematics and test data on the U.S. C-17 military transport. Soon after, China unveiled the Y-20-a striking look-alike, built faster and cheaper thanks to America's stolen playbook.

U.S. Steel

Hackers broke into U.S. Steel networks during a bitter trade dispute with Chinese state-owned companies. They made off with confidential strategies and technical data-digital espionage used to tilt the scales of global steel competition.

SolarWorld

In 2012, after U.S. regulators found Chinese solar firms were dumping products, hackers hit SolarWorld. They stole financial data, manufacturing secrets, and even attorney-client communications. The result? China crushed U.S. solar manufacturing, leaving only a handful of American survivors. (Not to be confused with the SolarWinds breach.)

F-22, F-35, and Stealth Technology

PLA hackers looted Lockheed and other defense firms, stealing design secrets of the F-35, F-22, B-2 bomber, missile systems, even nuclear submarine tech. Terabytes of data equivalent to *five Libraries of Congress were exfiltrated.* The result? China's J-20 and J-31 stealth fighters, uncannily familiar silhouettes in the sky.

China Telecom

For years, state-owned China Telecom secretly rerouted U.S. and allied internet traffic through Beijing. In one 2010 incident, it *hijacked 15 percent of global internet traffic, including U.S. government and military communications, for 18 minutes.* Imagine what was copied.

Satellites

In 2018, Symantec revealed Chinese hackers had infiltrated U.S. and Asian satellite operators, with access to systems that could change orbits. Civilian communications, military targeting, and missile warning systems were all one keystroke from disruption.

Submarine Technology

That same year, Chinese hackers stole 614 gigabytes from a U.S. Navy contractor tied to the Sea Dragon program, a classified submarine-launched missile project. Even the Washington Post withheld details at the Navy's request. That's how severe the breach was.

Elon Musk

In a damning 2025 lawsuit filed by Elon Musk's xAI against OpenAI in the U.S. District Court (Northern District of California), Chinese national Xuechen Li, a former xAI engineer, is accused of stealing the company's entire AI source code on July 25, 2025. Li is accused of uploading it to a personal cloud account, downloading it to his laptop, and deleting browser history/system logs to cover tracks. These actions were allegedly orchestrated by OpenAI recruiter Tifa Chen, a *Chinese national* who started her career interning at the communist state-owned Bank of China (per her bio on theorg.com) and actively recruited *visa-dependent foreign talent* like Cheng Lu (PhD from CCP-affiliated Tsinghua University in Beijing, whom she boasted about in 2023 as "joining our Frontiers research team" while supporting his U.S. visa processing). Chen initiated contact via encrypted Signal app on July 23, beginning a methodology that fits a pattern of CCP-enabled espionage.

As FBI Director Christopher Wray warned in 2023: China steals "hundreds of billions in IP annually" through cyber intrusions and talent programs, using similar visa-fueled thefts like Weiyun "Kelly" Huang's fake H-1B scams and ex-Tesla engineer Zhongjie "Jay" Li's alleged robotics blueprint heist. These incidents highlight how *H-1B programs (abused by 85,000+ annual Chinese/Indian applicants, per U.S.C.I.S. data) serve as CCP vectors to siphon Western tech for Beijing's AI dominance.*

And in 2025, a Southern California engineer, Chenguang Gong, pleaded guilty to stealing over 3,600 files of cutting-edge U.S. missile detection technology and seeking to sell it back to Beijing under a Chinese communist Party "talent" program. The stolen data included blueprints for space-based sensors designed to detect nuclear launches and hypersonic missiles, technology worth "hundreds of millions" of dollars in damage to U.S. security, according to the FBI.

Huawei, the gargantuan, thieving Chinese electronics company (Trojan Horse), represents a case of its own. Huawei was built via *IP theft* from Canada's oldest and largest employer, $30B Nortel - Northern Telecom, Canada's "AT&T." CCP espionage began in 2000, and Nortel was bankrupt by 2008.

Futurewei is Huawei's Trojan Horse in Silicon Valley, according to the House Select Committee on the CCP, a stealth proxy of the CCP hiding in plain sight. In a letter to the CEO of Huawei, the Committee identifies Futurewei's mission as embedding CCP operatives inside the very institutions that decide how the Internet itself will function.

Behind its polished claims of "building a more open and collaborative ICT industry" lies a darker truth: Futurewei's Chief Scientist chaired the ITU group pushing Huawei's "New Internet Protocol" to replace the free and decentralized web with a system *"enabling mass surveillance, user tracking, theft of IP, and content censorship."*

The Financial Times and others condemned it as "authoritarian" and "dystopian," yet rebranded versions now surface under new names like "Polymorphic Networking." The playbook is clear: keep pushing until Beijing's model becomes the global default.

Meanwhile, Futurewei has operated as a spy shop in Silicon Valley. DOJ indictments charged it with racketeering conspiracy, conspiracy to steal trade secrets, and "repeatedly making material misrepresentations" to U.S. regulators.

The Air Force suspended it from contracting, citing "adequate evidence of conduct indicating a lack of business integrity or honesty."

A civil complaint revealed Futurewei personnel "registered using fake U.S. company names to infiltrate into the meeting." When access was denied, they smuggled "confidential information" back to China.

Even more alarming, Futurewei spent a decade embedded on NVIDIA's Santa Clara campus - America's AI crown jewel - where it had daily proximity to the most advanced semiconductor breakthroughs available today.

This is pure infiltration and weaponization. As the Committee concludes, Futurewei "functions primarily as a vehicle to maintain Huawei's otherwise prohibited U.S. operations."

It is economic and cyber warfare in lab coats and conference badges-an enemy inside our gates, burrowing deeper while America looks the other way.

Overall, Cybersecurity Magazine states that "If it were measured as a country, then cybercrime - which is predicted to inflict *damages totaling $10.5 trillion USD globally in 2025* - would be the world's third-largest economy after the U.S. and China."

That is slow-motion looting of the U.S. economy. Make no mistake, Cybersecurity isn't just some IT issue, it's a matter of national survival. Every theft carries a human cost. Through the calculated theft of IP, the enemy follows no rules and becomes immediately competitive overnight by erasing the time and money investment. Not only does the CCP *steal decades of expensive research,* that crime strengthens the underpinnings of their totalitarian communist regime. Naturally, it kills jobs here, which means lost tax revenue and more children growing up in impoverished communities to underemployed and often drug-addicted dads. It deteriorates education, hospitals, national security, and other essential services. When it comes to IP theft, *their gain is directly our loss.* The CCP blatantly destroys U.S. companies, and even industries, by selling your product to your customers at 25 to 50 cents on the dollar.

The CCP executes its soft power as well as hard hacks to tap into our data.

Since 2018, for example, Apple *(who produces its cash-cow iPhones in China)* has complied with Beijing's data localization and national security law by storing all iCloud data of mainland users on servers in Guizhou, servers run by a CCP-linked company called GCBD.

That means:

- The encryption keys are in China, not at Apple HQ.
- Chinese officials have physical and electronic control of the servers.
- Apple made "a series of compromises," in their own words, to meet the Party's demands.

Chinese intelligence has physical control over your hardware. The human rights implications are staggering. Amnesty International warns that dissidents, journalists, and ordinary citizens now live under Beijing's shadow: their messages, photos, and contacts are all accessible to the state. Even Apple's own pop-ups tell users the truth: their data is subject to China's control.

In 2014, Chinese authorities almost certainly backed a man-in-the-middle iCloud hack, intercepting login credentials across the country. That was the test run. By 2018, Beijing didn't need to hack anymore - Apple gave them the keys.

Justice Hacked

Multiple government as well as corporate fronts have been breached, but that should surprise no one, at this point. The CCP has turned America's courts, the guardians of law and justice, into a one-sided battlefield. Relentless, organized, and strategic, CCP-linked hackers broke into the federal judiciary's case management system, going straight for sealed documents in espionage, money laundering, and cases involving foreign agents. They wanted the blueprints:

wiretap requests, search warrants, and cooperator names. With that intelligence, adversaries can preempt raids, silence witnesses, and dismantle investigations before they begin.

In other words, the very files meant to protect Americans from covert threats were stolen from under the judges' noses.

Think of what that means: informant identities, personal data, sealed evidence, sensitive trial strategies - all compromised. The intelligence treasure trove now in enemy hands empowers hostile states to shield their operatives, reroute their money, and sharpen their attacks against us.

Once discovered, the fallout was immediate. The Eastern District of Virginia, home to America's most sensitive national security cases, announced that all sealed documents must now be filed as hard copies only. Other courts from Brooklyn to Miami followed suit, scrambling to roll back the clock to pen, paper, and hand delivery.

This was targeted warfare. By infiltrating our judicial system, Beijing gains leverage over prosecutions, insight into intelligence operations, and the ability to intimidate anyone who dares cooperate with U.S. authorities.

FBI cyber officials admit the consequences: when hostile states seize this intelligence, they don't just keep it, they weaponize it. It equips their criminal syndicates, front companies, and covert networks to adapt faster, evade detection, and strike deeper.

The courts are the backbone of American sovereignty. Once adversaries can peer into sealed indictments and classified proceedings, justice itself becomes compromised. Every tactic, every investigative trick, every digital footprint the U.S. relies on is suddenly obsolete. Confidential informants can be burned. Ongoing espionage cases can be sabotaged. National security prosecutions can be gutted before trial. What we thought were safe havens of truth and law have become foxholes in a wider war. The courts, once the nation's safe repository of truth, have been turned into a weapon against it.

Another treasure trove of theft has been law firms where the motherlode of IP is stored, including innovation, future plans, negotiation strategies, even contact information for key executives, their spouses, at their primary home and even vacation homes.

Data theft, IP theft, and planting sabotage inside our infrastructure have all come into the light. But that's the tip of the iceberg. Roughly only 4% of the Internet is visible to the average user. The other 96% lies beneath the surface, hidden from standard search engines. This is the darknet - a vast, shadow network where weapons, data, and influence are bought and sold. Three years ago, 80% of the darknet was the domain of individual hackers and criminal groups. Today, 80% is controlled by nation-states, many of them hostile to America. They've absorbed those hackers into their intelligence services, turning what was once freelance crime into state-sponsored cyberwarfare.

As you are learning, Cyber is not a side show. According to the FBI, the CCP has a bigger hacking program than every other major nation combined. In fact, if each one of the FBI's cyber agents and intelligence analysts focused exclusively on the China threat, China's hackers would still *outnumber FBI cyber personnel by at least 50 to 1.* Cyber is the key accelerator - it amplifies all other unrestricted warfare methods. All of us are already on the battlefield. When you own a smartphone, use apps, drive a connected car, stream video, or log into a computer, you are part of the attack surface. Every American is wired into the war, whether they know it or not. In fact, 65% of Americans use a CCP-controlled TP-Link router in their homes acting as a data super-highway back to China.

That's why cyber is not only another weapon. It is the center of the CCP's modern unrestricted warfare strategy. It accelerates every other form of attack - economic, political, cultural, cognitive, and military - with efficiency, at low cost and high reward. It is a force multiplier for every other kind of CCP Unrestricted Warfare against us. As FBI Director Christopher Wray testified to Congress,

The PRC cyber threat is made vastly more dangerous by the way they knit cyber into a whole-of-government campaign against us. They recruit human sources to target our businesses, using insiders to steal the same kinds of innovation and data their hackers are targeting while also engaging in corporate deception-hiding Beijing's hand in transactions, joint ventures, and investments-to do the same. And they don't only hit our security and economy. They target our freedoms, reaching inside our borders, across America, to silence, coerce, and threaten our citizens and residents.

These attacks succeeded in large part because of the nature of our free society. Beijing has erected its formidable, centralized Great Firewall to actively filter out not only information they don't want reaching their people, but also to serve as a centralized sentinel on the lookout for hacks. Simultaneously, the West forbids exactly that kind of comprehensive, centralized monitoring. What's more, as of this writing, responsibility for cyber forces is fragmented across five different services. The U.S. Army, Navy, Air Force, Marine Corps - and soon, Space Force - are each separately responsible for the recruitment, initial training, promotion, and retention of their own cyber forces.

And while many good men and women are fighting the good fight, trying to create a more focused, effective Federal and international counterbalance to Beijing's cyberwar on us, they have been crippled by both political and technological obstacles. As Anne Neuberger has written:

Congress has shown little appetite for extending the legal authority and sustained investment that comprehensive cyberdefense requires. Private companies resist mandated security requirements that increase costs.Yet a wait-and-see approach has become unacceptable. If Washington does not move fast, artificial intelligence will only accelerate China's advantages.

Christopher Wray concurs, testifying to Congress:

> *I do not want those watching today to think we can't protect ourselves. But I do want the American people to know that we cannot afford to sleep on this danger. As a government and a society, we've got to remain vigilant and actively defend against the threat Beijing poses. Otherwise, China has shown it will make us pay.*

Fighting Back

As you are beginning to see, the CCP's cyber war on us is not something "over there." It is here, now, woven into the fabric of our daily lives. The devices in your pocket, the routers in your home, the Wi-Fi in your airport, hotel, and coffee shop. Every American is on the battlefield - whether you chose it or not.

We cannot wait for Washington alone. Every individual has a role to play. See what you can do now in Briefing Twelve and beyond.

The Red Tsunami is here.

The question is: *will we drown, or will we fight to survive it?*

BRIEFING SIX
The Battle For Your Child's Mind
Education War

The Chinese Communist Party crept into your child's classroom years ago.

It bribes your local school district. It recruits turncoats in your universities and steals the most sensitive technologies. It does its diabolical best to bend the minds that will inherit this nation, channeling them toward the lies, false utopia, and authoritarian nightmare of communism.

In short, education is the battleground for America's future brain trust and leadership, and right now, the CCP is winning it from the inside out.

The CCP knows something many American parents are just waking up to: the classroom and the developing mind is a "soft" and active battlefront. If you can shape the next generation, their values, their loyalties, their beliefs, their civic instincts, you don't ever need to ever fire a shot. You win the war from within.

The quiet invasion of our education systems began innocently, from our side, and with typical American goodwill. In 1978, Chinese leader Deng Xiaoping saw the need to shift China out of the blood-soaked wreckage of Mao's legacy and began reaching out to the West and to capitalism with his "Reform and Opening Up" policy. As part of that, he made an initial strategic decision to send 3,000 students and scholars from China overseas each year to further their education. U.S. President Jimmy Carter replied: "Tell him [Deng] to send 100,000!"

Carter, like the administrations that followed him, was making a fatal false bet that inviting China into the world would bring freedom, democracy, and abundance in its wake. And so, the flood of Chinese students to the U.S. began. By the 2018-19 school year, they numbered *369,548, comprising 33.7% of the 1.09 million international students in the U.S.*

But this flood has come with a deadly catch.

The CCP has treated American openness as an invitation to exploitation, thievery and treachery. An invitation to conduct its unrestricted war inside our borders. Inside our sovereign nation. They have sent countless waves of students, researchers, and "teachers" to covertly gather the tools and intelligence they need to undercut us, our intellectual property and trade secrets. All the while, they subvert our schools and campuses with socialist (communist) anti-freedom propaganda to destroy our fundamental cultural cohesion. The CCP considers every ethnic Chinese living abroad a national asset whose first and only loyalty is to the CCP, and can be called at any time to report back, or bring back any intelligence that will strengthen Beijing against its primary enemy.

FBI Director Christopher Wray stated, "the current Chinese regime will stop at nothing to steal what they can't create and silence the messages they don't want us to hear, all in an effort to surpass us ..."

He has warned repeatedly that China is engaging in a "breadth of theft and malign influence" that uses all tools and all sectors to steal what America has built, including within our labs and research institutions.

How pervasive is this thievery? In a speech made at the Reagan Presidential Library, Wray said that the FBI opens a new counter-intelligence case against the Chinese every 10 hours.

"When we tally up what we see in our investigations - over 2,000 of which are focused on the Chinese government trying to steal our information or technology, there is no country that presents a broader threat to our ideas, innovation, and economic security than China."_

Many of these cases are tied to researcher pathways and university-based joint ventures as much as cyber intrusions (Briefing Five), and corporate insiders (Briefing Six). This is a broad, diverse campaign of theft and malign influence, executed, in Wray's words, "with authoritarian efficiency."

We opened our doors in friendship. We offered exchange, scholarship, and free discourse. And in return, our educational institutions have been turned into channels for stolen research, shadow networks pushing communist ideology, surveillance, and often violent quashing of dissenting "freedom" voices.

It is first essential to recognize that the CCP commands that any Chinese national abroad is, de facto, an "asset," or "soldier" in the CCP/PLA matrix. Even the most reluctant Chinese nationals studying abroad are pressured to report progress back to their communist handlers, to identify innovation for theft, to monitor peers, to suppress voices, or face consequences for themselves and their families back "home."

Westerners don't fully comprehend totalitarian communism. When students depart China, they must sign a CCP "loyalty pledge" with their local government station to spy for the motherland. Disobey that pledge at your and your family's at risk.

If this slick and silent educational warfare continues unchecked, America will wake one day to find the unique intellectual engine of our universities, the once prodigious fount of our innovation and wealth, has been drained and rerouted, the trust in them eroded and the cultural foundations of liberty and free inquiry hollowed out. Because ultimately, what China is trying to steal at our schools and universities, is not our products and ideas, but our entire future.

K-12: Little Red Classrooms

The infiltration starts with our little kids.

Leading with big checks, the CCP planted "Confucius Classrooms" in 143 K–12 school districts across 34 states, subjecting more than 170,000 American children to pro-Chinese Communist Party propaganda. And the CCP's aim is often geographically and academically precise.

Over 20 of these schools sit within miles of U.S. military bases, posing, according to testimony in Congress, a national security risk. Thomas Jefferson High School for Science and Technology in Virginia, America's crown jewel STEM magnet, received over $1 million in CCP-linked funds for a "sister school" partnership to share its tech and techniques with Tsinghua University High School, which is connected to Tsinghua University, a Chinese military school "supervised" by the Chinese defense industry, according to the Australian Strategic Policy Institute.

Confucius Classrooms sound like innocent cultural and language sharing, but in fact execute carefully constructed ideological grooming. Think of them as educational time bombs, camouflaged in the name of the harmless, gentle ancient sage, Confucius (whose teachings, by the way, Mao tried to eradicate during the Cultural Revolution).

Congressional hearings, state investigations, and independent watchdogs have traced the money, contracts, and classroom content of the Confucius Classrooms back to Beijing's CCP and PLA propaganda ministries.

U.S. Representative Aaron Bean, a Republican in Florida and chair of the House Committee on Education and the Workforce's Early Childhood, Elementary, and Secondary Education Subcommittee, reported during a congressional hearing entitled, "Academic Freedom Under Attack: Loosening the CCP's Grip on America's Classrooms,"

> *Schools across the United States have allowed the CCP to establish itself in their halls under the guise of Confucius Classrooms. But when you pull back the curtain on these cultural exchange centers,*

you find a CCP-backed agenda that undermines the principles upon which our freedom and education system is built.

Let's look at the subtle and not so subtle ideas these generously funded "educational" implants into our children's minds execute. To start, they supply textbooks which glorify the CCP while forbidding all references to Tiananmen Square, human rights, state-run forced organ harvesting, Taiwan, and Tibet, and Uyghur "re-education," while planting seeds of sympathy for authoritarianism, wholly erasing democracy's noble, bloody yet failed struggle to emerge in greater China. All that is expected.

The propaganda goes beyond mere whitewashing of communist horrors. In order to keep the money flowing, school districts sign contracts with Confucius Institutes that include clauses that give Chinese government entities control over teacher hiring, curricula, and cultural programming, effectively importing CCP-dictated staff and lesson plans. And of course, no discussion of "sensitive issues" are permitted or funding would be pulled.

School districts in Texas, Oregon, and Kentucky accepted direct grants from the Chinese government (via the CCP's Hanban, now called "Confucius Institute Headquarters") to sponsor Chinese teachers, cultural events, and curriculum development, including lush "field trips" for staff to China, strictly for "cultural orientation." In one Texas suburb alone, with a population of approximately 300,000, there are 22 Chinese schools. In fact, a Senate Office investigation and HSGAC report documented that *China has invested $158 million+ into U.S. schools since 2006*, via Confucius Institutes/Classrooms.

A parade of witnesses testified to Congress that CCP-backed programs in elementary and middle schools promoted "heroic" portraits of communist leaders and normalization of autocratic governance. The propaganda is so obvious and so strong that the State Department eventually designated Confucius Institutes and linked K-12 programs as "foreign missions" directly identified as part of the CCP's overseas propaganda and influence operations.

Besides whitewashing Beijing's murderous totalitarian history, the following informational warfare examples have been presented in investigations and Congressional oversight hearings:

- Cultural projects or language assignments that require students to memorize or repeat proverbs or stories praising obedience, tradition, or loyalty, strengthening the idea of subservience, not individual sovereignty.
- Compositions/speaking prompts for students to write or talk about "why China is our friend" or "what we learn from Chinese culture" amid strictly censored and biased information.
- Investigative reporting and parent groups have found contracts stipulating "joint decision making" in classrooms between CCP-linked officials and American school administrators.
- Documents that reveal direct involvement of the CCP's United Front Work Department (which leads China's international propaganda campaigns) in curriculum approval and staff selection for American K-12 programs.
- During "Confucius Day" events, American elementary students reported activities promoting "national pride" in China, complete with red flag-waving and CCP slogans under teacher instruction.
- Schools in Montana, Pennsylvania, and California have received documented offers of Chinese government funds and mandatory cultural curriculum "co-developed" with visiting CCP officials. Materials and maps present China's territorial claims (Taiwan, Tibet, South China Sea) as uncontested fact.
- Parent advocacy groups tracked "sister-school" arrangements where American students correspond with Chinese peers using carefully screened, pro-CCP content and storytelling as "cultural exchange," with classroom teachers required to censor discussion of Western democratic principles.

This CCP initiative has been so blatant that Senior Fellow at the Heritage Foundation, Michael Gonzalez, reported to the Congressional Early Childhood, Elementary, and Secondary Education (ECESE) Subcommittee:

> *"By allowing the Institutes and the Classrooms to continue, the U.S. government is allowing not only a foreign government, but a communist party, to dictate what our children learn about an adversary."*

The CCP's strategy is neither subtle nor deniable: it is a persistent, well-funded campaign to shape and control our young minds. Fortunately, thanks to the hard work of leaders like Gonzalez, the pushback has begun.

In 2023, Florida Gov. Ron DeSantis signed a law prohibiting public schools from entering into any agreement with or accepting any grants from "a foreign country of concern," specifying fears over the Chinese communist Party's influence on American schools. Further, he barred four private schools that he claimed had "direct ties to the Chinese communist Party" from receiving funds through the state's private school voucher program, which allows families to use public money for private school tuition.

DeSantis understands and speaks up on what most leaders are afraid to, pledging to "go after the cultural power [China has] in our country."

As part of that, he also banned the CCP from buying land in his state. "We should do that all across these United States," he said. "We shouldn't have them in our universities. We shouldn't have Confucius Institutes."

Similarly, in late 2024, The Texas House Select Committee on Securing Texas From Hostile Foreign Organizations also flagged Confucius Institutes and Confucius Classrooms as hostile and detrimental to the children of their state. Said the committee:

Adversary-controlled cultural exchanges and financial gifts to school systems may serve as avenues for infiltration. Through these means, adversaries could embed narratives or collect data in ways that circumvent local oversight, influencing curricula and fostering dependency on external educational providers.

Yes they "could" - and they, in fact, do.

The pushback has worked. Several Confucius Classroom programs have been shut down although the CCP has been engaged in rebranding them under new names, pushing the same programs, the same CCP funding streams, the same hidden strings.

And their attempt to own the minds of your youngest and most impressionable stretches beyond infiltrating America's public K-12 schools...

CCP Buying Our Private Schools

While slipping its tentacles into the minds of our public schoolchildren, Beijing is simultaneously quietly buying up America's private K-12 schools and colleges. In 2015, for example, a mysterious Chinese company bought the New York Military Academy, yes, the very prep school President Donald Trump attended, with its U.S. Army-aligned JROTC program. A Chinese-backed firm also scooped up Florida Preparatory Academy, which runs a U.S. Air Force JROTC track. Parents thinking they were escaping leftist indoctrination by turning to private schools walked straight into the CCP's trap.

Congressman and former National Security advisor Mike Waltz (FL) blew the whistle:

It's incredibly concerning that there are American private schools owned by companies with strong ties to the Chinese communist Party (CCP). From Florida to New York, there is clear evidence that the ownership of these schools are linked to our greatest adversary and it's ridiculous that we are developing potential future military leaders through JROTC programs where the CCP could be shaping school curriculum and activities.

Let that sink in: JROTC cadets - our future officers - are being trained and tracked inside schools controlled by the CCP. The buying spree extends beyond military academies to other elite private schools where America's future leaders study. As of this writing, the CCP now owns or controls or is linked to the owners of:

- **Stratford School:** Majority-owned by Primavera Capital Group, a China-based private equity firm led by Fred Hu, who has documented ties to the CPPCC, a key "united front" organization under the CCP's umbrella, designed to co-opt elites, intellectuals, and business leaders into supporting party goals.
- **BASIS Independent Schools (New York and Other States)** With campuses in New York and beyond, BASIS Independent Schools were purchased by a company backed by Chinese investors, specifically through a Hong Kong-based entity.
- **Busche Academy:** Established after the sale of Chester College of New England to a private Chinese group (Jiahui Education Group) in 2015.
- **Florida Preparatory Academy:** Purchased in 2017 by Newopen U.S.A., a subsidiary of Chongqing, China-based Newopen Group, which has a major education presence in China and operates other U.S. programs.
- **Chesterbrook Academy, Nobel Learning Communities, Laurel Springs School, and Paladin Academy:** All operate under the umbrella of Spring Education Group, primarily owned by Primavera Capital Group, the Hong Kong/China-based investment firm founded and run by Fred Hu. Spring Education Group manages over 200 private schools of varying levels across 19 U.S. states.

Money and geography make this strategy surgical. Stratford lists 30 locations, including San Jose, Palo Alto, and San Francisco, the key U.S. tech hubs where influence and access matter. And wealthy Chinese families pay premium prices to fast-track entry into these schools and other elite U.S. higher education institutions and its networks. The investors behind the purchases are not amateurs: Primavera counts Goldman Sachs alumni and graduates of Harvard, Columbia, NYU.

Beijing's reach is not limited to the U.S. Across the Atlantic, they've bought 17 private schools in the UK - nine directly controlled by senior CCP members, according to the Daily Mail.

Mao spelled out the strategy: young minds, in all their fragility, were a primary target. The CCP turned internal Chinese schools into brutal indoctrination factories during the Cultural Revolution. Millions died, often at the hands of radicalized students, and Mao considered it all a success. CCP officials often quote Zhou Enlai's 1963 Ten Theses on the necessity of reshaping the next generation's worldview through education. These include the following principles which happen to be directly hostile to our core social values, yet they are being filtered into our system:

- **Weaponize Intellectuals:** Redirect teachers, professors, writers, and scientists to serve the Party's ideological goals.
- **Replace Family & Tradition:** Dismantle inherited values, replacing them with Party-approved "truths."
- **Exploit Authority:** Use the prestige of educators and professionals to lend credibility to Party ideology.
- **Prepare Successors:** Systematically raise a new generation of leaders loyal only to the CCP and Mao.
- **Perpetual Struggle:** Education as a battlefield and every generation must be won over.

Mao's formula and Zhao's theses haven't changed; they have been imported into our own schools.

Do we want the CCP holding files on America's future soldiers, engineers, business leaders, and lawmakers? Do we want Chinese-controlled institutions guiding the "school choice" movement, so parents desperate to flee failing public schools unknowingly hand their children over to Beijing's long game?

Of course not.

China is buying the minds of America's next generation of leaders. Primavera Capital Group, which also holds investments in ByteDance, the parent of TikTok, the CCP's wildly successful cultural and cognitive warfare weapon has also bought Tutor.com and Princeton Review (SAT, ACT, AP, PSAT, GMAT, LCAT, MCAT, GRE, CPA, CISA). The CCP now has access to student data across the board. It should be noted that Tutor.com is widely used by our military families.

If our republic values the civics and character that schools once reinforced, this market-driven, foreign-funded buying spree demands immediate reversal before another generation is routed through CCP-controlled corridors of influence.

While the CCP's infiltration of sensitive university labs and departments has raised public concern, few people realize how many Chinese students have been sent to our high schools overall.

Since 2016, the number of Chinese secondary students studying in the United States on F-1 visas has seen huge increases. This is soft power weaponized: steadily filtering CCP-friendly students (remember, Chinese nationals have no choice but to pledge loyalty and supply intel to their communist regime masters) into our educational institutions. In 2016, there were 59,392 secondary students on F-1 visas, of whom 33,275-about 56 percent-were from China. By 2018, this number increased by nearly 17 percent to 39,904 Chinese F-1 secondary students, reflecting rising demand and deepening educational ties.

More recent reports indicate the number of Chinese students in American high schools has continued to climb markedly, with a 48 percent increase since 2013.

The numbers at our university are far higher… and carry far more immediate consequence and danger.

Marxist Destruction of American Universities

"No nation has targeted Western research, science and technology as aggressively as China."

That is the conclusion of the National Counterintelligence and Security Center's recent 40-page report, "Safeguarding Academia: Protecting Fundamental Research, Intellectual Property, Critical Technologies and the U.S. Research Ecosystem."

Let the following words from that same report burn into your consciousness: "The Chinese Communist Party (CCP) and Chinese intelligence services represent the broadest, most active and persistent espionage threat to the U.S."

Universities, the supposed sanctuaries of open inquiry and critical thinking have become the CCP's softest underbelly for attack. The scale of this attack is astounding. At the peak in 2018, there were an estimated 405,000 Chinese students at U.S. universities.

Despite pandemic disruptions, the 2023-24 academic year saw approximately *277,000 Chinese students enrolled in U.S. colleges and universities,* accounting for roughly 24.6 percent of total international enrollments. Chinese students largely concentrate in fields like mathematics, computer science, engineering, and business, paying significant tuition often at international rates, which makes it difficult for universities to say no.

The result? Direct espionage through intelligence officers posing as students, IP theft, and coercion of faculty and students, harassment of dissidents on campuses, as well as recruitment of key professors, researchers, and graduate students under the notorious "Thousand Talents Plan."

These visiting students are not studying feminist resistance poetry or indigenous basket weaving. They register overwhelmingly in technology fields that reads like a blueprint for 21st-century dominance: AI, machine learning, quantum technologies, semiconductors, optics, hypersonics, energy systems, genetics, medicine.

And again, under China's 2017 National Intelligence Law, Article 7, *every single one of them is treated as an intelligence asset and compelled to cooperate with the CCP's intelligence apparatus.*

Some of these students are here to learn, of course. But others, handpicked by Beijing, are here to conduct espionage and steal. They are embedded in labs working on AI, robotics, quantum computing, and military-grade technologies. Even as I was researching this book, at Stanford insiders revealed that Chinese international students are reporting directly to CCP handlers, spawning a national scandal.

The FBI has repeatedly warned that Chinese Students and Scholars Associations (CSSAs), operating on nearly 200 U.S. campuses, answer directly to Chinese consulates. They monitor, intimidate, and control their fellow students, and funnel information back to Beijing.

Evidence shows that many of China's so-called "Seven Sons of National Defense" universities, which operate as feeder schools for the PLA, developing hypersonic weapons, drones, UAVs, and cyber warfare tools, have formal and informal student pipelines directly into American research programs. According to a report from the Select Committee on the CCP (previously: The Congressional Select Committee on Strategic Competition Between the United States and the Chinese Communist Party): "Over 400 Chinese nationals-enough to crew two Arleigh Burke-class U.S. Navy destroyers-are conducting sensitive research at just one U.S. university, all at the expense of hardworking American taxpayers."

Joint institutes and research collaborations between leading U.S. and Chinese universities facilitate the direct transfer of critical technologies to Chinese state-security and defense entities. For example, the University of Illinois Urbana-Champaign's "Zhejiang University - University of Illinois Joint Engineering Institute" was flagged as a pipeline for sensitive U.S. technological expertise into an institution co-administered by China's top defense research agency, SASTIND. A congressional report warned: "Joint institutes pair prestigious U.S. universities with Chinese counterparts under the guise of academic cooperation, but in practice, they serve as sophisticated conduits for transferring critical U.S. technologies and expertise to the PRC, including to entities linked to China's defense and security apparatus."

The infiltration operates through multiple channels including direct student and faculty exchanges, joint research labs, sponsored professorships, and informal faculty-level collaborations. The scope of collaboration is so broad and deep, it remains frequently unclear to university administrations. For example, the University of Maryland conceded that it "does not maintain complete insight into what, exactly, [Chinese students] are researching" and "does not comprehensively track the type of research students are conducting," despite many participating in federally funded projects.

Congressional investigators have highlighted how lack of clear oversight and insufficient enforcement of visa and export-control laws has allowed the CCP to embed itself "in the heart of America's top universities." The Select Committee's findings warn that "failure to establish effective guardrails and due diligence standards has created a pipeline through which the CCP can accelerate its military-industrial ambitions using American science, American systems, and American openness."

One flagrant program that has caught the concerned attention of American officials is The Thousand Talents Program, which we've mentioned earlier in brief. The Thousand Talents Program is designed to weaponize American openness. Through this program, Chinese national and U.S. trained professors and researchers are offered money, status, and labs in exchange for funneling American innovation to the CCP/PLA. In 2019, U.S. Attorney General William Barr declared at a U.S. Attorney's Conference:

The Chinese communist Party's Thousand Talents Program encourages theft by commissioning Chinese nationals studying at U.S. universities to acquire and steal U.S. intellectual property and research. We've seen cases where participants in this program hid their Chinese affiliations while applying for U.S. grants, effectively turning our own funding against us.

Former Director of National Intelligence John Ratcliffe confirmed...

China's Thousand Talents Program is a blueprint for stealing our ideas and talent. It preys on the ambition of brilliant minds, tempting them with lucrative offers to share-often secretly-our cutting-edge research. This isn't collaboration; it's a systematic assault on American innovation that endangers our technological edge and military superiority."

Rep. Mike Gallagher (R-WI), Former Chair of the House Select Committee on the CCP and a true warrior committed to protecting American interests, testified in committee:

The Thousand Talents Program is the velvet glove over the iron fist of CCP espionage. It recruits our brightest minds with promises of prestige and paydays, but the real goal is to hollow out American R&D and supercharge China's military-industrial complex. We've lost count of the dual-use technologies siphoned off- from AI to biotech-that now threaten our alliances and way of life. (House Select Committee hearing on "China's Exploitation of Global Technology," March 2023)

Let's be clear: *the Thousand Talents Program is the largest state-sponsored talent-recruitment and IP theft operation in history.* And it's just one part of the broad battle front. Here's a tiny sampling of what's been going on in our ivory towers:

- A U.S. professor handed genetic data to Chinese researchers. Beijing's Ministry of Public Security weaponized it to build a DNA database of Uyghur minorities, used to track and suppress dissidents. The data was used to build a comprehensive DNA database that enabled the CCP to identify and track Uyghur dissidents, sparking widespread criticism from human rights groups. This is genocide assistance imported through American research.
- A Chinese student in the U.S. was sentenced to prison for stalking a fellow student who dared post pro-democracy flyers. He threatened to "chop off the student's hands" and report her family to Chinese security services. On sovereign U.S. soil, free speech is persecuted and silenced by Beijing's long arm.
- Ji Chaoqun, a Chinese student recruited by the Ministry of State Security, infiltrated a U.S. university, then joined the Army aiming for citizenship and access to CIA or FBI jobs. He was arrested in 2023 and sentenced to eight years in prison as an unregistered foreign agent.
- Harvard star scientist Charles Lieber secretly took CCP cash while running $15 million in U.S. taxpayer-funded research for the Pentagon and NIH. He became a "Strategic Scientist" at Wuhan University of Technology while hiding Chinese income. He was convicted in 2021.
- Several U.S. universities have been fined six-figures for secretly taking CCP money - even from notorious Huawei (see Briefing 6) - while applying for federal grants.

How does the media report all this, if they bother to at all? They downplay it.

The media, if they report this at all, downplays it as isolated incidents of theft. But it is WAR.

And the CCP tightens the noose every day. Economic "links" to the CCP/PRC induce self-censorship and obedience since so many American universities receive huge donations from Chinese government entities, companies, and individuals. The U.S. Department of Education General Counsel asserts that "the evidence suggests massive investments of foreign money have bred dependency and distorted the decision making, mission, and values of too many institutions."

Universities in the United States were given more than $56 million from Chinese sources in 2017 alone, according to Stein Ringen in "Totalitarianism: A Letter to Fellow China Analysts," (That's Democracy blog, September 19, 2018).

Two notable examples of this: Stanford University "received $32,244,826 in monetary gifts from China" during six years, while Harvard University "received $55,065,261 through a combination of contracts and monetary gifts."

Other American universities have refused to cooperate with a federal investigation into their CCP/PRC income sources.

The CCP has infiltrated our campuses, compromised administrations with huge checks, corrupted our professors and fellow-students by stifling their free-speech, stolen our most innovative technological breakthroughs, and, worst of all, converted American taxpayer-funded advanced sciences into the bristling arsenal of a relentless adversary bent on global domination.

If America does not wake up immediately to these infiltrations, the Red Tsunami will wash away our technological edge, our national security, and our freedom itself.

"Useful Idiots:" Marxists with Tenure

Across campus from the science departments, our universities' liberal arts classrooms have become a tragic joke.

Three generations of neo-Marxist professors hiring ever more extreme Marxist junior professors have turned our elite campuses into incubators of virulent anti-American ideology. Whereas students may have once productively analyzed cultural, social, or economic challenges in the U.S., a quick search turns up current course titles that make the core curriculum all sound like variations of a declared major called: "Wow! I Hate America!"

- "Decolonizing the American Empire: Marxist Perspectives on U.S. Imperialism"
- "Critical Race Theory and the Critique of American Capitalism"
- "Whiteness as Property: Anti-Colonial Readings of U.S. History"
- "The Exploitation of Labor in the Neoliberal University: A Marxist Analysis"
- "Imperialism and Resistance: Unlearning American Exceptionalism"
- "Capitalist Patriarchy: Feminist and Marxist Critiques of U.S. Gender Politics"
- "From Manifest Destiny to Mass Incarceration: Marxist Views on American Racial Capitalism"

Wouldn't you love to pay $80,000 a year for your kids to absorb all that? Recently, one professor, at the University of Minnesota, draped in a terror-support scarf, told her students: "I hope you seek to dismantle the United States!" She is not alone. Here's a small smattering of the Super-Villains teaching our kids:

- **Ward Churchill, University of Colorado Boulder** (former professor of ethnic studies): In a 2001 essay titled "Some People Push Back," Churchill referred to victims of the 9/11 attacks as "little Eichmanns," comparing them to Nazi bureaucrat Adolf Eichmann and accusing the U.S. of being a "technocratic corps" enabling global imperialism. (Source: Churchill's essay in Pockets of Resistance; covered in The New York Times and Chronicle of Higher Education.)

- **Angela Davis, University of California, Santa Cruz** (emerita professor of history of consciousness): A self-identified communist and former Black Panther, Davis stated in a 2016 interview that "capitalism has no moral or ethical foundation" (Source: Davis's memoir, "Freedom Is a Constant Struggle" and interviews with The Nation, 2016–2023.)
- **Cornel West, Harvard University and Princeton University** *(former professors of African American studies and religion):* In his 2020 presidential campaign and book Race Matters (updated editions), West described the U.S. as a "corporate plutocracy" built on "the gangster style of American capitalism," urging "prophetic resistance" to dismantle it through democratic socialism influenced by Marxist thought. (Source: West's "The Cornel West Reader" and CNN interviews, 2016–2024.)
- **Robin D.G. Kelley, University of California, Los Angeles (UCLA)** *(professor of American history):* In his 2020 book, "The Long Student Movement," Kelley portrays the U.S. as a "racial capitalist empire" that must be "abolished" through Black radical traditions, drawing on Marxist and Frankfurt School critiques of how American democracy perpetuates exploitation. (Source: Kelley's writings in Boston Review and Jacobin magazine, 2015–2024.)
- **Nikhil Pal Singh, New York University (NYU)** *(professor of social and cultural analysis):* In his 2004 book, "Black Is a Country," Singh argues that American nationalism is inherently "imperial and genocidal," calling for a "decolonization" of U.S. institutions to reject Western liberal values as tools of racial capitalism. (Source: Singh's book and a 2019 panel at the American Studies Association critiquing U.S. exceptionalism.)
- **Mohamed Abdou, Cornell University** *(visiting assistant professor of anthropology, 2023–2024):* In a November 2024 TIME magazine op-ed, Abdou described the U.S. as a "settler-colonial empire" complicit in "genocide" and urging the abolition

of Western academic structures as tools of imperialism. (Source: TIME op-ed, November 2024; covered in The Cornell Daily Sun and Inside Higher Ed.)

- **Rabab Abdulhadi, San Francisco State University** *(professor and director of Arab and Muslim Ethnicities and Diasporas Studies, 2023):* Advocated for "intifada" against American imperialism. (Source: Hearing testimony transcript via House Committee on Education and the Workforce; covered by Fox News and the San Francisco Chronicle, May 2023.)
- **Noura Erakat, Rutgers University** *(associate professor of Africana studies):* In a November 2023 public lecture and subsequent op-ed in The Nation, Erakat called for the "dismantling" of American institutions that uphold Western liberal values as covers for imperialism and advocated for global anti-capitalist solidarity. (Source: The Nation op-ed, November 2023.)
- **Sunaina Maira, University of California, Davis** *(professor of Asian American studies, 2024):* In a March 2024 faculty statement supporting pro-Palestine encampments, Maira described the U.S. as an "imperial power" built on "settler colonialism" at home and abroad, critiquing American democracy as a "myth" that masks racial capitalism, and calling for universities to reject Western "Enlightenment" values in favor of decolonial resistance. (Source: UC Davis faculty letter archived on the AAUP website; Maira's statements in Jacobin magazine, April 2024.)
- **Keeanga-Yamahtta Taylor, Princeton University** *(professor of African American studies, 2023):* In her June 2023 book "Until We Are Free: Black Feminism, Marxism, and the Abolition of the Carceral State," Taylor portrayed the U.S. as a "racial capitalist empire" whose policing and prisons must be "abolished" to end Western exploitation.

- **Marc Lamont Hill, City University of New York (CUNY)** *(professor of urban education, 2023):* In a December 2023 CNN appearance and subsequent Substack post, Hill urged the "dismantling" of American foreign policy and institutions to achieve "global liberation" from Western imperialist legacies, drawing on Black Marxist traditions. (Source: CNN transcript; Hill's "On the Spot" Substack, December 2023, reported by Mediaite.)
- **Jeong Eun Annan, Duke University** *(associate professor of the practice in gender, sexuality, and feminist studies, 2024):* In an April 2024 op-ed in The Chronicle of Higher Education, Annan critiqued U.S. universities as "complicit in empire-building" through their endowment investments and curricula, calling for a "decolonial reckoning" that rejects Western liberal arts as perpetuating capitalist and patriarchal violence, (Source: Chronicle op-ed, April 2024; Annan's Duke faculty page and related panel discussions at the National Women's Studies Association.)

This is all right out of the communist playbook. Yuri Bezmenov, the high ranking Russian defector, laid out the strategy in his famous 1984 interview with G. Edward Griffin. He said the communists have a clear goal: in place of forming disciplined, competent citizens who can build and defend a nation, the Marxist subverter seeks to make them incompetent:

> *...in terms of young people, it is very important to distract them. Distract them from learning something which is constructive, pragmatic, efficient. Instead of mathematics, physics, foreign languages, chemistry-teach them the history of urban warfare, natural foods, home economy, sexuality-anything as long as it takes you away from the useful skills. And this is the most important part of demoralization: to make the young people useless.*

Marxists have taken over our universities, replacing hard knowledge with soft, ever more divisive dogma. Replacing excellence with ideology. Replacing a generation of builders with a generation of angry froth-mouthed activists.

America, with positive intentions, opened its campus gates to China, but what has flowed through is not cultural exchange, it is education warfare. The CCP has made America's youth despise democracy, capitalism (economic freedom) and America itself and to sympathize with the communist facade.

When defenders of freedom who can spot CCP subterfuge call out this infiltration, those who have been swallowing CCP-funded "woke" propaganda rise to their feet and accuse anyone - journalists, concerned parents, educators, clerics, any critic of being a racist. Or a Sino-phone. Or Islamophobe. This is how they are able to shut down real debate and distract your attention from unrestricted warfare activities like education inversion, cognitive debilitation, the creation of social chaos and division, inducing Western self-loathing and anomie, money laundering, drug trafficking, election meddling.

It's like a secret weapon: scream "racism" - and you shut down dissent. Sadly, it works all too often.

If we do not regain control over our universities and research institutions, if we do not teach the truth about Western values vs. Marxist values and history, the CCP will gladly continue to fund and inject its poisonous venom. It may be too late. The sad truth is that *our ivory towers are no longer ivory, but blood red.*

BRIEFING SEVEN

The Battle For Your Livelihood
Economic War

"We allowed ourselves to be repeatedly duped into building the most lethal, diabolical, and determined enemy in history."
~ T. Casey Fleming

"The CCP has used capital to literally dangle in front of politicians and business people, and people that we should trust have been subverted subtly."
~ David Murrin, Global Forecaster

"Xi Jinping's plan is simple: make the world dependent on China, then use that dependence as a weapon. Rare earths. Chips. Batteries. Medicine. If we don't act now, the CCP will decide what and when America can build."
~ U.S. Congressional Select Committee on China, Oct 5, 2025

No longer fiction…now reality. Imagine with me for a moment, the sobering week of destruction the CCP can unleash upon you and your family. A week where no bombs are dropped, no missiles fired, no EMP pulses released to wipe out our electrical grid. But a week, nevertheless, solely of economic levers pulled, that can spiral us into hell on earth.

Sunday: The Opening Salvo - Rare Earth Stranglehold and Initial Cyber Probes

The CCP declares an "emergency export ban" on rare earth elements and refined magnets, citing "national security." As the world's 70% miner and 85-90% processor of rare earths, this instantly halts supplies for U.S. EVs, wind turbines, and defense technology. Bans on lithium, cobalt, and nickel precursors follow suit, choking battery production. Tesla lines halt. Within days, utilities can't replace failing grid components, and defense contractors like Lockheed Martin scramble: F-35 jets and drones - grounded. Panic buying surges; electronics prices spike 50% overnight.

To probe defenses, CCP hackers launch DDoS attacks on port logistics and financial exchanges through pre-embedded backdoors, delaying shipments and sowing confusion. Social media bots, amplified through U.S.-based influencers, flood feeds with "supply chain sabotage" conspiracies, blaming domestic "corporate greed" and pitting workers against elites. Union protests erupt in American factories, framing the crisis as "billionaire betrayal." Cities erupt.

Monday: Infrastructure Assault - Cyber Blackouts on Grids, Pipelines, and Water Systems

Escalation hits critical infrastructure. Building on Sunday's probes, the CCP unleashes targeted cyberattacks: spear-phished through vulnerable IoT devices in U.S. utilities (recall the 2021 Colonial Pipeline hack's blueprint). Electric grids in key regions (e.g., Texas, California) suffer cascading failures: substations overload, blacking out cities. Water treatment plants in the Midwest glitch, contaminating supplies with chemical imbalances. Boil water advisories are issued, hospitals divert patients. No explosions, just code: Volt Typhoon variants exploit unpatched SCADA systems, imported from China-dependent suppliers now offline. Economic *damage ripples: factories halt without power, costing $100 billion in lost productivity. Social media psyops intensify: deepfakes of "government neglect" circulate, inciting rage. Urban liberals blame "climate-denying" red states for grid failures; rural conservatives decry "federal overreach." Both are stoked by CCP-fed social media bot farms. Flash mobs and riots strike in powerless neighborhoods, dividing communities along partisan and racial lines as blame games escalate.*

Tuesday: Health System Collapse – Pharma Export Halt and Amplified Division

With infrastructure reeling, the CCP weaponizes health dependencies. They impose a total ban on active pharmaceutical ingredients (APIs) (90% of U.S. generics derive from China). Antibiotics, insulin, cancer drugs vanish from shelves; hospitals lock up and ration ventilators and chemotherapy, leading to 10,000+ preventable deaths in the first week (per HHS estimates of vulnerabilities). Emergency rooms overflow with untreated infections; black-market pills flood streets, laced with fentanyl from CCP-tied sources.

Cyberattacks follow: hackers disrupt CDC and FDA databases, leaking falsified patient data to expose "elite privileges" (e.g., VIP vaccine access rumors). Disinformation campaigns explode. WeChat-sourced bots on X and Facebook claim the shortages are a "Deep State plot" or "immigrant-driven demand surge." Social conflict soars: Anti-vaxxers clash with healthcare workers in protests; racial tensions flare as shortages hit minority communities hardest, with narratives of "systemic bias" vs. "welfare abuse" flooding the socials. The economy hemorrhages another $200 billion in healthcare disruptions, as businesses shutter amid worker illnesses.

Wednesday: Semiconductor Starvation - Bans on Gallium, Germanium, and Graphite

Momentum builds as the CCP expands bans to gallium, germanium (critical for chips and 5G), and synthetic graphite (for batteries and EVs). U.S. factories like TSMC's Arizona plant starve; Intel and NVIDIA halt production. Auto giants (Ford, GM) idle lines as supply chains halt. Job losses hit 500,000 overnight, with ripple effects in solar and defense (no infrared optics for missiles). Building on Tuesday's chaos, cy-ops target chip suppliers' logistics, faking "embargo compliance" delays. The CCP's global reach surges: they pressure allies like South Korea, Japan, the EU via trade threats.

Domestically, bots stoke more class warfare like "tech bros hoard while workers starve," fueling riots in major cities. Economic nosedive: Stock market plummets 40%, as $400 billion in tech/defense output evaporates and tech giants freeze up. Social fractures deepen: Tech hubs vs. manufacturing towns, with viral videos of layoffs igniting "economic civil war" rhetoric.

Thursday: Food Weaponization and Financial Tremors

Starvation fears edge in. The CCP cuts exports of pharmaceuticals, vitamins, amino acids, and feed additives - 80% of the U.S. supply. Grocery shelves empty; prices quadruple, farms cull herds. Shortages compound Monday's water woes; contaminated crops rot.

Simultaneously, Beijing dumps $200 billion in U.S. Treasuries (a quarter of their $800 billion holdings), spiking yields and interest rates. Mortgage and loan costs soar; banks freeze lending. CCP-linked investors (e.g., via Belt and Road partners) pull from U.S. startups and agribusiness, drying capital flows. Cyber hits amplify: Attacks on ag exchanges manipulate futures, crashing commodity prices.

Disinfo pivots to food scarcity-"globalist hoarding" vs. "farmer negligence"-sparking urban lootings and rural militias. The economy dives into freefall: $1 trillion GDP hit, inflation at 20%. Divisions harden: City-dwellers hoard vs. rural self-sufficiency myths, with race-baiting narratives blaming "migrant labor" for shortages. Violence spreads.

Friday: Global Isolation and Psyops Onslaught

The CCP drops the hammer: leans on its 120+ top trading partners (Africa, Latin America, Southeast Asia), issuing ultimatums: halt U.S. trade or face immediate reciprocal bans. Brazil freezes soy exports; India curbs pharma reroutes. Western unity fractures, EU hedges, Taiwan quivers. U.S. leverage evaporates; NATO wavers amid energy and supply shortages. Psy-ops go nuclear: state actors flood U.S. networks with tailored disinformation: AI-generated videos of "civil unrest" in swing states, exploiting divisions to incite election-year violence. AI bots amplify Thursday's riots, framing them as "Second Civil War." Social chaos: Armed standoffs between protesters and police; partisan militias clash over resources. Economic ruin compounds: markets halt trading, unemployment soars past 15%. The U.S., isolated and divided, begs for concessions.

Saturday: The Reckoning – Total Submission

By week's end, the U.S. is a husk: Grids flicker unrepaired, hospitals triage the dying, shelves barren, markets in meltdown, streets ablaze with fury. Social division has metastasized: racial riots in cities, secessionist murmurs in heartland states, trust in institutions shattered. The CCP, unscathed, dictates terms: give up Taiwan peacefully or else, cede South China Sea claims.

No invasion needed. Unrestricted warfare has rendered America a vassal.

This scenario represents what's waiting for us on the other side of an already ticking clock. One that has been constructed meticulously by the CCP.

For the first time in its history, the U.S. finds itself with limited international economic leverage. The CCP can now dictate terms, from war-fighting posture to trade concessions to foreign policy retreats to domestic submission.

Game over.

The question is: how did we get here?

The answer is complex but not complicated. In a recent discussion with the Red Tsunami team, David Murrin, the leading Global Geopolitical Strategist, pinned the danger to a key year:

> *In 1996, China was frustrated when they were trying to go and reach across to Taiwan. But Americans sent two carriers and they realized they could not overtly challenge America. Its power was absolute. So they came up with a really cunning plan. 'A' was to seduce the west to invest in its industrial base to give it an industrial base. The promise was you'll lower your inflation because we'll manufacture more cheaply. So every industrialist and everyone from Wall Street said 'yeah we'll do that,' money flowed in.*
>
> *At the same time they grew 200,000 hackers that stripped IP from everything that moved – which should have been the first sign it wasn't going the way we thought it was going. They educated their people. The system grew and when Xi came along in 2012, they had already built a monster and they knew they had a monster. It was still very covert but he moved to a more overt identity for China's next expansion. Since then it's become worse and worse. The West got weaker because it prints money. Its real productivity has decreased. It's been de-industrialized voluntarily and it doesn't*

make the things it needs. It's super codependent with China which has inhibited our responses."

In other words, we built Satan. We opened our arms and they snatched our tech, our military blueprints, our IP, our data, our industrial base, keys to our food supply and essential industries and they sold us back electronics and essential service equipment containing "time bombs" to destroy our water and power grids. It's a military play. Classic Sun Tzu: "Let your plans be dark and impenetrable as the night, and when you move, fall like a thunderbolt."

Their plans have now come into the light - at least enough to raise urgent alarms, but our leadership, seduced by sweetheart deals and the ol' bowing and scraping, humble CCP cosplay, can't or won't do anything to stop them. That's how we got here. But let's walk through exactly how it happened, step by step, so we know exactly what actions we need to take to reverse the process

The Gate That Opened and Never Closed

In 1972, Richard Nixon shook hands with Mao Zedong. A new door was opening. Decades of Cold War separation were ending. America and China, it seemed, would become friendly partners, trading with each other, growing together, building a shared, prosperous future.

Few people at that moment understood that what was actually being opened was not an innocent front door, but a deadly trap door. What sounded like cooperation was the start of predation. What appeared to be commerce was the gearing up of slow, methodical conquest. It was the beginning of China systematically dismantling American prosperity, stealing American innovation, and weaponizing American capital against America's own economic and physical security. And they did it while we watched, often while we helped.

This has never been about normal economic competition. This has been unrestricted warfare, where economics, finance, and technology are turned into weapons of mass destruction.

Program 863: Closing the Gap

In 1986, under the direction of paramount leader Deng Xiaoping, the Chinese Communist Party unveiled Program 863: a written master strategy with one goal: to catch up and replace the United States as the world's dominant power by any means necessary.

Former U.S. Director of National Intelligence John Ratcliffe summarized the strategy in three brutal words: "Rob, replicate, and replace." In other words, we will take your money. We will steal your secrets. We will use both to destroy you.

Program 863 was the blueprint for the CCP's systematic theft of Western technology and military advancement. Named for its approval date (March 1986, or "86/3"), Program 863 explicitly tasked Chinese scientists, students, and businesses with acquiring advanced foreign technology in fifteen critical areas including biotechnology, space, information technology, automation, energy, advanced materials, and marine technology, not through innovation, but through espionage, forced technology transfer, and academic infiltration.

What makes Program 863 particularly insidious is its dual-use Commercial-Military Fusion doctrine: every "civilian" technology acquired is immediately funneled to the People's Liberation Army for military application, meaning that American universities collaborating with Chinese researchers, corporations entering joint ventures with Chinese partners, and defense contractors hiring Chinese nationals are arming America's primary adversary. The program's success is why China went from technological backwater to AI superpower, from regional military to near-peer competitor, and from dependent client state to existential threat so quickly. All enabled, funded, and handed over on a silver platter courtesy of Program 863.

"Made in China 2025" Achieving Dominance

By 2015, riding the success of Program 863, the CCP stepped up its strategy and goal. The Communist Party officially adopted a new plan called "Made in China 2025." The title said exactly what it meant: by 2025, China would aim to dominate the global economy in 10 strategic sectors. Again, those sectors weren't random. They were deliberately chosen for their dual-use military and economic applications: Semiconductors. Artificial intelligence. Robotics. Aerospace. Biotech. Power equipment. Rail transport. New-energy vehicles. Advanced materials. And biopharma.

Every one of these sectors is directly tied to military capability. Every breakthrough China has achieved in these areas becomes a weapon pointed back at the United States.

Former FBI Special Agent Don McGahn highlights how this plan has not been hidden: "China's five-year plans are public 'shopping lists.' If your company is on that shopping list, please beware. Because whatever means possible will be utilized."

By 2019, the bellicose President Xi Jinping declared: "The eventual demise of capitalism and the ultimate victory of socialism will require a long historical process to reach completion." This was open warfare, and China was going to win it. In 2020, Xi became even more explicit:

> *[We] must forge some 'assassin's mace' technologies. We must sustain and enhance our superiority across the entire production chain... and we must tighten international production chains' dependence on China, forming powerful countermeasures and deterrent capabilities based on artificially cutting off supply to foreigners.*

Matthew Pottinger, who served as Deputy Director of the National Security Council, understood what Xi was really saying: "Xi's deterrent capability is better viewed as an offensive capability."

China hasn't been building defenses, it has been building and leveraging offensive weapons.

The Greatest Theft in Human History

In 2012, General Keith Alexander commanded both the National Security Agency and U.S. Cyber Command. He had access to classified intelligence on Chinese espionage operations. What he revealed shook Washington when he exposed that what the CCP was up to was "the greatest transfer of wealth in history." Alexander explained the math. The annual loss of intellectual property to Chinese theft was approximately $500 billion (2012). But that number captured only the immediate damage. When you multiply that by ten years - the typical innovation and production cycle - you realize that China was stealing not just the product, but the entire future value of that innovation. The jobs, the profits, the advancement, the competitive advantage, but also the tax base, the national security, the societal prosperity of the West.

The actual total damage he estimated to be *$5 trillion per year.* That was 2012. It has only accelerated since then. By 2020, FBI Director Christopher Wray testified before Congress and delivered that stunning statistic: "The CCP's deep and wide and persistent ability to influence American sectors prompts the agency to open a China-related probe about every 10 hours."

That means on average, the FBI opens more than two China-related counterintelligence cases per day.

Every. Single. Day.

The FBI's "official estimate" of the current annual damage: $600 billion in intellectual property theft, with China as the overwhelming culprit. FBI Intelligence Analyst Nikki Floris sums the reality up yet again: "By far and away the greatest immediate and long-term threat to our information, our innovation, and our national and economic security is the one posed by the People's Republic of China."

China, for decades, has been a theft machine. They didn't innovate. They infiltrated. They stole. Then they copied at fractions of the price to destroy industries in the West. The CCP's methods are planned, systematic, sophisticated, and relentless.

Cyber Espionage

Because I work in cybersecurity every day, I know it 's hard for the average citizen to appreciate the devastation "silently" caused by the CCP's army of cyber-hackers. As mentioned in Briefing Three, in 2014, Chinese hackers stole the personal health records of 80 million Americans from Anthem Insurance. The data included Social Security numbers, dates of birth, and medical histories: essentially a complete blueprint of American citizens' vulnerabilities. This gives Chinese intelligence permanent blackmail leverage over government officials (cross-referenced with the OPM hack, explained below), the ability to create 80 million synthetic identities for espionage and fraud, detailed epidemiological maps showing which U.S. populations are most vulnerable to biological threats, and targeting data on who has chronic illnesses, genetic weaknesses, expensive medical dependencies, or family members that can be exploited.

You can cancel a credit card, but you can't change your DNA, your medical history, or your Social Security number. And that stolen data is still being weaponized against us today, over a decade later, in ways most Americans will never see but may already be experiencing through identity theft. What's coming? Espionage operations, perhaps, or targeted future biological and economic warfare.

In 2015, even more devastatingly, the U.S. Office of Personnel Management (OPM) was breached. Chinese hackers stole biometric data and security clearance files for 21 million federal employees, including everyone with a security clearance, from the military and CIA officers to nuclear facility workers. They stole fingerprints, retina scans, and polygraph results. These files contained everything: their financial problems, mental health issues, affairs, family vulnerabilities.

Let me explain why that matters: it means China can now identify undercover spies (even those using fake names), blackmail people with secrets, track agents anywhere in the world using biometrics at airports and borders and target individuals for recruitment based on their weaknesses. Unlike stolen passwords, you can't change your fingerprints or erase what China learned about your personal life. This single hack compromised an entire generation of U.S. intelligence personnel permanently, making their jobs more dangerous, operations harder to conduct, and creating a blackmail and recruitment database that China will exploit for decades.

The silent attacks never stop. In 2020, the DOJ indicted two Chinese nationals for hacking into Moderna's COVID vaccine research. They were specifically targeting the genetic data of the vaccine. In other words, they were stealing genetic intelligence. By mapping American DNA, China can better develop targeted bioweapons designed to affect specific ethnic populations. These attacks are never just about economics, they are also about military conquest. As former Director of National Intelligence John Ratcliffe has warned: "The People's Republic of China poses the greatest threat to America's biosecurity (as well as) economic security."

The Thousand Talents Program

I have mentioned in previous chapters that Beijing runs a program called "Thousand Talents" that directly targets American scientists, engineers, and researchers. The pitch is simple: generous cash bonuses up front, a fully-equipped research facility, and unlimited funding. All you have to do in return is share the intellectual property you're working on for your American employer.

This happens at universities as well as corporations. Former Air Force and Space Force Chief Software Officer Nicolas Chaillan has been emphatic about the destruction: "Insider threat" is probably the most underestimated threat of all these top organizations on the commercial side. The fact is, the Chinese Communist Party is sending a lot of people to our universities and to our most innovative companies. The result: "exfiltration of data from within." These aren't simply students or junior employees. They're embedded operatives with access to classified projects, cutting-edge research, and strategic defense information. And they bring it all back to Beijing.

Intellectual Property (IP) Theft

Intellectual property (IP) represents the lifeblood of American innovation, fueling our economic strength which helps safeguard our freedoms and national security. Yet the CCP has too easily treated it as easy pickings, opting for brazen theft over domestic innovation. This not only massively cuts billions in R&D, it catapults them ahead by years. Straight out theft is how Beijing gained their ever-growing edge in corporate competitiveness, military might, and global economic power. Our naive hope that trade and engagement would "tame the dragon" and foster democracy has backfired spectacularly. We've allowed the CCP to plunder our ingenuity through a web of insidious tactics including:

- **Recruitment via Social Engineering:** Foreign operatives prowl social media, LinkedIn, and even dating apps to befriend and lure targets, turning casual connections into pipelines for sensitive data.
- **Infiltration of Corporate R&D:** CCP agents embed themselves in U.S. corporate, government, and academic research teams, posing as collaborators to siphon proprietary designs from the inside.
- **Cyber-Espionage and Hacking:** Sophisticated malware and state-sponsored breaches infiltrate networks, as seen

in attacks on defense contractors, giving Beijing footholds in critical sectors like oil, pharmaceuticals, and national security.

- **Honeypot Operations and Blackmail:** Deceptive romantic entanglements, sometimes laced with drugs like GHB ("date rape drug"), are used to compromise targets; in one chilling tactic, American women are lured at bars, recorded, coerced or paid to engage in honeytraps to extract secrets from their partners, echoing the infamous American Superconductor case (see below) where stolen tech gutted a large U.S. firm.
- **Physical Stalking and Eavesdropping:** Innovators, especially boastful PhDs at conferences, restaurants, flights, hotels, or bars, are tailed and overheard. Academics prove particularly vulnerable, with spies exploiting the thrill of road life under the adage, "If you're not a 10 at home, you're not a 10 on the road."
- **Reverse Engineering:** Once acquired, pilfered prototypes are dissected and replicated at scale, erasing the victim's head start overnight.
- **Forced Technology Transfers:** Joint ventures with Chinese firms demand handing over core IP and data as the entry fee, locking U.S. companies into one-sided deals.
- **CCP National Security Laws:** Require all companies doing business in China to hand over their IP and data to the CCP.
- **Academic Partnerships as Trojan Horses:** Seemingly benign university collaborations serve as gateways for espionage, funneling cutting-edge research straight to CCP handlers.

These sinister methods reveal a regime that is relentlessly predatory, eroding America and the free West's technological edge. Let me show you three of thousands of case studies so you know how it works, and begin to get a sense of this thievery's cost:

Case Study 1: Nortel - Destruction of a Global Telecom Leader

We'll now dive deeper into the Nortel scandal mentioned in Briefing Three. Nortel (Northern Telecom) was once the pride of Canada, an A-list telecom superpower headquartered in Ontario, with roots stretching back to the AT&T empire in 1895, was Canada's largest employer. But in the early 2000s, the company suffered a sustained, silent onslaught that destroyed it: cyber-espionage from the Chinese Communist Party (CCP).

Brian Shields, Nortel's top systems security advisor, repeatedly warned management as early as 2004, "We tracked the theft of over 1,400 documents from the LiveLink server... China is the source of all extractions we are aware of," Shields explained to CBC in 2012. "When they see what your business plans are, that's a huge advantage. It's unfair business practices that really bring down a company of this size." He called the evidence of the hands of the CCP "indisputable."

Here's how it worked: The hackers, operating out of Shanghai and Beijing, used seven stolen executive passwords, including the CEO's login, to siphon off business plans, R&D documents, internal emails, and proprietary technical reports. The breach went undetected for years. As Shields said, "technicians in China could send encrypted packages of stolen Nortel data to Shanghai and Beijing...by sending Internet commands to a 'backdoor' buried in a Nortel computer."

The result? Massive technological hemorrhage. By 2008, Nortel was bankrupt, getting undercut at every turn by Huawei, China's new telecom juggernaut, which was built on Nortel's stolen secrets. Nortel went bankrupt the next year, and Huawei dominated the industry with $30 billion in global contracts using the very tech Nortel had spent billions and decades pioneering.

One Canadian intelligence expert confirmed, Nortel "was being systematically compromised, and everything was being taken." It's hard to imagine the scale of devastation: tens of thousands of jobs lost, Canada's tech leadership erased, and a Chinese state-backed giant - Huawei - now controlling much of the global internet backbone, powered by what was once the best of the West. Huawei is now the CCP's backbone for espionage.

Case Study 2: American Superconductor and the Destruction of an Industry

American Superconductor (AMSC) was a Massachusetts-based innovator whose breakthroughs in wind turbine control software were destined to lead a renewable revolution. The nucleus of their genius was source code, locked away and guarded; only seven people worldwide knew it. Enter Sinovel, a Chinese "partner" turned predator, and their sinister trap: According to the U.S. Department of Justice, an Austrian employee of AMSC's subsidiary downloaded proprietary source code from a secure system in Wisconsin and sold it in exchange for millions, an apartment, and a new life in China. And so, CCP-linked agents got their hands on the "digital crown jewels" of wind energy.

Once Sinovel had the source code, the Chinese quickly reverse-engineered AMSC's turbine hardware and, with AMSC's own training, rapidly scaled up factory robotics and manufacturing know-how that U.S. companies taught them. AMSC CEO Daniel McGahn reported to the Wall Street Journal, "They ordered a billion, took $100 million, then started canceling orders," with Sinovel slashing $900 million in "inventory" immediately after the theft.

The crime didn't just kill off orders; Chinese competitors flooded the market with cloned turbines, quickly stealing 20% of global share. That market is now over 90% filled by Chinese-manufactured, American-stolen tech. The financial results for AMSC? A devastating stock collapse: shares crashed from a high of $690 to slump under $10 a share for over a decade. Hundreds of millions in shareholder value and years of research, lost over booze, bucks and the alluring smile of a pretty face.

But the final gut punch: this theft gave the Chinese state a high-tech wind arsenal, with profits now weaponized to fund the CCP regime's critical clean energy technologies. As McGahn put it, this "now directly funds and powers the regime that is programmed to destroy America."

The U.S. Attorney at the time referred to it as "corporate homicide."

Case Study 3: Motorola and the Creation of the Monster: "Huawei"

In the 1990s, Motorola, the pioneering American telecom giant, invested billions to build manufacturing plants and R&D centers in China. Their advanced mobile phones were status symbols for China's new elite, but Motorola's generosity came with a brutal price. State policy demanded technology transfer as the price of market access, and Motorola was forced to train legions of Chinese engineers, imparting the "Motorola Way" of manufacturing and innovation, know-how that incubated their own demise.

One particularly keen student was Huawei, a company that started as a reseller but quickly leveraged Motorola's training and technology transfers to develop its own telecom gear. By the early 2000s, Huawei was manufacturing network equipment and selling it under Motorola's own brand.

Mark Duval, a former Motorola executive, recalled how Beijing's "all-of-nation approach to acquiring every possible technology" aggressively extracted supply chain secrets and product know-how under the guise of partnership.

The Chinese government systematically tilted regulations and industry standards to favor Huawei, pressuring Motorola to adopt Huawei-developed battery technology and other standards, continuing to undermine Motorola's market position.

The result was catastrophic. Motorola's core mobility division eroded and was sold off-first to Google, and later ironically to Lenovo, a Chinese tech giant based on purchasing the IBM PC division. By 2011,

Motorola America had basically ceased to exist as a global telecom leader. Its collapse not only marks the loss of a tech giant, but epitomizes how the CCP harnesses IP theft, coerces technology transfer, and uses regulatory manipulation to demolish Western innovation and replace it with Chinese state-backed entities. The Motorola saga is another dark lesson in how Chinese strategic economic warfare leverages Western ingenuity and diminishes our power, prosperity, and global leadership, all in one move.

Stolen Swords

In Briefing Five, I showed you how "Borrowed Swords," that old Chinese military stratagem found in the "Thirty-Six Stratagems," advocating using an opponent's resources, weapons, or strength to strike and defeat them, is applied in the CCP's cyber war against us. They have upgraded this strategy into "Stolen Swords" as everyday, they acquire and weaponize U.S. and allied technology to integrate into its own military machine.

This goes beyond mere dual-use acquisition; it is often also single-purposed theft aimed squarely at advancing the People's Liberation Army (PLA). One of the most alarming cases of insider theft involves United States' nuclear weapons research. In the summer of 2021, China tested a nuclear-capable hypersonic missile. Evidence supports that this technology traces back to the Department of Energy's Los Alamos National Laboratory. A Strider Technologies investigation revealed that 162 scientists from Los Alamos were systematically recruited by the CCP, with at least 59 brought into its flagship Thousand Talents Program. The report concluded that their work advanced Chinese capabilities in "hypersonic, missile, and submarine programs" and contributed to systems including jet engines, deep-earth penetrating warheads, stealth submarines, and unmanned autonomous vehicles.

Simply put, the CCP is leveraging taxpayer-funded American research to build weapons that can be deployed against U.S. forces in a future conflict. With infiltration in the supply chain, bribery of employees, covert part substitutions in Pentagon contracts and hacking of government agencies, the net effect is that America's most advanced military technologies are being systematically siphoned to empower the PLA. The result is a clear and present danger not only to U.S. national security, but to the stability of the international order.

"Be careful raising a baby tiger. One day, it will grow up and eat you."
~ Chinese proverb

During a recent conversation I had with a senior U.S. Military Counterintelligence officer and colleague, who requested to remain anonymous, he asked me to emphasize to you that it's not the stolen weaponry that should alarm us, but that all the stolen tech underlying our entire global security lifelines also represents a military threat.

> *I believe what they openly say - dominating and controlling the network fiber, the whole infotech ecosystem we live in - from submarine cable to satellite above - will be owned by the CCP, and remember - there is no company in China that is not CCP-run. The CCP controls all the economic levers financially and means of transport, from storage to maritime ports. They're not doing it to make money: they want to control the economic ecosystem. Also, they didn't build the largest navy in history for decoration; the biggest peacetime military expansion on Earth is not a budgeting accident. Beijing is buying at scale because it plans to use it. This is global coercion: ports in the Atlantic, influence over Africa, presence in the Arctic and Antarctic, not local skirmishes but a global chokehold. If you want to push Europe and America around, you don't build bases in your own neighborhood; you build them where you can strangle commerce and influence decision-making.*

Your Wake-Up Call: Civilization at Stake

The CCP laughs at our gullibility. The formula has been devastatingly simple: dangle the fantasy of selling products to 1.4 billion consumers while promising that market access will expand "any day now."

CCP law says if you're going to do business in China, you must surrender all of your intellectual property, all of your trade secrets, and all the data that goes through your company. And if you're a consulting company, you also must provide your intellectual property, IP, trade secrets, and the same for all of your clients.

Beijing's psychological manipulation has worked so completely that American businesses salivating over the overblown Chinese market have surrendered critical technology as simply the cost of doing business.

Every major American company, especially the tech giants, are thus compromised. Executives ignore the regime's fundamental murderous brutality, systematic human rights violations, even when fellow American investors get arrested on fabricated charges whenever it serves Beijing's interests.The siren call of cheap labor and the massive Chinese market has birthed many a deal with the devil in a thousand ways.

"The Chinese government has weaponized our own capitalist system against us," writes former United States Under Secretary of State for Economic Growth, Energy, and the Environment, Keith Krach.

"Ultimately, the winner of the innovation / technology war will win all wars."
~ T. Casey Fleming

Through Wall Street, retirement funds, and index products, the CCP has turned America's most powerful engine of prosperity into a war chest for authoritarianism. He points out that we are all complicit: roughly 100 million Americans are unknowingly invested in CCP-linked companies through 401Ks, ETFs, and index funds. That means average citizens are financing Beijing's military build-up, surveillance state, and repression campaigns globally without knowing it.

"It is past time for all free nations to decouple from China. The CCP has been selectively decoupling from the U.S. and our allies over the past few years in a move to war-footing. We must immediately create a counter supply system of freedom-based allies to combat the hostile communist Chinese system."
~ Paul S. Boardman, Executive Director, Decouple China PAC

What's worse, confesses New Jersey Rep. Chris Smith, "I think we've been naive or complicit in the extreme." "The U.S.," he says, has been "selling and conveying to a malevolent power the ability to destroy us and destroy like-minded Western democracies."

The CCP's "whole-of-state / whole of society" onslaught leaves no more room for our complacency. The gate opened in 1972; now, it's time to lock it before the house is completely gutted. Our innovation, economy, our security, and our very freedom depend on it. As former Chairman of the Select Committee on the CCP, Rep. Mike Gallagher (WI) has written: "U.S. companies need to choose: are you with us, or are you with this genocidal communist regime?"

BRIEFING EIGHT

The Battle For Your Loyalty
Culture War

"Give me four years to teach the children, and the seed I have sown will never be uprooted."
~ Vladimir Lenin

"The reality is evil does exist in this world, and it is persistent in its efforts – we cannot ignore it, hide from it, or defeat it unless we act with purpose and remain resolved. Too many Americans take our freedoms for granted, have short memories, do not study history, and quickly fall into one or more of the four buckets of despair – they become complacent, compliant, complicit, corrupt, or a mixture of the latter. Any mixture of the latter leaves the doors wide open for tyranny."
~ Ed Haugland
Retired Intelligence Community Executive & Author of "The Cognitive War"

Divide and Conquer: How the CCP is Killing America From Within

America is built on a set of core values that the CCP is committed to undermine, destroy, and replace, one-by-one, cherished values such as...

- Government **by the people**

- The sacred centrality of the **family** hearth
- The frontier spirit of self-reliance and **individual rights**
- Unified civil society grounded in **constitutional rights** and debate
- Freedom to **worship** as you choose
- Freedom to **speak** as you choose
- A meritocratic **free market**

By slowly capturing our teaching and media institutions, twisting and pushing inverted historical narratives, funding radical agitators and mobs (2023 U.S. State Department reports on CCP cultural influence ops estimate $1B+ annually) and amplifying chaos, the CCP is attacking the free world's moral architecture from within. "Propaganda isn't a side hustle in China," as my colleague, Ken Cao, founder of The Center for Asian Democratic Resilience, emphasized in a recent conversation,

> *It's a full-time industry. From Beijing's central ministries down to village offices, there's a 'Propaganda Department.' Let's call it what it is: the 'B.S. Department:' armies of full-time myth-makers with budgets, KPIs, and quotas for deception. Their job? Manufacture illusions. And it's not just officials anymore. The self-media crowd joined in too: Fake-news farms, patriotic trolls, and paid influencers spinning the same recycled fantasies. Some do it for clicks. Some for cash. Some for free, like unpaid interns in hell. You're fighting a multi-billion-dollar disinformation machine.*

As you will see in this Briefing, we are ensnared in this deadly moral and spiritual siege, where Beijing's blood-soaked, totalitarian, atheist regime is driving daily daggers into the heart of what makes America free, great, and prosperous, softening the ground for communist conquest. As the CCP works daily to undermine our economic strength, our political sovereignty, our spiritual and religious foundations, our cognitive clarity and our physical bodies, it is running a full-on assault on cultural values, a civilizational psy-op designed to induce our own self-destruction. They are seeking to destroy our confidence in ourselves and our institutions, eliminate spiritual and moral resistance and paralyze our civil society.

We are talking about a targeted dismantling of what makes us "us," piece by piece.

"The purpose of propaganda is to make one group of people forget the other groups are human."
~ T. Casey Fleming

The Communist Masterplan: Four Stages of Ideological Subversion

In a chilling 1984 interview, Soviet defector and ex-KGB agent Yuri Bezmenov detailed the long-game strategy of communist ideological subversion, a "slow process" he called "a great brainwashing," designed to demoralize and collapse Western societies from within.

As he described, this four-step process creates a new reality where "no one is able to come to sensible conclusions in the interest of defending themselves, their families, their community, and their country."

The process he revealed should be taught in every school in every free society, and memorized by every adult.

Citing established Marxist-Leninist tactics, he outlined four progressive stages taking roughly twenty years to fully erode a nation's moral, economic, and defensive fabric. Here's the blueprint; you can see it at work all around you today.

Stage 1: Demoralization (15-20 years)

Corrupt the mindsets of a generation through education, media, religion, and social institutions. Infiltrate schools to promote relativism, discredit patriotism, and sow division. "A person who is demoralized is unable to assess true information; the facts tell nothing to him… The facts tell nothing to him. Even if I shower him with information, with authentic proof, with documents, with pictures; even if I take him by force to the Soviet Union and show him [a] concentration camp, he will refuse to believe it, until he [receives] a kick in his fat-bottom," Bezmenov warned. The result: A population detached from reality, vulnerable to propaganda, where "exposure to true information does not matter anymore."

Stage 2: Destabilization (2-5 years)
Accelerate chaos by targeting the economy, foreign relations, and defense. Radicalize labor, incite ethnic tensions (e.g. BLM, pro-Islamism), and undermine law enforcement (e.g. "defund the police"). Bezmenov described it as exploiting the demoralized to create "disorientation," where societal pillars like free markets and alliances crumble under engineered crises – no shots fired, just systemic rot.

Stage 3: Crisis (weeks - months)
Precipitate a violent upheaval – revolution, civil war, or even invasion, as the destabilized society implodes. "The time is ripe," Bezmenov said, because radicals violently demand radical change and the demoralized, resentful masses go along. This stage justifies the subverter's intervention, turning desperation into takeover.

Stage 4: Normalization (a few months)
Install a compliant regime under the guise of "restoration." Dissenters are liquidated (murdered) or re-educated (tortured); the new communist order becomes "normal." Bezmenov emphasized, "It will not be violent in the sense of guns, but it will be a steady process of changing the perception of reality." The conquered nation accepts its chains as progress.

Stages 1 and 2 are being actively waged by the CCP, who are using the growing pro-socialist Left for their purposes. But the disdain that communists actually have for leftist agitators, "political prostitutes" as Bezmenov revealed his communist overlords back home called them, is total:

> *Your leftists in the United States, all these professors and all these beautiful civil rights defenders, are instrumental in the process of the subversion - only to destabilize a nation. When their job is completed, they are not needed anymore. They know too much... [and] when they get disillusioned, when they see Marxists and Leninists come to power, they obviously get offended. They think that they will come to power but that will never happen. Of course, they will be lined up against the wall and shot. They may turn into the most bitter enemies of Marxist Leninism when they come to power -that's what happened in Nicaragua. It's the same pattern everywhere. The moment they serve their purpose, all the useful idiots are either executed or exiled or put in prisons like in Cuba."*

Here's a quick reference of the four stages of communist ideological subversion:

1. DEMORALIZATION (15-20+ years)
    - Target: culture, education, media
    - Goal: weaken shared values & confidence
    - Result: confusion, division, cynicism

2. DESTABILIZATION (2-5 years)
    - Target: economy, foreign relations, defense
    - Goal: disrupt systems & institutions
    - Result: growing tensions and dysfunction

    ** **You are here**

3. CRISIS (weeks-months)
    - Rapid, destabilizing event

(another virus, electrical or internet blackout, etc., COVID-19 was a test run)
- Goal: break normal governance
- Result: panic, conflict, urgent demand for change

4. NORMALIZATION ("new normal")
    - Power consolidates new order
    - Goal: impose stability under new authority
    - Result: acceptance of the new system

The mechanism the CCP uses to deploy these four stages, they call the "Three Warfares" doctrine. They include:

1. Public Opinion/Media Warfare
2. Psychological Warfare
3. Legal Warfare

Elsa B. Kania of the Center for a New American Security explains that the Three Warfare Doctrine is "intended to control the prevailing discourse and influence perceptions in a way that advances China's interests, while compromising the capability of opponents to respond."

This hybrid strategy weaponizes media, information, emotions, and societal rules to fracture Western resolve to reshape global narratives in Beijing's favor. Public Opinion/Media Warfare is the doctrine's propaganda spearhead, Kania explains, hijacking public discourse to "weaken the adversary's 'will to fight' while ensuring strength of will and unity" on China's side. They use social media, films, television programs, books, the internet, and the global media network, boosting anti-U.S. content to alienate American youth from democratic institutions. The CCP takes advantage of the freedoms of the United States and other democracies to advance its ideologically-driven narratives, while using its domestic restrictions on freedom to prevent the reverse.

This represents a relentless campaign to rewrite our inner reality, one viral post at a time, until we question our cultural foundations. The doctrine's objectives amount to a psychological siege:

- Control of public opinion manipulates narratives to sway masses against their governments, as seen in CCP-orchestrated social media campaigns amplifying U.S. racial divides.
- Blunting an adversary's determination saps fighting spirit through doubt, like flooding Taiwan's online spaces with despair-inducing memes to *undermine military morale* ahead of potential conflict.
- Transformation of emotion shifts judgment into *compliance,* evident in Xinjiang propaganda videos that recast Uyghur internment camps as "vocational harmony" to soften international outrage.
- Psychological guidance steers individual mindsets toward pro-China views, such as Confucius Institutes embedding favorable curricula in Western campuses to *groom future elites.*
- Collapse of (an adversary's) organization *dismantles institutions from within,* like by transferring power from elected officials to non-elected organizations.
- Psychological tactics prevent domestic unity, exemplified by China's Great Firewall blocking critical COVID-19 reports to *maintain party loyalty* amid global scrutiny.
- Restriction through law *exploits legal systems* to intimidate and constrain victims, foes and challengers.

The goal of information warfare: *control us, demoralize us, and break down our resistance to communism.*

The process: *make us hate our families, our religions, our country, our values, ourselves, and each other.*

The Trojan Horse: TikTok & Social Media

"TikTok is a weapons platform. Full stop."
~ Shawn Chenoweth, Director of Cognitive Advantage at the National Security Council

Air dominance. Sea dominance. Information dominance.

A 2024 Rand report revealed that China views information as the most important of the "three dominances," it is constructing on its march toward global rule. Even by 2018, the CCP established a PLA cyber force of as many as 300,000 soldiers, as well as a netizen "50 Cent Army" of perhaps 2 million individuals "paid a nominal fee to make comments on social media sites in favor of [CCP] propaganda," (Keoni Everington, "China's 'Troll Factory' Targeting Taiwan with Disinformation Prior to Election," Taiwan News (Taipei), 5 November 2018.)

The "tip of the spear" of this battle for dominance has been TikTok. TikTok, ensnaring over 170 million U.S. users in its endless, dopamine addictive, mindless scroll stands as a masterstroke of the Chinese Communist Party's (CCP) cultural warfare: *a digital Trojan Horse* smuggling subversion into the heart of Western society. One sign of the danger: a 2023 Pew Research study found *62% of teens view the communist TikTok app as a primary news source.*

Since its explosive U.S. launch in 2018, ByteDance-owned TikTok has harvested vast troves of personal data under CCP laws mandating cooperation with Chinese intelligence agencies. Its full devastation stems from its algorithmic alchemy, engineered to corrode American values and confidence from within.

TikTok has excelled here, bombarding youth - its core demographic - with algorithm-driven content that amplifies fleeting consumerism, gender fluidity, anti-authority, anti-capitalism, racial and social division, rebellion, and social chaos.

For instance, during the 2020 Black Lives Matter protests, TikTok's feeds boosted anti-police narratives. Meanwhile, internal leaks reported by The New York Times in 2022 showed ByteDance engineers suppressing U.S. content critical of CCP policies like Uyghur concentration camps and at the same time, promoting viral dances that trivialize historical atrocities, simultaneously demoralizing users and replacing moral anchors with mindless entertainment. As one former ByteDance employee told Forbes: "The algorithm is designed to keep users hooked, but it's also a tool for influence."

The trail of destruction is damning. During COVID-19, TikTok, according to a 2024 Oxford Internet Institute analysis, CCP-linked accounts flooded U.S. feeds with misinformation on COVID-19 origins, blaming America and fueling vaccine confusion, destabilizing public health trust. TikTok also ignited division before and during the January 6, 2021 Capitol riot, where #StopTheSteal content was amplified by 40% more views than fact-checks, per an MIT study. And following Oct 7, 2023, TikTok promoted anti-Israel protests, mobilizing mobs by omitting crucial context on Hamas, all documented in a House Select Committee on the CCP report.

But the app works in other, secretive ways. Peter Schweitzer reports that In 2022 ByteDance admitted that employees accessed app data to track reporters' locations, a live operation against American journalists. The CCP also used TikTok to track military personnel. TikTok has your data even if you don't have the app. Using tracking pixels, the CCP can follow users and non-users alike across the internet, measuring usage and building profiles.

An investigation released in March by the cybersecurity firm Feroot Security revealed that tracking pixels from ByteDance were embedded in 30 different state government websites in the U.S. This means that Americans could have had their personal information accessed simply by visiting their local government's webpage, without downloading or using the app at all.

There are darker, personal crimes committed by TikTok. In Schweitzer's incisive book, "Blood Money: Why the Powerful Turn a Blind Eye While China Kills Americans" (2024), the company was revealed to have keylog capability, meaning that the app records all of a user's keystrokes on the device they are using. They track what you're texting, who you're texting, passwords, email accounts, everything else on your phone, and anything that you're typing in emails. That's right: keylogging is recording each word and each *password.* This is whyTikTok is so much more than a mere distraction machine; it is a ruthless "espionage application" for the CCP. In the same vein, Andrew Thornebrooke reported in the Epoch Times, quoting a U.S. Government official: "TikTok surveils everything and everyone. Names, ages, locations, what you do outside of TikTok, apps used, texts, who you talk to, contacts, passwords, browsing history, photos, biometric data like your face, voice, fingerprints, and more."

But, and perhaps this is the most morally repugnant revelation of all, Schweitzer reveals how the CCP directly attacks our children...

> *Independent tests built fresh accounts and clicked like ordinary teens. Within minutes the feed accelerated toward self-harm, eating disorders, sex, and drugs. The machine learns the vulnerability, then feeds it. This is dopamine engineering at industrial scale. In China, the sister app Douyin enforces a strict youth mode with daily limits and study content for under-14s. Chinese students get guardrails. American kids get mania, esteem attacks.*

Schweitzer concludes, "TikTok is not entertainment. It is a weapon that smiles. The friendlier the feed, the sharper the blade."

The CCP doesn't restrict this cultural assault to TikTok; it weaponizes the entire U.S. social media ecosystem for what the Center for Strategic and International Studies (CSIS) called a "Machiavellian" strategy to "influence public opinion and policy debates." In its 2023 report,

"Fortifying the United States Against Adversarial Influence Operations," the CSIS identified how the CCP exploits Section 230's broad legal immunities across social media "to disseminate state-sponsored narratives that erode trust in democratic institutions and sow division among Americans."

TikTok Sale: Real or Illusion?

As you already probably suspected, now that you are learning more deeply how the CCP's China operates, TikTok is built on stolen IP from the U.S. In a scathing analysis, investor Ken Cao exposes the TikTok "spinoff" as nothing more than a sophisticated Trojan Horse. "We didn't rescue TikTok," Cao warns, "we bought a hollow shell" - a $14 billion illusion of victory that leaves the most dangerous components firmly under Chinese Communist Party control.

As Cao meticulously shows, ByteDance's strategic retreat preserves its most potent weapon: the algorithm - "TikTok's brain" - which remains in Beijing's hands. "Modern cyberwarfare" he warns, "is about controlling narratives."

With the ability to viralize content, amplify divisions, and flood feeds with strategically selected information, TikTok represents a psychological warfare platform more insidious than any traditional espionage tool. The real peril lies in TikTok's weaponized ability to "capture your data, study your behavior and influence what you think, all while reporting back to a company under complete CCP control," as Cao exposes.

ByteDance "doesn't need to hack your data to harm you. It just needs to nudge the algorithm: boost certain videos, bury others. Amplify division during an election. Flood feeds with anti-war content during a Taiwan crisis."

TikTok, Cao says, unlike any espionage technology before, "can spy on your thoughts - and change them," eroding American unity one swipe at a time in service of Beijing's "Strategy of Sowing Discord."

That's why the 2025 $14 billion "sale" is nothing more than a calculated maneuver, allowing ByteDance continued control of the recommendation engine while neutralizing the threat of a complete ban. India's decisive action had it right: ban TikTok, foster local alternatives, and keep your data safe, a decision that stands in stark contrast to America's naive capitulation. It needs to be reversed.

"TikTok is a weaponized enemy military application in the hands of our youth.
The U.S. must immediately and completely replace TikTok with a 100% U.S. app.
It is a matter of national security."
~ T. Casey Fleming

Beyond TikTok

TikTok, though, is only the tip of the iceberg. Social media has been serving as a multi-headed hydra, pouring misinformation and inflammatory ideological content into the minds of the free world at every turn.

In 2022, Meta removed 7,704 accounts, 954 pages, and 15 groups linked to efforts to promote pro-China talking points and attack the Chinese government's critics. According to Meta's analysts, Chinese influence operations targeted at least 50 other platforms and apps, including YouTube, Reddit, Pinterest, TikTok, Medium, and X, the company formerly known as Twitter.

On Twitter (now X), CCP state media like CGTN and Global Times maintain accounts with millions of followers. A 2022 Graphika study exposed over 3,000 bot accounts amplifying anti-U.S. sentiment during the Taiwan Strait tensions, reaching 100 million impressions.

X is no anomaly. Facebook faces similar infiltration: Meta's 2021 transparency report revealed CCP-run pages targeting U.S. elections with 2020 interference, including fake ads on racial division viewed by

150 million Americans, while WeChat, ByteDance's domestic Chinese sister app, censors dissent domestically but exports propaganda abroad via 1.3 billion users. YouTube, too, hosts CCP-affiliated channels with a 2023 Stanford Internet Observatory analysis tracking 500+ videos pushing propaganda to Western audiences.

And, now of course, with AI and deepfakes, this tsunami is getting worse. "We are seeing an ability to both develop and deliver [disruptive AI disinformation] at an efficiency, at a speed, at a scale that we've never seen before," Gen. Paul Nakasone, former head of the NSA and U.S. Cyber Command, told reporters at a recent DEF CON hacker conference.

In short, Beijing has turned America's open social media platforms into weapons against us. The wake-up call is clear: TikTok's destructiveness has created a cesspool of self-hate but the CCP's full arsenal across all social media demands we comprehensively fortify our cultural defenses before the subversion normalizes surrender.

In Briefing Four, I spoke about the Four Goals of Cognitive Warfare. One of those was to cause us to hate ourselves. Now let me break that down into what I call "The Four Hates" that the CCP is actively engendering among us:

The Four Hates

CCP Cultural Goal 1: Hate The Family

"The greatest threat to communism has always been the traditional family unit. As long as there exists an entity outside the state that raises, rears, and educates young people, communism can never really fully take hold. It is essential to the success of the totalitarian agenda that each individual stand naked and alone against the machine."

~ Sam Faddis, Former Central Intelligence Agency (CIA) operations officer

On July 4, 2025, the Democratic Socialists of America (DSA) published a panel discussion from its annual Socialism Conference that featured open calls for the abolition of the nuclear family and traditional family structure in the U.S. The DSA provided this summary of its content: the nuclear family is "an inherently repressive, racist, and heterosexist institution that functionally reinforces and reproduces capitalism."

The family is the first line of defense for communism to break down traditional society and replace it with something that can be molded, manipulated, and controlled. Reviewing the DSA annual conference, retired CIA operations officer and U.S. Army Judge Advocate General officer Sam Faddis, the DSA stands "for the radical, Marxist takeover not only of our government but of society. They stand for total totalitarian control, and in order to make that a reality, their first target is the family."

Michael Pillsbury, author of "The Hundred Year Marathon: China's Secret Strategy to Replace America as the Global Superpower," calls this "civil engineering," stating, "The family is the primary transmission mechanism of cultural values. Destroy the family, and you destroy a society's ability to reproduce its core beliefs across generations."

Marxist theory views the family as a "mini-bourgeois" institution that must be weakened to free individuals from so-called capitalist oppression. So communism does everything it can to reduce the traditional authority of fathers, create single-parent households, raise divorce rates and hinder children growing up without stable family units.

Colleague Xi Van Fleet, who suffered growing up during the horrors of Mao's Cultural Revolution, sees the CCP's playbook now playing out in America. She writes in her book, Mao's America…

> *I know what is happening here because I've seen this on both fronts: far-left progressive forces, using weapons such as CRT, woke-ism, BLM, and cancel culture, in order to root out conservatives and any resistance to their radical agenda… Watching the Floyd-inspired riots in 2020 and seeing the*

> *parallels to China's Cultural Revolution was an epiphany for me...*

A mother herself, she noticed that beginning especially during the George Floyd riots, local parents...

> *...Were...now being scorned by their sons and daughters whose confrontational attitude and unprecedented disrespect went well beyond the usual teenage angst and rebellion. Chalk this up to the promotion of CRT in schools, where the teachings are designed to violate and disrespect the sanctity of family and usurp parental values. Many students now questioned their parents' attitudes about race and oppression, accusing them of being racists. What I had seen... remained so vivid for me that I was determined to not let people dismiss this as not happening, as unreal. It was a full-blown Marxist revolution, American style. Enough is enough. I felt a personal urgency to get involved politically and to do my part in my small slice of this world, in order to help keep America from going over a cliff.*

She has experienced the communist devil at work, so to speak, and so has no illusions. Through the attack on the family unit, "Our freedom is under attack. Our country is under attack."

CCP Cultural Goal 2: Hate God

Though we cover the CCP's war on Religion and Spirit in Briefing Ten, I want to make sure you understand how this is also part of the CCP's war on all the foundations of our culture. CCP's venom laser-targets America's Judeo-Christian core, from the Ten Commandments' moral compass to the Sermon on the Mount's call to forgiveness and personal redemption, seeking to replace it with Marxist facsimiles of "collectivism" that facilitate state worship only.

Through their propaganda machine, Christian values are branded "oppressive" relics to be silenced in the name of "progress." Through Belt and Road-funded academic exchanges and Confucius Institutes. Beijing seeds curricula that equate biblical family with "patriarchy" and charity with "exploitation," while TikTok videos (algorithmically boosted 300% for anti-faith content, according to the 2023 Network Contagion study) amplify atheist influencers decrying churches as "colonial holdovers." The CCP wishes to replace the first commandment by replacing "no other God before me" with "no other God than the communist State." They are working to normalize submission over salvation, state over soul, and they are succeeding with our children and on the Left.

CCP Cultural Goal 3: Hate America & Its Core Values

Welcome to the Upside Down.

The technical term for it is a calculated "Inversion Matrix" wherein the CCP twists America's heroic saga - the Lewis and Clark frontier, unprecedented prosperity, Apollo's lunar leap, the Allied victory over fascism - into a unitary tale of "imperialist aggression."

This unitary and dualistic, reductionist myth of "oppression/oppressed" feeds today's communist narrative in the U.S. (e.g. white skin bad/brown skin good) and demands endless apologies.

Leaked United Front docs (2021 Australian Strategic Policy Institute) reveal CCP directives to fund "decolonization" studies that recast:

1. Manifest Destiny as "genocide"
2. The space race as "militarism"
3. WWII heroism as "white supremacy"
4. Capitalism-created abundance as "theft"

By co-opting the ever-popular, totalizing European/U.S. "colonization" narrative of the left, the CCP re-narrativizes our imperfect, yet always improving free society as an irredeemable "evil empire."

The term "Inversion Matrix," describes how authoritarian regimes like the CCP psychologically invert Western self-perception to foster internal decay. The tactic is to target those fortunate enough to grow up in the bubble of the West's freedoms, prosperity, and democratic abundance and systematically condition them through media, education, and algorithms to despise these very gifts, much like a child resenting their nurturing parents for perceived flaws.

This inversion breeds ingratitude and self-loathing, portraying economic freedom (capitalism) as exploitative, individualism as selfish, and Western history as uniquely oppressive, while glorifying collectivist alternatives (which are exploitative, coldly selfish and uniquely oppressive)!

The danger is profound: it *demoralizes societies from within,* eroding national confidence and unity. As Bezmenov noted, such inverted mindsets pave the way for normalization of communist demagogues and the quiet surrender of individual and national sovereignty.

Foreign communists are funding this inversion and training violent leftist radicals in the U.S. and Europe. Mike Gonzalez, Senior Fellow at the Heritage Foundation, sums it up:

> *BLM, The Palestinian conflict, the climate, transgenderism, immigration, and abortion are all proximate causes for protests and now terrorism. But they are all also part of an amalgamated "omnicause" whose real purpose is to bring down the United States and the West... The CCP has zero interest in transgender and gender politics, which their communist leaders recognize as depraved. What they care about is revolution in our streets.*

He points out that China's funding of these causes flows because they "benefit when chaos weakens us. It doesn't matter what issue gets thousands out on the street to riot, or now, even kill. That's why it's an omnicause."

One cause. One party. One goal: the elimination of Western freedoms and sovereignty to be replaced by communism.

Elon Musk reposted a video that has garnered over 40M views which shows an ANSWER Coalition demonstrator telling a journalist in 2024 at a pro-Hamas rally, what the purpose of the demonstration really was. "Getting rid of America, getting rid of the West. This is what this is for. Yes. Everyone here understands that, at some level, we need to get rid of America, completely."

This carefully stoked hatred of all things America defines Antifa as well. President Trump issued an order identifying it as a terrorist organization. "Antifa is a militarist, anarchist enterprise with communist roots that explicitly calls for the overthrow of the United States Government, law enforcement authorities, and our system of law," the order reads. "It uses illegal means to organize and execute a campaign of violence and terrorism nationwide to accomplish these goals."

What the order didn't mention is that Antifa has been doing the CCP's bidding, wearing all black, their faces covered, harassing reporters, photographers, and camera crews working for the anti-CCP, The Epoch Times and its sister media outlet NTD. In at least one notorious incident, they chased down and strangled Andy Ngo, author of "Unmasked, Inside Antifa's Radical Plan to Destroy Democracy" who had to relocate to England for safety.

The CCP's decades of narrative warfare is paying off: division has been strategically seeded, funded, nurtured, viralized, and is bearing poisonous fruit everywhere you look. For the first time in American history, a majority of Democrats view socialism more favorably than economic freedom (capitalism). According to Gallup, only 42% of Democrats see economic freedom (capitalism) positively, while 66% openly embrace socialism.

The same poll shows that only 31% of Democrats under 50 still support economic freedom (capitalism), compared to 54% just fifteen years ago. Figures like Bernie Sanders and Zohran Mamdani are proof of this shift. Sanders built his career by railing against "capitalist oligarchy," giving socialist ideology a friendly American face. Mamdani, the self-described democratic socialist (communist), weaned on preening, self-righteous, and comically reductive Marxist postcolonialist dogma, draws crowds by openly calling capitalism a system of exploitation. He has declared globalist "international law" (prelude to communism) for New York City over U.S. law.

If he were a true communist, he wouldn't identify so strongly with Islam because both communism and Islam are equally absolutist in claiming the sole right to represent the only god. Communists are non-believers and Muslims cannot be atheists. His campaign and persona represented a well-crafted charade to fool the 'useful idiots' (Lenin's term) to lead the sheep to go to slaughter.

Xi Van Fleet, who grew up as a little girl amid the blood-soaked mass murder of the Cultural Revolution in China has been raising the alarm about how nonstop Marxist propaganda has destroyed the minds of the Western Left...

> *They are taught to hold America to a standard that is impossible. They see shortcomings and faults everywhere, and then they conclude that the system is not fair and in fact, so evil, so racist that it needs to be overthrown. They want the government to determine what should be distributed. But with communism, they will find out that there is no way to generate new wealth, and then everyone will be poor, just like every communist country in the world. Reality is the best teacher. That's why I tell the American people, please listen to me: 'I've been there, and I've seen that, experienced it. By the time you discover that you were lied to, and you vote the communist Party into power, it will be too late. You will not be able to vote them out.'*

The CCP has hammered the message globally: capitalism equals oppression, America equals imperialism, China equals justice and historical inevitability. Through TikTok, state media, and its vast influence networks, Beijing has been injecting these narratives into U.S. discourse. As a result, for millions of young, deluded Americans and other Western youth socialism isn't just tolerated, it's the new orthodoxy. It has gotten so bad that James Fanell, former Intelligence Chief of the U.S. Pacific Fleet says "If you are a CCP propagandist trying to disparage America, you do not have to invent your own material anymore. All you have to do is retweet the Americans who say it."

CCP Targets Freedoms and Symbols of Freedom

In the CCP's grim calculus, America's liberty is the ultimate foe, a virus to be killed through cultural subversion. Through an estimated $100M+ in CCP-linked donations (U.S. House Select Committee 2021), schools once echoing with Patrick Henry's "give me liberty or give me death" now peddle "equity" over excellence and "micro-aggressions" and phony "hate speech" rules over free speech.

Knowing they can't militarily overthrow the U.S., Marxist violent revolutionary strategy has had to morph into a slower, steadier, subtler form, costumed in the language of equity, American hegemony, and colonialism. Marxist brutalities across the globe have been sanitized and removed from curricula, media, and social campaigns, framing Marxism instead as the enlightened response to Western injustice. They contort and reduce everything to that same old tired Marxist/Leninist binary logic of "victim vs oppressor," and treating any divergence from that as some kind of horrible moral transgression.

Core to this attack is the CCP's focus on the free market system despite the obvious irony that Deng's opening of China to capitalism is responsible for its new prosperity. The free market system, rooted in Enlightenment ideals championed by John Locke and Adam Smith, forms part of the interlocking web of human freedoms, including the connection between material abundance to spiritual flourishing found in 3 John 1:2: "Beloved, I pray that you may prosper in all things and be in health, just as your soul prospers." (NKJV)

This root of prosperity flowing from a soul aligned with divine design was affirmed by Jefferson's immortal words, who enshrined it into the Declaration of Independence. In his words, "life, liberty and the pursuit of happiness" have been "endowed by our Creator" as inalienable rights, which includes the sacred right to property as a natural extension of human dignity and sovereignty.

The Founding Fathers, steeped in these thinkers' works, viewed government not as an all-powerful wealth redistributor (another "King") but as a guardian of private property rights to foster innovation, voluntary exchange, and individual agency. In this Divine order, the free market liberates politically represented individuals to create wealth ethically, while curbing tyranny.

That makes one recent public betrayal of America's foundational principle in Philadelphia so shocking and repulsive. There, in the birthplace of the Declaration of Independence and the Constitution, city officials raised the Chinese Communist Party flag at City Hall, transforming our symbol of freedom into a monument of oppression. Tibetan activist Tsering Jurme denounced this grotesque spectacle with searing moral clarity:

"The red flag of the Chinese Communist Party is not a symbol of culture; it is the emblem of a brutal, totalitarian regime responsible for the persecution and murder of millions, the destruction of thousands of monasteries, and the ongoing cultural genocide of my people in Tibet and the Uyghurs in Xinjiang."

The flag-raising, co-organized with Beijing-linked groups, represents more than a mere diplomatic gesture. It was part of a strategic psychological operation designed to normalize a totalitarian regime. Republican state Senator Doug Mastriano correctly identified "the cradle of liberty flying the banner of tyranny," as a moment of deep civilizational surrender. https://dailycaller.com/section/us/

But really, should we be surprised? After all, in England, it's suddenly become a "provocation" to raise the Union Jack or St. George Cross flag for fear of hurting the feelings of their growing, militant Muslim population. And city institutions in Dearborn, Michigan and Patterson, New Jersey fly the Hamas-terrorism-associated Palestinian flag. While I laud the prevalent American ethos of "peace on Earth and good will toward all men" that we repeat so often around Christmas, not all men have good will toward us. And if we want peace, we must actively and fiercely resist those that would do us harm.

Another core Western cultural value the CCP attacks are the voluntary and elected community and civil society bonds that hold our diverse society together in order to replace them with State dependence. The natural ties between neighbors, families, churches, and civic groups make a free society resilient. But as defector Yuri Bezmenov explained, the Marxist goal is to:

...replace traditionally established institutions and organizations with fake organizations [and] take away the responsibility from naturally established links between individuals, groups of individuals and society at large, and replace them with artificially, bureaucratically controlled bodies.

This way, instead of a bottom-up community, you get state dependency. Instead of the neighbor who helps shovel your driveway, or brings you food when you are sick, motivated by human care, you get a half-interested "social worker" whose loyalty is not to you or your family, but to the totalitarian government paycheck.

The bond of free citizens joining together in brotherhood and sisterhood gets stripped out and replaced with faceless bureaucracy. People no longer turn to each other. They are forced to turn to state-paid intermediaries, clerks in a system that prioritizes itself.

CCP's Grip on Hollywood: Censorship From Abroad

The (CCP) wields control over Hollywood through economic leverage and enforced self-censorship, turning Tinseltown into a propaganda arm, as documented in Ben Schwartz's 2022 book "Made in Hollywood, Censored by Beijing: How China Influences Film and Television."

With China's internal box office surging from $1.6 billion in 2010 to a projected $7.5 billion in 2025 (per Statista), studios like Disney and Warner Bros. have caved to Beijing's demands to secure access, altering scripts, casting, and narratives to align with CCP propaganda. A 2021 U.S.C. Annenberg report reveals that since 2014, over 20 major U.S. films were modified for Chinese release, with the Motion Picture Association (MPA) advising studios to preemptively excise content offending the regime.

Follow the money. Former MPAA China consultant Matt Damsker admitted openly in a 2019 Hollywood Reporter interview, "We don't want to antagonize the Chinese government... it's about protecting our market."

In the 2013 Sony hack, for example, executives were shown discussing CCP-approved propaganda for films like Skyfall, where Shanghai scenes were designed to glorify the city. They also revealed the MPAA's internal guidelines mandating removal of "sensitive" topics like Tibet or Taiwan independence. The direct influence is on the surface, omnipresent, and obvious and extensive

- In Marvel's "Dr. Strange," Tilda Swinton was cast as the "Ancient One" - originally (and obviously) a Tibetan character - reportedly to *avoid offending China* (The Guardian).
- "World War Z's" film adaptation downplayed or *removed the book's explicit Chinese origin* of the viral outbreak to avoid implicating China.
- "Looper" had a line referencing "living in China" that was altered/omitted in some versions amid *sensitivity to Chinese audiences.*

- Tom Cruise's jacket in "Top Gun: Maverick" had a Taiwan flag patch removed in initial marketing to *appease Chinese censors* and accommodate Tencent Pictures, a Chinese company that was initially involved as a financial backer for the film's China release (when Tencent pulled out, to Paramount's credit, they replaced the flag).
- "Seven Years in Tibet" led to a *de facto ban on Brad Pitt and Sony* in China, serving as a cautionary example to studios (1997).
- Critics argued the live-action "Mulan's" villains and production choices *echoed Chinese state narratives* and raised concerns about marginalizing Uyghurs.
- Producers attempted to change a "Spider-Man" film's third act to avoid depicting American symbols such as the Statue of Liberty *to placate Chinese sensitivities.*
- "Red Dawn" (2012) - the remake of the Chinese invasion of the U.S. - was pressured to portray the invaders as *North Korean rather than Chinese.*
- "Transformers: Age of Extinction" (2014) omitted Taiwan's flag and added *pro-CCP product placements* after Beijing's intervention, later earning about $320 million in China.
- South Park's 2019 episode "Band in China" mocked Hollywood's self-censorship to appease China, leading to the show's **total ban in China.** Apple forced the creators to issue at least an (of course) satirical "apology."

Studios have been warned against making films about sensitive topics like Tibet, Taiwan, state torture, and organ harvesting in China. But that's only part of the problem. Chris Fenton is a Hollywood executive and producer who worked on behalf of the CCP's Hollywood censors for years, until he had enough. Their censorship extends beyond China's market: by capturing a few elites and pressuring Hollywood to self-censor, they can export propaganda and reshape the U.S. and global entertainment landscape in ways they could not achieve overtly.

He says of the CCP...

They have amazing influence over Hollywood. There are a couple of versions of it. One is a premeditated version of what is censored even before it was written or scripted, which is this idea with any sort of sensitive topics, whether it has to do with Taiwan, or Hong Kong or Tibet ... things that have something to do with human rights. Those are essentially taboo in Hollywood.

And regarding shows or films that are not even planned for Chinese release, "If China does find out about those movies and knows about them, even if that particular film does not get into China, China will penalize the studio or filmmakers involved with that particular movie, so that they can't get other movies in."

The 2023 RAND Corporation study quantifies the chilling effect: today, 80% of U.S. studios now consult CCP censors pre-production, fostering "preemptive compliance" that sanitizes history. Schwartz quotes a studio exec: "China's the golden goose. We kill the one that lays the eggs at our peril."

Through economic leverage, the CCP's cultural warfare launders authoritarian narratives into global pop culture, eroding Western values. This "soft power subversion" normalizes the CCP's human rights abuses and sows division. America's storytelling engine has become Beijing's megaphone. This is ideological surrender to the CCP's cultural war on us all.

The CCP operates to destroy free speech in American professional sports as well. A brief look:

- **NBA & Daryl Morey (2019):** After Morey's pro-Hong Kong tweet, China cut NBA broadcasts and sponsorships; the league distanced itself to protect its multibillion-dollar China market.
- **Enes Kanter Freedom:** Criticized CCP human rights abuses, leading to Celtics games being pulled in China and his effective blacklisting from the NBA.

- **LeBron James:** Dismissed Morey's Hong Kong support as "misinformed," avoiding criticism of Beijing amid deep personal and brand ties to China.
- **Peng Shuai & WTA Standoff (2021):** After accusing a senior CCP official of assault, Peng disappeared; WTA suspended China events, while CCP propaganda deterred other sports groups from speaking out.

CCP Cultural Goal 4: Hate Each Other

The CCP's masterstroke over the past years has been to fuse ancient resentments to current political rifts, fueling a frenzy of street mobs, wealth-class wars, race/gender re-education and rich vs. poor schisms, creating chaos and talk of civil war. It's all centrally planned and amplified, for example, through TikTok's divisive algorithms (700% surge in U.S. polarization content, 2023 MIT study) and proxy funding of violent agitators (e.g., $5M+ to Black Lives Matter-linked groups alone via CCP shells, per 2022 Washington Examiner).

The CCP gleefully pits neighbor against neighbor, Democrat vs. Republican, White vs. Black, the Wealthy vs. the Middle Class, Men vs. Women, Generation vs. Generation, the very idea of Man/Woman vs. the Heinz 57 flavors of brand new gender variations all in relentless psyops. It's Mao's Cultural Revolution all over again, creating a splintered tinderbox where unity burns away. In Peter Schweizer's words, "part of China's strategy toward the United States is to divide the country, to encourage conflict in division because they believe that it saps the United States of its energy to be able to operate internationally."

As a patriot who genuinely loves my country, I feel no deeper grief than watching America's melting pot boil over into manufactured hate. Bezmenov warned us that "there are always unhappy people in a society" to be exploited; communist cultural warfare weaponizes them to break all social bonds. CCP's ever-inverting bot farms turn criminals into victims, guardians into villains, and honest labor into the "theft" of owners. It creates hatred and mistrust of police and the military, floods media and campuses with "resistance," and "class struggle" oppression frames which leads to mob rule and the harassment of students, faculty, and administration alike. It enforces DEI/equity dogma to detach people from personal responsibility and meritocracy. In short, the CCP splits and inflames public opinion over every issue, domestic and foreign.

In this inverted Orwellian world, the CCP trains a population to parrot that vice is virtue, freedom is slavery, prosperity is an illusion, weakness is moral superiority, victimhood is something to brandish as a weapon rather than fix, and safe and social order is "oppression."

Once that's accomplished, the playbook assures that violence and intimidation follow. So what looks like grassroots fury is actually coordinated and well-funded escalation: cinderblocks and bricks stacked near planned protests, free and abundant signage and megaphones, lavishly paid street rioters, smashed storefronts, families threatened. In the mayhem, the established social contract breaks down and the public loses faith both in the institutions that support social order and in each other as co-citizens.

None of this "looks" like a foreign invasion at first. It looks like disconnected phenomena - innocent domestic social feeds, grants, curricula, NGO programs, "research," glossy documentaries, and attractive (paid or AI) influencers simply speaking their mind. But over time, the cumulative effect results in a population that no longer knows what is true, what is sacred, or what needs to be defended.

Case Study One: Marxist Roots and the Poison of BLM

Few recent social issues have ripped apart the American populace and wrought as much violence as the George Floyd case and its aftermath.

BLM was founded in 2013 by three African American women: Alicia Garza, Patrisse Cullors, and Opal Tometi in response to the acquittal of George Zimmerman and has been a Marxist organization from the start. Cofounder Patrisse Cullors called herself and other BLM founders "trained Marxists" in an interview on Real News Network.

BLM receives support from the CCP the same as the Black Panthers did from Mao in the 1960s. According to Mike Gonzalez, author of "BLM: The Making of a New Marxist Revolution," the Black Futures Lab and the Black To The Future Action Fund, both associated with BLM founder Alicia Garza, were founded as Maoist organizations in 1972 and have been doing pro-CCP work in America ever since.

Xi Van Fleet, a close observer (and former victim) of the CCP's strategy and tactics during the Cultural Revolution, observes that supporting Black lives is not the organization's priority.

> *Since the organization came into being in 2013, BLM has done nothing in terms of making the lives of Black Americans better. More than 90 percent of Black homicide deaths are at the hands of Black offenders. Have you ever heard anything whereby BLM addressed all the Black people killed in 2020, even a simple statement of sincere grief? You didn't, because those Black lives did not matter to BLM. The death of Floyd amid the COVID pandemic lockdown created the perfect storm. It was in the year 2020 that BLM activism turned the protests against police brutality into a full-blown Marxist upheaval aimed at destroying our society.*

Indeed, as reported by the Federalist, a study has shown that up to 95 percent of the 2020 U.S. riots were linked to BLM.

Apostle Tommy Quick, a prominent Black leader, Project 21 Ambassador, and Founder of Christian Families Against Destructive Decisions (CFADD), is not fooled. He recently told me...

> *We have seen the impact of BLM. It camouflaged its real purpose in the form of social justice. That has to be exposed. In the Black community, we must emphasize family and self reliance first, not color. We must get past the complexion of our skin to see what's right and wrong. BLM - that's a Trojan Horse of communists and the progressive left to create division and subjugation of our people. The complexion of my child is not as important as the soul of my child.*

The educational group, Every Black Life Matters, concurs, declaring,

> *The most effective way to build Black wealth for individuals, families or businesses is to educate and train the community how to embrace innovation and leverage free markets and entrepreneurialism. Free markets are the least racist of all systems. A manufacturer of goods or provider of labor cares not what color their repeat customers are, only that their interactions are freely engaged in, mutually prosperous and beneficial.*

At the financial center of this corrupt nexus is Neville Roy Singham, the notorious Chicago-born billionaire now based in Shanghai, whose web of nonprofit funding channels has been highlighted as bankrolling a significant number of left-wing U.S. protest groups and mob actions, while spreading pro-CCP messaging.

House Oversight Chairman James Comer (KY) and Declassification Taskforce Chairwoman Anna Paulina Luna (FL) confirmed in June 2025 that Singham's network - including the Party for Liberation and Socialism (PSL), The People's Forum, and the ANSWER Coalition - advances Beijing's explicit "Strategy of Sowing Discord" strategy by deepening

American social divisions. Senators Marco Rubio and Lindsey Graham had previously urged the DOJ to investigate Singham's CCP ties.

The CCP-linked network, with no organized examination or pushback, festers and spreads. The People's Forum, based in New York City, has hosted classes like "Lenin and the Path to Revolution" and events glorifying the Chinese revolution, while also justifying Hamas' barbaric October 7, 2023 pogrom against Israeli civilians.

A New York Times investigation found that Singham sold his software firm ThoughtWorks for $785 million in 2017 and now shares Shanghai office space with Maku Cultural Communications, a CCP propaganda entity. His money - funneled through opaque donor-advised funds - has sent over $20 million to The People's Forum and at least $275 million to a global network pushing pro-Beijing, pro-Marxist agendas. Singham's wife, Jodie Evans, co-founder of CodePink, co-authored "China Is Not Our Enemy" with staff from CCP-aligned institutes, and funds multiple society-fraying militant groups as well as serving CCP-funded outlets like Tricontinental Institute and Dongsheng News. The International People's Assembly, also tied to Singham-funded Tricontinental, platformed PFLP terrorist Leila Khaled, normalizing extremism in protest spaces.

If anyone needed a smoking gun about how money has been behind the hysterical street mob violence of the past few years, the citizen journalist @NateFriedman97, discovered on camera that a protester holding "a large flag that said Allah is the only God" was making $75,000 per year protesting- and the money led back directly to Neville Roy Singham. A September 4, 2025, letter from Ways and Means Chairman Jason Smith (MO) demands records from Code Pink, citing its justification of Hamas' October 7 attacks, incitement of anti-ICE riots and campus occupations, and role as a "CCP-funded propaganda arm."

Marxist rhetoric within BLM-affiliated circles echo CCP propaganda themes to the letter: casting Western capitalism as the global system of oppression, disparaging the "Western nuclear family" as oppressive, elevating "resistance" movements abroad and framing all politics in binary revolutionary terms. These groups have merged domestic social justice causes with foreign policy stances uniformly favorable to Beijing, twisting Western civil rights language to legitimize anti-U.S., anti-allied positions and pro-Party positions.

In effect, with this and other dark funding, the CCP's Marxist ideological exports have found fertile ground in the United States' protest culture, embedding itself in activist groups like BLM under the banner of justice.

Alex Goldenberg, senior adviser to the National Contagion Research Institute, warned in The New York Post, "The Singham network operates as a coordinated movement incubator," amplifying disinformation on social media to fracture American unity. He has demanded Attorney General Pam Bondi's scrutiny to expose and dismantle this foreign enemy subversion of U.S. civil society.

With this dark money and CCP backing, Marxist rhetoric has seeped ever more deeply into the fore of Black activism. April Chapman, Project 21 Ambassador, in a case study on BLM narratives, highlights pastors like Jamal Bryant using "blatant Marxist language," referring to congregants as "comrades" and viewing the Black church's mission as "socio-political" infiltration.

> *Bryant's New Birth logo, a clenched fist holding a cross-echoes revolutionary symbolism, with Bryant, a longtime NAACP member, employing "old school communist" tactics, she says. Apostle Quick calls it "a Marxist communistic training camp [pushing] spiritual abuse and the mishandling of God's Word.*

Marxist infiltration into the Black Church community goes back to Civil Rights days, according to Vince E. Ellison, Project 21 Ambassador, author and political commentator. He traced the history with me during a recent conversation:

The Civil Rights Movement was led by Marxists who came against the black community: the structure of the family, making you hate your own nation and becoming permanent victims. The Black community before the Civil Rights Movement, it was patriotic! But after the Civil Rights Movement, we became this victim class. They set up the S.C.L.C. - the Southern Christian Leadership Conference for Martin Luther King, Jr. to go into the Black church, and turn the community away from its own nation. We rejected capitalism, we got an apostate religion and what happened? The Black community becomes completely dysfunctional. Positive things are looked upon as negative and negative things are looked upon as positive. How do you get to where calling your women bitches and hoes is popular? How do you get to calling yourself the N-word as popular? Hip hop culture? How do you get where the worst elements of Black society set the markers for the rest of society to be elevated?

This "complete dysfunction" started with the arts, which he points out, creates culture.

"They use public education, music, TV, hip-hop, all the arts to press their agenda forward. And they hold up all these socialist heroes, the Black Panthers and the SCLC - and the ones who stood up for righteousness, the right thing, who loved America, were looked upon as Uncle Toms and buffoons."

The end result? Says Ellison:

"To put businesses and individual associations under the hand of the government. When you took away capitalism and incentive, when you separate citizens from God, to say that you can't pray here, and you can't pray there. When they gaslit the American people into believing that something was happening in America that just wasn't true with these setups, like Birmingham - finding the worst of the worst in Bull Connor and saying that was America. All planned. And now? You can't get patriotism now from the Black

community anymore because they've destroyed this country in the minds of the young people. And it all came from the Civil Rights Movement. It was a plan. We were lied to. We were told to reject and resist rather than embrace the best of this country and rise. People don't get that it's Marxism pure and simple. They created complete dependency on the state. Make the state god. And it worked."

Case Study 2: Funding Islamist Fury and Western Collapse

In the wake of the savage Hamas attack on Israeli civilians, the CCP ratcheted up both its anti-Israel and anti-Semitic propaganda and funding to drive a further wedge into the American public - as well as to promote its narrative of Western imperialism vs. third world victimhood.

Says Ofir Dayan, a Research Associate in the Israel-China Policy Center at INSS, China doesn't promote anti-Israel narratives in order to harm Israel directly, but rather it seeks to damage the United States both internally and internationally. So all the funds and violence and bile Beijing has poured forth on the Jewish state and people is a way for Beijing to advance its claim that it's Washington that destabilizes both the international system and the regions where it operates.

This paves the way for the CCP to take the role of international hegemon.

As always, the CCP strategy is multi-pronged. The CCP has allowed, tacitly endorsed and funded social media posts scurrilously equating Jews with Nazis, describing Israel as a "terrorist organization" when defending its people from genocidal jihadis, praising Hamas and Palestine, and spreading conspiracies.

Post-October 7, Chinese social media platforms Weibo and Bilibili teemed with libels and propaganda equating Israelis with Nazis, praising Islamic terrorists, and reviving the book "Currency Wars" - a Chinese bestseller blaming Jewish bankers for everything from JFK's assassination to random global woes. China's state-controlled internet search giants Baidu and Alibaba literally erased Israel from their map services. Pro-Hamas/Terrorist media cheered this topographical "Final Solution" of Israel, fulfilling their genocidal call of "from the river to the sea."

[Important note: The National Education Association (NEA), the largest teachers' union in the United States, sent an email to its 3 million members in October 2025 that included a map of the region that labeled all the territory of Israel as "Palestine," enforcing this same territorial Final Solution.]

Graphika Research showed that TikTok, ByteDance's CCP-owned psyop machine, promoted pro-Hamas content post-October 7, algorithmically amplifying it to drown out Israeli, American, and Pro-Western, Pro-Christian voices while, U.S. intelligence revealed, the CCP's Houston consulate used big data to seed tailored riot videos into the feeds of vulnerable Americans.

State-owned Chinese Central Television repeatedly spread antisemitic conspiracy theories since the outbreak of the war. One Chinese TV report stated absurdly that "Jews represent a mere 3% of [U.S.] population but control more than 70% of its wealth." CCP outlets have resuscitated and spread all the old, tired anti-semitic tropes from Nazi and Soviet propaganda mills about Jews running the world, etc.

Meanwhile, the CCP's favorite cash-rich toadies, Singham and Code Pink, promoted mass protests in cities across the country, funding Anti-West/Anti-Israel mob violence. The ANSWER Coalition, fat with Singham's money, didn't just convene post-October 7 to create culturally dividing mega-rallies; it demanded America abandon its allies while glorifying Hamas as "resistance" (New York Times, 2023 investigation). Universities, once bastions of Enlightenment inquiry, now fester as CCP-Singham incubators of hate, where the "Shut It Down for Palestine" hashtag - launched from The People's Forum's

CCP-infused lair funds blockades, classroom takeovers, and chants that veer from anti-Zionism into outright Jew-bashing.

Let's be clear: protests that block ambulances, burn cars, and beat up Jewish students aren't liberation; they're Beijing/jihadi victory laps, dividing Americans, radicalizing debate, and priming America for paralysis and takeover.

If the danger wasn't so serious, the irony would be a joke: a totalitarian regime interning over a million Uyghur Muslims in torture camps pretends to champion Palestinian Muslims, recycling Nazi playbooks to project U.S. "dysfunction" abroad. But politics makes evil bedfellows; the unholy fusion of Marxism and Islamic jihadism serves their shared goal: sapping Western will, especially support for Israel, the frontline against jihadist tyranny. Woke ideologues borrow Marxist anti-imperialist rhetoric to "decolonize" Israel into oblivion, while jihadists leverage left legitimacy to mainstream their death-cult fever dreams.

Divide and conquer, the oldest political trick in the book

Again, Beijing maintains a relationship with Israel, so their arrows are not really aimed at Jerusalem, but rather at Washington and American society. It took the Germans, who have learned the lessons of spreading this kind of divisive hate the hard way, to call out China's anti-Jewish hate propaganda. The German Beijing Embassy didn't hold back, *"Those who deliberately combine the Israeli flag with Nazi symbols in their profile pictures are either ignorant idiots or shameless bastards!"*

All this reveals the CCP's Cultural Warfare at work: divide a society against itself until it can no longer tell friend from foe. What looks like organic public outrage or street theater is, in reality, well-funded strategic destabilization. While Americans tear each other apart at rallies, in classrooms, and on social media, Beijing quietly fuels the fire and the rot spread. It is calculated. The CCP wants America culturally fractured, morally confused, and politically paralyzed. And it is using tech, wealthy sympathizers, dark money networks, and ideological Trojan horses to make it happen.

A review of *only a few* culture war methods financed and used to divide Americans:

- Corrupt district attorneys and other public figures (campaign payments and kickbacks)
- Education system: schools, colleges, universities
- Election fraud, voting machines
- Open Society Foundation's network of groups, activists, and their activities
- Antifa rioters (designated as a terrorist organization)
- Black Lives Matter (BLM)
- The Color Revolution
- WEF, WHO, CDC
- Online porn, pedophelia sites, and sex sites
- EU penetration (campaign payments and kickbacks)
- Child trafficking
- Entertainment industry
- **Much more**

Global Forecaster David Murrin likens the process to a slow death...

> *The danger of gray-zone warfare, especially its cultural dimension, is that it deliberately corrodes a society's immune response, delaying collective reaction times by normalising incremental assaults. Victims get used to subtle attacks and fail to recognise or respond to the next phase of escalation. So the target is cooked slowly, like a frog in warming water. That, to my mind, describes what the 'axis of autocracy' (China and its allies Russia, North Korea, and Iran) has been doing to America, Europe, and Israel-and now the water is finally beginning to boil and we are still in the cooking pot.*

The brilliance of America was not only its structure, but its grounding in natural law and biblical wisdom. John Adams's observation is timeless: "Our Constitution was made only for a moral and religious people. It is wholly inadequate to the government of any other."

If we wish to save the republic, we must restore the things that make self-government possible: the family, the church, the community, and the conscience.

We fight for the freedom to live virtuously. We must reclaim what is ours: the right to exist as a sovereign people under God.

Politics alone is not enough. It is not enough to win elections if we lose our culture. It is not enough to pass laws if we do not form strong individual souls.

BRIEFING NINE
The Battle For Your Country
Political War

The CCP's Systematic Assault on Western Institutions and Sovereignty

The Stakes: Who We Are (the West), Who They Are (the CCP):

A quick review...

The West embodies a unique legacy of individual freedoms, democratic sovereignty, constitutional protections, and market-driven prosperity - values rooted in Judeo-Christian and Enlightenment principles that prioritize individual dignity, human rights, free enterprise, and self-governance.

By dark contrast, the CCP is a totalitarian, mafia-type, violence-based, regime, built on failed Marxist-Leninist ideology, where one Party exercises absolute control, viewing Western democracies as "soft" ideological targets to be subverted through unrestricted warfare, defeated and ruled over. In the accurate, unfiltered words of retired U.S. Navy Captain James E. Fanell testifying before Congress:

> *The PRC is a coercive, expansionist, hyper-nationalistic, militarily powerful, brutally repressive, fascist, and totalitarian state, where people are subjects, simply property of the state, and ideals such as democracy, inalienable rights, limited government, and rule of law have no place. [Hearing on China's Worldwide Military Expansion,*

before the House Permanent Select Committee on Intelligence, 115th Congress. (2018)]

In short, communism is a nightmare, from Moscow to Caracas to Havana to North Korea, as you will see detailed in a few pages. Marxism/socialism/communism have killed hundreds of millions of people and have proven they can only fail, as we will chronicle later in the four coming case studies.

Colleague Ken Cao, Executive Director of the Center for Asian Democratic Resilience, an expert who publishes a regular insider look at China, wrote in September 2025, regarding those who cling to a fantasy of a "socialist paradise" or "false utopia"...

Behind the propaganda and glittering skyscrapers is a society built on radical selfishness, where altruism isn't rare - it's dangerous. Helping your neighbor isn't noble. It's stupid. This isn't just cultural. It's engineered. For decades, the communist Party has rewired an entire society, systematically destroying trust and cooperation: villagers forced to denounce their neighbors. Children rewarded for reporting their own parents. Temples, churches, and independent communities crushed into dust. Over time, people learned a brutal truth: "If you trust anyone but the Party, you're dead. Even today, helping others can backfire catastrophically: A man helps an old woman who fell - she sues him, accusing him of causing the accident. Donations to the Chinese Red Cross after disasters vanish into luxury cars and villas for insiders. Kindness becomes self-destructive. So people stop helping. They retreat inward, teaching their children to only look out for themselves. Generations later, empathy atrophies, replaced by a permanent culture of radical egoism and mistrust. The result? Education becomes a war zone. Workplaces devolve into snake pits of betrayal. Politics becomes pure self-service.

And yet, despite communism's abject catastrophe as an unmatched historical generator of human misery, some Westerners still dream of emulating this collectivist, atheistic, surveillance state nightmare. At home, we see "democratic socialists" clawing their way up onto our own urban, state, and national tickets. They can call themselves what they want, as long as we remember Ayn Rand's words: *"There is no difference between communism and socialism, except in the means of achieving the same ultimate end. Communism proposes to enslave men by force, socialism by vote. It is merely the difference between murder and suicide." (Ayn Rand, Textbook of Americanism, 1946.)*

Open societies vs. communism. Two vastly opposite systems. Two diametrically opposite worlds. It's not some "friendly competition" of economic structures. It's an existential showdown, a case of "We Must Live. You Must Die." - the sentiment reflecting CCP hardliners' conviction that coexistence with the U.S. is ultimately impossible.

Nevertheless, the CCP and its lackeys (including hard-core domestic communists dedicated to doing Beijing's bidding) who live in the comfort of the West, continue to recycle and weaponize their failed, murderous doctrines. They work day in and day out to erode the West's core identity, compromise our political leaders, take over our organizations and turn our strengths (rights-guaranteeing institutions, freedom, tolerance, and diversity) into vulnerabilities for their assault on our way of life.

How Did We Get Here?

I: They Deceived Us: The Wolf in Panda Clothing

Throughout the 90's and early part of the 20th Century, when the CCP was seeking acceptance in the WTO and looking to steal as much Western technology and manufacturing as possible, it put on a humble, foot-shuffling, meek show: a deceptive charm offensive. But where Beijing once hid their motives, as Professor Kerry K. Gershaneck, former U.S. Marine Officer and NATO Fellow writes...

The CCP no longer hides its disdain for concepts such as democracy, rule of law, freedom of speech, and human rights, nor does it conceal its intent to create a new world order based on its totalitarian model. Political warfare is a primary tool that the CCP employs to defeat the United States. It is the PRC's magical path to victory, to win not so much without struggle but without having to resort to open kinetic conflict. The PRC's intent is not a theoretical conjecture. Beijing demonstrates on a daily basis its eagerness and ability to subvert and defeat-or, to use CCP parlance, to "divide and disintegrate"-the United States and other foreign nations.

And, I'm sorry to say, at the political leadership level, the U.S. has been sleeping on the job. The fall of the U.S.S.R. made us over-confident, fat, and happy. We dismantled our externally-facing political influence machine as well as our defenses against outside influence. We believed communism was done. Doomed. Defeated. And it would only be a matter of time before China and other communist states would fall. We thought it was, in the words of Francis Fukayama's notoriously shortsighted book, "The End of History."

But it was only the beginning for the CCP.

In their book, "Embracing Communist China: America's Greatest Strategic Failure," retired U.S. Navy Captain and intelligence specialist James E. Fanell and Bradley A. Thayer meticulously dissect how American national security elites, driven by wishful thinking, financial temptation, corruption, and strategic incompetence, surrendered the strategic initiative inside a process they call "threat deflation." As Fanell, also Former Director of Intelligence, U.S. Pacific Fleet, testified to the House Oversight Committee:

Through elite capture, psychological warfare, deception, disinformation, and propaganda, the CCP misled and enculturated our government as well as other American elites. The intelligence community and the Department of Defense were deceived into

> *buying the lie of China's 'peaceful rise' and failed to fulfill their most basic function. The CCP has classified America as its main enemy since its inception. They seek to defeat us first through political warfare - protracted Maoist struggle - before kinetic war.*

The "panda huggers" - as Michael Pillsbury and others call them - politicians, academics, and think tank experts who advocate for China, not only ignored mounting evidence of China's aggressive multi-front political infiltration, but actively suppressed serious strategic assessments and resistance. Two brief stories illustrate our submission...

- Colleague James Fanell, CAPT U.S.N. (ret.), tells of giving two public, unclassified speeches in 2013 and 2014 exposing the PLA's expansionist activities in the South and East China Seas. Though he was the U.S. Navy's most respected China expert, he was shut down because the Obama administration didn't want to publicly emphasize that the CCP/PRC was a threat. Fanell was soon fired.
- Colleague Robert Spalding, PhD, BGEN USAF (ret.), similarly tells of how he was "routinely rebuffed" for raising security concerns, being told that assisting the NSC "might anger... Chinese funders or business accounts." As he recalls, "the list of organizations that refused to engage with me publicly in my official capacity was stunning. Top white-shoe New York law firms. Organizations with mandates to promote democracy, freedom, and human rights would refuse to support my mission."

By consistently downplaying China's military modernization, economic warfare, and global influence operations hoping not to poke the (panda) bear and keep the money flowing in, our elites facilitated the most damaging geopolitical power transfer in modern history. Kershaneck writes:

> *The CCP is quite good at employing political warfare. By contrast, the United States is not. Yes, we mastered it pretty well during the Cold War, but we then declared victory over the Soviet Union... Consequently, we shut down our cornerstone political warfare institutions and capabilities and dropped our guard for nearly three decades, during which our offensive and defensive political warfare skills atrophied. Despite some effort devoted to combating radical Islam and a nod to Russia, we paid little focus to the greatest threat: the PRC... One consequence I have observed firsthand is that many U.S. government officials and bureaucrats cannot recognize political warfare at all.*

Fanell and Thayer call this malfeasance a catastrophic strategic failure, and I agree. The result: a resurgent, emboldened, arrogant CCP, positioned to challenge American global leadership across the globe.

II: They Compromised Our Leaders

The CCP targets U.S. and other global politicians through sophisticated influence operations, funding campaigns, and embedding agents. How effective is it? Well, 239 Socialist (communist) and extreme leftwing candidates were elected to federal and state legislatures in 2020, winning 90 percent of their races according to The Heartland Institute. CCP money, coercion, and backroom dealings started slowly and now exercise leverage everywhere.

To give you a taste

- In 1996, PLA intelligence officer Gen. Ji Shengde provided Johnny Chung, a fundraiser for the Democratic National Committee, with $300,000 to donate towards President Bill Clinton's reelection. Chung visited the White House over fifty times during the 1996 presidential campaign, and was responsible for at least $400,000 of contributions to the DNC.

- The Biden Family: senior FBI counterintelligence officer Charles McGonigal detailed a critical U.S. probe into CEFC China Energy, a Xi Jinping-linked oil conglomerate with deep ties to the Biden family. CEFC served as a CCP front for influence operations, bribery, and smuggling, funneling illicit funds through New York banks to corrupt African officials, traffic Iranian oil, and groom American politicians. DOJ documents reveal CEFC chairman Ye Jianming wooed Hunter and James Biden with payments and gifts, touting his proximity to communist Chairman Xi.

Through political slush funds, luxurious junkets, lobbying leverage, and post-political job opportunities, Beijing has turned Capitol Hill and Washington power into a revolving door.

- Senator Diane Feinstein's husband, Richard Bloom, was an early investor in Lenovo, the Chinese tech giant founded by military scientists from the Chinese Academy of Sciences.
- U.S. Representative Lee Terry joined Huawei after leaving Congress.
- Montana senator and U.S. ambassador to China, Max Bacus, has served on advisory boards of Chinese tech firms, endorses Confucius Institutes, and appears regularly on Chinese state television, where he's compared U.S. policymakers to Hitler and McCarthy.
- Neil Bush's foundation receives millions from C.U.S.F, the China United States Exchange Foundation, a known CCP United Front proxy, while echoing Beijing's rhetoric at every turn.

Peter Schweitzer, the indefatigable detailer of the CCP's hold on elites in the West, pointed out that the collusion crosses the political aisle:

> *Joe Biden's family has received tens of millions of dollars from the Chinese government. He (did) not condemn their work on Fentanyl.*

He (did) not challenge them on COVID. He does not even want to get to the truth. If you look at Mitch McConnell, his family's business through (former Transportation Secretary) Elaine Chao and her father, owns a shipping business that is wholly dependent upon the good graces of the Chinese government. They build the ships for them. They finance the construction of those ships. Were Mitch McConnell to say or do anything offending the Chinese government, they could destroy the family business overnight. Hence, he will occasionally say something kind of tough, but he will never support any action to actually deal with it.

Democrat, Republican, Independent - to the CCP, it doesn't matter as long as they can get you to do their bidding. As Brigadier General Robert Spalding PhD, USAF (ret.) says,

The three political parties in the United States are the Democratic Party, the Republican Party, and the Chinese Communist Party. The Chinese Communist Party is against the other two, and the other two are against each other. So who do you think's going to win that?... The Chinese Communist Party convinces them that they're actually mortal enemies, (wanting them to) fight between themselves to the point of destruction of the United States. That is pure communism. How do I destroy a society? I destroy it from within. I create distrust. I create division. This is the Chinese Communist Party way. These two are going to be fighting while the Chinese Communist Party [uses] that partisanship to destroy patriotism, faith, and confidence in our system of government.

Quietly, the CCP has identified an additional critical vulnerability in the United States' political infrastructure by targeting state and local leaders, who are relatively free from federal oversight and international security concerns. As a recent National Counterintelligence and Security Center report states, "The PRC understands U.S. state and local leaders enjoy a degree of independence from Washington and may seek to use them as proxies to advocate for national U.S. policies Beijing desires."

Their report further emphasizes that "targeting state and local entities" is an "effective way to pursue agendas that might be more challenging at the national level. "By presenting seemingly benign business opportunities and local people-to-people exchanges, the CCP masks its political agendas, using financial incentives to entice local leaders, then coerce them. FBI Director Christopher Wray's January 2022 statement to Congress sums up the long-term strategic approach:

> *The Chinese government understands that politicians in smaller roles today may rise to become more influential over time. So they look to cultivate talent early-often state and local officials-to ensure that politicians at all levels of government will be ready to take a call and advocate on behalf of Beijing's agenda.*

The infiltration strategy is fundamentally about patient, strategic manipulation. As the report chillingly concludes, this approach represents a sophisticated form of political warfare, exploiting the complex, decentralized nature of the United States' governmental system to create hundreds of backdoor channels of influence and potential control. Some of the higher profile cases include the case of New York Governor Andrew Cuomo.

The New York Post exposed Dr. Lining "Larry" He, a mayoral campaign aide to Cuomo as having deep ties to CCP-controlled entities. Records reveal he was director of asset management at state-owned Guangxi Beibu Gulf Investment, aggressively pushing California and Australia toward deeper economic entanglement with China. He chaired Guangxi Beitou Petrochemical Company, a Sinopec joint venture for 2 years, with an embedded CCP cell in its leadership.

He was also listed as a partner at Chongqing-based Penshare-Banyu Technology - a regulatory firm that scrubbed his profile after

Post inquiries-while owning InterStellar Enterprise, importing plastic bottles from Shenzhen, with his wife Jing Lei's firm shipping 8.5 tons in May alone.

Underlining the CCP's close ties with organized crime, he was photographed chummy alongside John Chan, the 70-year-old Brooklyn ex-gangster convicted of heroin and human trafficking. Chan, a key player in the CCP's New York machine, has attended CCP events in the U.S. and China and is featured on China's Ministry of Foreign Affairs site.

These ties are a small part of a surging CCP offensive against New York and other politicians.

- Federal prosecutors charged Linda Sun, a Cuomo-Hochul liaison, as an unregistered communist CCP agent.
- In 2024, two Chinese agents were arrested for sabotaging Taiwan-born activist Xiong Yan's congressional bid.
- In February 2024, the FBI raided Winnie Greco's home, a Chan ally and Adams aide.

Human rights expert Yaqiu Wang says, "at this point, it's hardly surprising that individuals with close ties to the Chinese Communist Party are working for politicians in New York."

That's where the financial center of the world lives. As do so many ex-pat Chinese nationals fighting for human rights back home.

Over on the West coast...

- Los Angeles Mayor Karen Bass welcomed CCP-tied Dominic Ng (East West Bank) and Simon Pang (Royal Business Bank) onto her transition advisory team after those same men, their banks, and related outfits funneled big money into her campaigns and the Mayor's Fund. A Daily Caller investigation tied those donors to CCP United Front–linked organizations and documented their cash donations.

- The PRC has financed a number of political candidates through its agents in the U.S. Katrina Leung, a Chinese spy, contributed to the campaign of Richard Riordan, the former mayor of Los Angeles. He lost his primary to Bill Simon Jr., Leung then contributed to Simon's campaign so at the direction of her Chinese handlers, Leung also contributed to the 1992 campaign of George H.W. Bush.

CCP influence has no U.S. party loyalty. Anyone who can be compromised is fair game.

The pattern reveals exactly how Beijing operates its political-warfare playbook: use political and civic actors (as well as business and cultural leaders) as vectors for influence, while at the same time deploying organized crime money and brute force behind the scenes.

Indeed, the criminal element gets darker. According to a report by the The National Counterintelligence and Security Center inside the Office of the Director of National Intelligence (ODNI), a March 2022 U.S. Justice Department criminal complaint alleged that a PRC operative allegedly instructed a private investigator to physically attack a Chinese American candidate for Congress in Brooklyn, noting "violence would be fine...beat him until he cannot run for election."

While the CCP targets national, state, and local political leaders, sometimes it end-runs them.

Schweizer emphasizes that CCP operatives seek to entrap financial leaders, which gives them enough power to pressure them to politically fight against America's best interests. So when Trump imposed tariffs on China, he explains by example, "China didn't go to Washington to lobby on it. They went to Silicon Valley and they went to Wall Street, and they told their biggest investors in China, and said 'look, if you still want access to our market, you will go and you will do everything in your fiber to get these policies reversed.'"

III: They Influence Our Elections

Regardless of your political beliefs, it is core to our democracy and freedom to ensure free and accurate elections. Citizens must trust in the process.

According to the New York Times, Chinese operatives were elbows deep in the 2024 elections, running fake accounts on X, Facebook, Instagram, Threads, masquerading as ordinary Americans.

You didn't know it then, but thousands upon thousands of Chinese operatives posed as your next-door Trump enthusiasts on social media, stirring up hate to rig from afar the 2024 U.S. vote. The CCP's slick "Spamouflage" network deployed troll farms that push division, boost extremists, and most of all, aim to erode trust in democracy. Meta spotted it early, calling its 2023 takedown the biggest influence op ever, but CCP voices-in-disguise kept resurrecting on X, TikTok, Facebook, etc. under new names. Here's a fraction of the hard evidence of their assaults:

- **Fake Profiles Masquerading as Americans:** On April 1, 2024, The New York Times revealed Chinese operatives running pro-Trump accounts across socials, posing as "doting fathers, husbands, and MAGA die-hards" yelling "MAGA all the way!!" to promote conspiracy theories, attack Biden as a "Satanist pedophile," and recycle Russian propaganda videos.
- **Rapid Amplification of Lies:** A Chinese-linked "MAGA 2024" account shared a Russian propaganda clip, and the next day, Alex Jones blasted it to his 2.2 million followers, showing how Beijing's disinformation races from China to mainstream U.S. politics in less than 24 hours. These ghosts reappear on TikTok, X, and Blogspot, mutating to dodge bans.
- **Green Cicada:** A Massive X Onslaught: In August 2024, cybersecurity firm CyberCX uncovered "Green Cicada," a Beijing-based network with over 8,000 accounts on X, suspected of direct election interference to sway public opinion and votes.

- **AI-Powered Division on Hot-Button Issues:** Graphika's September 2024 report tied Spamouflage to AI-generated fake U.S. users on X and TikTok, denigrating Biden, Trump, and Kamala Harris while questioning election legitimacy and inflaming debates on gun control, homelessness, drug abuse, racial inequality, and the Israel-Hamas conflict.
- **Coordinated Fake Networks Everywhere:** Meta's August 2024 threat report detected eleven China-linked "coordinated inauthentic behavior" operations across platforms, while Microsoft flagged increased Chinese efforts to stoke campus protests, deepen divisions, and meddle in elections.
- **Down-Ballot Dirty Tricks and Antisemitism:** By October 2024, The Washington Post exposed Spamouflage targeting "dozens" of local races with antisemitic smears and conspiracies-like calling non-Jewish Rep. Barry Moore a "Jewish dog" backed by a "bloody Jewish consortium" after he supported China sanctions. It also ramps up rage on police violence, Black Lives Matter, immigration, and Taiwan policy to twist U.S. foreign affairs.

This is mass, deliberate, partisan warfare emanating from Beijing, designed to sow doubts about U.S. leadership, undermine democracy, and extend influence. It looks to polarize families, taint ballots, and spark violence. China's digital daggers will continue to carve up our society into frothing, hateful factions for good if left unchecked. We either fight back together or lose our civil society together.

IV: Undermined Elected Power

Yuri Bezmenov, the celebrated KGB defector, detailed the exact communist political plan to undermine faith in the institutions that hold a society together. Part of that method is "institutional takeover," saying, "The natural bodies of administration which are traditionally either elected by people or appointed by elected leaders of society are being actively substituted by artificial bodies."

By that he means that communist agents work day and night to gradually transfer democratic power and authority to unelected committees, advisory boards, NGOs, panels and self-styled guardians of public opinion that answer to no ballot, no civic mandate, nor to the people. "Bodies of people... who nobody elected," he says, gradually claim authority over what is true, who is respectable, which policies are acceptable and should be funded. "That substitution," he warned us, "is political takeover dressed up as expertise." These unelected cadres "have so much power, almost monopolistic power on your thoughts," he says, "they can rape your mind."

Case in point: ever heard of WHO? The World Health Organization? Did you elect them to dictate how to live under COVID? I know I didn't. WHO cares about your health and mine about as much as arms dealers care about global harmony: zero. It's a massive lobbying group bankrolled by Big Pharma, an unelected entity where tycoons buy influence to dictate what's "healthy" for the masses.

So why, you ask, would governments hand over their authority to this cabal? Dead simple: COVID taught politicians that they couldn't ram through the harsh restrictions they wanted without voters booting them out of office. So to shield themselves from the ballot box backlash, leaders outsource the tough calls to this shadowy body. Then, they can shrug and say, "We wouldn't have quarantined your homes or shuttered schools ourselves-it was the WHO's orders, and our hands are tied." That's the scam in action.

As communists work to steal power from elected officials and place it in unelected organizations, the message sinks in: you don't matter. Decisions no longer reflect popular will. Voters lose a sense of agency and participation. Democratic institutions lose legitimacy. Talking heads and protected technocrats call the shots.

This demise kills confidence in the foundations of a free society. When people believe authority is exercised without consent, democracy becomes reduced to a theatrical shell. And the disaffected, disempowered populace gives up or looks to extreme solutions for answers.

V: They Weaponized Our Courts Against Us

Like our politicians, our elected bodies, our local authorities, and our business leaders, America's judiciary is under siege, and the enemy is using our own laws as weapons against us. The Chinese Communist Party, combined with allied antagonists, have turned American courtrooms into battlegrounds where they silence critics, steal technology, and escape justice, all while we foot the bill for our own destruction. Kerry Kershanek describes the CCP's Lawfare successes as exploiting:

> *...all aspects of the law, including national law, international law, and the laws of war, in order to secure seizing 'legal principle superiority' and delegitimize an adversary. Tools used in lawfare operations include domestic legislation, international legislation, judicial law, legal pronouncement, and law enforcement, which are often used in combination with one another.*

Congressional testimony revealed how Beijing systematically exploits "U.S. entities that have been co-opted by dependence on or resources from the PRC" to reshape American laws from within.

They seek to rewrite our rules, and when they can't, they just break them. In the words of Emily de La Bruyère of the Foundation for Defense of Democracies, "Beijing's scheme exploits U.S. courts through proxy lawsuits that drain targets with crippling fees, while gaming laws to protect bad actors... [It] works to shape U.S. laws and regulations via U.S. entities that have been co-opted by dependence on or resources from the PRC."

She says that the regime ruthlessly "use[s] the U.S. legal system to punish those who stand in its way," treating Chinese firms not as private entities but a colluding "cartel or arms of the Chinese system." Dissident Chinese nationals living abroad are threatened or bankrupted through expensive lawsuits to shut them up.

Defense and economic experts warn that China ruthlessly weaponizes "the U.S. legal system to punish those who stand in its way."

Rep. Darrell Issa (R-Calif.) decried this as a "particularly disturbing" escalation. Issa, Chair of the House Judiciary Subcommittee on Courts, Intellectual Property, and the Internet, read into the congressional record that we can see this abuse...

> *...in criminal operations, in human trafficking, in drug smuggling, in commercial fraud... not limited to any one country [and] backed by a powerful country... This is over and above the 10,000 attacks a day that occur on the internet. This is over and above their spying. This is over and above the abuses that occur on companies in China. This is, in fact, using our patent system, our trademark system, and our courts to their advantage.*

The damages are real and devastating. For only one example, Charlotte Pipe and Foundry burned through $7 million fighting CCP-backed rivals who flooded markets with impossibly cheap, tariff-evading products. When the company discovered blatant trademark theft - fake business cards copying their name and logo traced to Shanghai - Chinese courts simply stonewalled their lawyers, ensuring the American firm's destruction. Charlotte Pipe and Foundry's story is one of thousands.

Additionally, through intellectual property lawsuits, the CCP can gain access to valuable technology IP through the discovery process, where parties exchange evidence before trial that it can't steal outright.

Beijing's legal warfare isn't limited to business; they're using lawfare to obstruct U.S. military operations in Japan and Pacific territories as well, literally hampering our national defense through court manipulation.

China has figured out that *you don't need to win shooting wars when you can capture the legal system that defines victory and defeat.* They're turning our own courts into weapons of mass suppression, and every lawsuit they file makes confronting China harder and more dangerous. While we debate justice, they're redefining and destroying it.

Chilling legal attacks target those who dare even speak the truth about China's brutality. Shen Yun Performing Arts, founded by persecuted Falun Gong practitioners, faced a coordinated assault after Xi Jinping personally ordered officials to corrupt U.S. courts and spread disinformation. Chinese agents bribed an IRS official to strip Shen Yun's nonprofit status and conducted surveillance of their New York headquarters to manufacture bogus environmental lawsuits, later thrown out by judges who saw through the fraud.

The strategy is devastatingly effective. As one expert who chooses not to be named, warns, people simply stop speaking out because it's too expensive and worse, "too dangerous." Chinese diaspora communities, already vulnerable, are being terrorized into silence. Chinese nationals are blackmailed, doxxed, followed, poisoned, beaten, forcibly repatriated, and sometimes "disappeared." There are over 40 CCP "police stations" on sovereign U.S. soil used as bases for espionage, training, and persecution of anyone speaking out against the CCP. Now, imagine the CCP allowing 40 FBI stations in China. It will never happen.

The Political End Game

Political Warfare isn't something to expect later; as you've seen, it's well underway. The CCP's campaign has a crystal-clear destination: your complete political subjugation.

The CCP's ultimate vision is simple: total government control over every aspect of production, consumption, legislation, and judicial decision-making in America. Jan Jekielek, who has done harrowing research on forcible organ harvesting in China reminds us that "no matter how harsh they are with their own people, America's always the number one external enemy." Xi Van Fleet concurs, saying that America is enemy #1 because it represents their "trinity" of evils: capitalism, Christianity, and imperialism. "It's baked," she says, "into the CCP's DNA and it has been from the start."

Through economic leverage and engineered crises, the CCP has created dependencies so deep, so irreversible, that resistance becomes nearly impossible. When China controls your supply chains, your technology, your energy, your politicians, courts, and journalists, they don't need to invade, they already own you.

Let's call it what it is: colonization. Every factory moved to China, every critical domestic resource made dependent on Beijing's whims, every trade deal our leaders make that favors their interests over ours, every Western voice squelched or business driven to destruction, it's all contributing toward their intended collapse of American civilization. The motivation runs deep. In the words of Professor Kerry Gershanek:

> *To the leaders of the CCP, this (political) war is meant to "rejuvenate" China to its former imperial grandeur as the "Middle Kingdom," to once again be "everything under the sun," the all-powerful hegemon power. It is a war to ensure the CCP's total control over China's population and resources, as well as those of foreign nations that the Chinese have historically called "barbarian states," both nearby and throughout the world.*

The final stage of this vision is the most terrifying: the complete elimination of constitutional protections and sovereignty throughout the free world. When economic dependency meets digital surveillance (Digital ID, digital dollar, CBDC mass surveillance with AI) meets compromised leadership, constitutional rights become meaningless pieces of paper. You can't exercise free speech when speaking out could cost you your livelihood. You can't petition for redress when the system already knows your every move and is prepared to destroy you. We must resist this kind of digital centralization from both domestic and external sources.

This is how republics die - through the systematic erosion of every institution, every protection, every principle that made freedom possible in the first place. Nations become vassals through a thousand small compromises that seem reasonable or prudent at the time, until it's too late to resist.

Every day that we delay our own personal and political pushback, every month we pretend this is normal competition, every year we allow this infiltration to deepen, we move closer to a point of no return where American independence will become an historical curiosity.

The choice is stark and immediate: fight back now, while we still can, or accept that our children will grow up as persecuted victims in a CCP-dominated world order where the very concept of individual liberty has been permanently erased.

This is political warfare's endgame. And we're losing.

"Freedom is never more than one generation away from extinction."
~ United States President Ronald Reagan

Five Case Studies on Communism

LET THESE BE A WARNING

Russia: The Red Terror

Yuri Bezmenov, the noted KGB defector, laid it out decades ago: communism destroys your country in four stages: demoralization, destabilization, crisis, normalization.

He warned that "Americans say, 'it will never happen here.' But it is happening. And it is already far gone." Bezmenov warned that it takes 15-20 years to reeducate a generation, as it did before Lenin took over Russia in 1917 - year-by-year, radical intellectuals infiltrated universities, newspapers, media, and cultural circles. Every one of the foundations of society were maligned. They mocked the Church as feudal superstition. They painted the family as a prison, condemning property as theft. Grievance and victimhood replaced hard work and merit. The "bourgeoisie," - the doctors, businessmen, farmers, and professionals who built prosperity - were labeled "enemies of the people."

A culture that once revered productivity, faith, family bonds, and patriotism was taught to despise itself. The communists stoked class envy, glorified violence, and promised utopia. Emotion replaced reason.

Sound familiar?

By the time World War I bled Russia dry, the foundations had already cracked and the Bolsheviks exploited it. Bezmenov's stage two - destabilization - is never an accident. It follows stage one, demoralization, long-term psychological warfare that cripples the opposition, by enacting engineered chaos.

The February Revolution easily toppled the incompetent Czar's monarchy as the Bolsheviks struck with ruthless precision. What followed was Bezmenov's stage three: Crisis. A radical minority with ideological zeal in a demoralized, war-weary society, quickly seized power.

What did they deliver? A worker's paradise as promised? Nope. Russia got famine, mass executions, and the world's first monstrous communist totalitarian regime - a model to be exported across the globe.

Bezmenov sums up this third stage: "When the country reaches crisis, it is too late to save it. All that remains is normalization."

In the U.S.S.R., stage four "normalization" meant purges, censorship, collectivization, indoctrination, surveillance, and punishment, rebranded as "building socialism."

For families, normalization meant betrayal to the regime. It meant children raised to believe that truth was whatever the Party declared. It meant violence and fear etched into daily life.

The permanent lie of hell replacing the promised paradise had become "reality."

Even after the Soviet flag fell in 1991, the system didn't die. The security services rebranded. The propaganda modernized. The lies persisted. For the vast majority of the population, Russia continued to descend into despair, stagnation, corruption and fear.

The real fruit of communist subversion is not just control of politics and economics, but exhaustion of the human spirit.

You don't need gulags to lose freedom. You only need to teach a generation to hate their own country, distrust their families, and censor or "cancel" their own thoughts and better judgment.

You don't need tanks in the street, you only need what the CCP is working so hard to sow today into the Western mind: stage one demoralization:

- Schools teach children to loathe their nation, faith, and history.
- Attacks on police, courts, churches, family, free enterprise.
- Censorship, intimidation, political demonization, marketed as "equity."

As Lenin said in 1920:

"A revolution is impossible without a revolutionary situation. All objective changes must be accompanied by a subjective change-the ability of the revolutionary class to take mass action strong enough to break the old government."

Despite its global failures, the communist playbook slithers into our institutions today, trying to make this subjective change.

Yuri Bezmenov lamented, "I often reflect on what Russia might have become had its people understood the true nature of the ideological cancer that would consume them. I wonder if we would still have fallen so easily for the comforting lies."

Like Venezuela and Cuba, Russia didn't lose their freedom overnight. It was dismantled carefully, methodically, in these four distinct stages.

His warning was clear: "The process is irreversible at the point when the subverter gains access to power. Then, there is no turning back."

But we are not yet past that point - yet. Which means his warning still matters.

The question is not if the West can fall. The question is whether enough people will wake up and take action before it does. As he reminds us, communist tyranny does not always wear a uniform and brandish a gun. It arrives wearing a smile, a diploma, and a seductive fantasy of human paradise and utopia - that swiftly descends into an inhuman hell.

China: Famine, Fratricide, and Death of Freedom

It's not easy to wrap one's mind around the magnitude of misery and mass murder that the CCP has inflicted upon the Chinese people. To get personal insight, I turned to Katherine Hu, the award-winning television journalist and director who grew up in mainland China. She is now an independent investigative documentary filmmaker and serves as a judge for the News & Documentary Emmy Awards. Her notable works include: "Tracking Down the Origin of the Wuhan Coronavirus" and "The Final War." The following is based on what she told me...

Why Communism Is Not the Miracle

The single most successful propaganda lie of the 21st century is this: that the Chinese Communist Party (CCP) rescued China from poverty and built its economic miracle.

It is a lie.

From the beginning, communism in China wasn't about prosperity. It was about total control. Mao Zedong himself declared: "Political power grows out of the barrel of a gun."

China didn't rise out of poverty because of communism. It rose in spite of it. When pockets of economic freedom (capitalism) were finally allowed to breathe under Deng, prosperity blossomed. Everywhere else, where the Party ruled, all was misery, murder and ruin.

China had a long, prosperous history which collapsed in the 19th Century. By the early 20th century, China emerged, bruised but alive. The Republic of China was unstable, but it had a free press, intellectual pluralism, and room for religious tolerance, business growth, and civil debate. Then, in the 1930s, the brutal Japanese invasion brought devastation, humiliation, and panic.

After years of the Japanese bleeding the Nationalist army and with the backing of the Soviets, Mao stepped in and seized power with a militaristic fervor as violent as Imperialist Japan. In fact he idolized violence, writing that "revolution is not a dinner party… it is an act of violence by which one class overthrows another."

Mao and his communists disregarded the fundamental value of human life: "We are not afraid of sacrifice. Ten or twenty million people may have to die."

That was an underestimation of the horror to come. Murder became Mao's legacy. He executed millions as "landlords." The notorious Great Leap Forward forced rural collectivization, creating the deadliest famine in human history with an estimated 30-45 million dead. The equally brutal and misguided Cultural Revolution left many more millions killed, countless families broken, ancient Chinese heritage burned, and students turned into mobs screaming "Long Live Chairman Mao!"

Mao's communism was nothing less than the engineered collapse of civil society. The economy lay decimated. By the time Mao died, China was broken. Deng Xiaoping cracked the door open to capitalism and a margin of freedom. As he said, "It doesn't matter whether the cat is black or white, as long as it catches mice."

He tolerated "catching mice" with limited capitalism because communism had failed so completely. Farmers farmed again, markets reopened, and economic growth stumbled into new life.

Capitalist prosperity? Yes. But liberty? No. When students demanded freedom in Tiananmen Square in 1989, Beijing ordered the army in: tanks crushed unarmed citizens, thousands were killed, and the freedom movement was murdered at its birth. Deng's excuse? "Stability overrides everything."

The Party was clear: limited capitalism can be permitted under strict control, but freedom cannot.

Xi Jinping intensified that lesson. His mantra: "The Party leads everything." Under him, communism tightened its grip even as elites prospered and forged whole new expressions of soul-killing horror:

- **The Surveillance State:** Nearly 3 billion cameras watch everything...even facial expressions. AI scores every citizen. The "Great Firewall of China" blocks the international internet from outside Western influence.
- **Speech Police:** The Great Firewall deletes forbidden history. Dissidents vanish. Journalist Zhang Zhan was jailed simply for reporting on COVID in Wuhan.
- **Religion Strangled:** Xi declared: "We must insist on the Sinicization of religion... so that religions serve socialism." Mosques, churches, temples, and their symbols are banned and now carry Party slogans, not prayers.
- **Economic Control:** Billionaire Jack Ma disappeared after criticizing regulators. Ant Group's IPO was crushed. Xi reminded entrepreneurs: "No matter how big a business is, it must always love the Party."
- **COVID Tyranny:** Shanghai locked down for months. Families sealed inside apartments, some literally welded inside. Drones barked from the sky: "Control your soul's desire for freedom."

The CCP represents the most advanced technological tyranny in human history. It weaponizes everything to lock in party control at every level.

The skyscrapers are real. The money miracle is real. The human "miracle" is not.

Less than 20% of bank deposits belong to ordinary Chinese. The rest is hoarded by Party elites. 70% of rivers are poisoned. 20% of farmland is contaminated. Six of the world's ten most polluted cities are in China. Food safety scandals, crumbling infrastructure, a terrorized populace desperately trying to get their money, and children abroad are all symptoms of communist ideology that rewards total obedience, not competence.

As China demonstrates, the communism playbook never changes. It begins with subterfuge, promising justice, liberation, and utopia. Then it moves into capture - taking control of guns, schools, media, courts. Then it creates total dependency, replacing self-reliance with rations, work units or, in the Chinese case, digital scores. It then keeps tightening the screws of control: surveillance, censorship, persecution, disappearances, assassinations, and executions. In the end, all is destruction: families torn to shreds, religions banned, a vibrant culture replaced with soul-deadening propaganda.

Katherine Hu reminds us that this is the story of every communist policy: divide, destroy, dominate.

The lesson for the West should be clear: communism does not save nations: it hijacks them. It weaponizes resentment, erases culture and lives off fear.

The CCP's legacy will not be the prosperity it brandishes, but the destruction of the human soul that accompanied it, all in the name of control.

And if the West doesn't wake up, the same tyranny, sold as social justice, equality, stability, productivity or "order," will seep into our own homes and families.

Cuba: The Lie That Won't Die

The downfall of Cuba has been so catastrophic that even nearly 70 years after Castro's coup, what was once a vibrant, prosperous country crawls on its knees in impoverished squalor. Communism has been such an abject failure there that an estimated 20% of the population has fled since 2022 alone.

To review this descent into despair, I turned to Dr. Orlando Gutiérrez-Boronat, author, spokesperson for the Cuban Democratic Directorate, member of the Assembly of the Cuban Resistance and lecturer at Georgetown University and elsewhere.

Dr. Orlando Gutiérrez-Boronat recalls a pre-Castro Cuba that boasted a growing economy, expanding industrialization, and a construction boom. Before Castro, Cuba had…

...a class of statesmen who ran the economy well and were kept in place by different governments, including those with ideological differences. Municipal governments were well run and efficient. The Cuban Congress tended to balance budgets and pay off foreign debts. The currency was very stable and strong, and an efficient independent banking sector, both foreign and domestic, had developed. Cuba was a rapidly industrializing, growing economy with a first-world capital, Havana, which was a magnet for foreign and domestic investment. Cuban public and private education was good and the country had one of the highest literacy rates in Latin America. In addition to the above, by the 1950s, Cuba had become a world cultural powerhouse.

But as he describes below, the good times were not to last. His family had been a typical success story with his grandfather finishing only fourth grade, his three sons graduating from the University of Havana. It seemed to be going well.

As Gutiérrez-Boronat reminds us, communist takeovers can be slow and insidious; Castro's takeover didn't result from a sudden armed insurrection. It was achieved through a mixture of complex factors that free peoples, including us, need to be on alert for every single day. Here is what he told me...

In 1958, Havana was a rising first-world capital, a city of neon lights, entertainment and world-class culture. Cuban families worked hard, built businesses, pooled resources, sent their kids to college. Municipal governments balanced budgets. The Congress paid debts. Banks were solid, both foreign and domestic. Despite Castro's hysterical claims, this was not poverty waiting to be saved. It was prosperity primed to expand.

Castro didn't storm into Havana with an army. He didn't have to. Batista's regime grew corrupt, discrediting republican institutions.

Castro moved slowly, with a campaign of promises of redistributed wealth, urban terrorism, assassinations, and limited guerrilla warfare. Washington wavered, but the Soviets were laser-focused: they saw Cuba as their beachhead in the Western Hemisphere and they made Castro stronger.

Eventually, Batista fled. Castro took over and the lies began. He promised elections within 18 months but they never happened. Instead, he crushed rivals, silenced moderates, and hijacked the "people's" revolution. Exactly like Lenin, he converted a moment of social collapse into permanent dictatorship.

The new regime executed the Soviet communist playbook: erase memory, indoctrinate, intimidate, kill. Foreign advisors from the U.S.S.R. and Eastern Bloc showed Castro's men how to brainwash and control. Schools rewrote history. Families were fractured by surveillance and informants. Anyone who resisted paid in blood. Firing squads echoed during mass executions in La Cabaña fortress. Thousands of political prisoners rotted in cells. Concentration camps and forced labor camps sprouted where dissenters were "reeducated."

This totalitarian laboratory landed hard: an Iron Curtain outpost only 90 miles from Florida.

The Soviet Union desperately needed a revolutionary poster child. Stalin's crimes, tanks in Budapest, waves of worker revolts in East Germany, violent protests and reforms in Poland and mounting unrest across the Eastern Bloc showed the world that Soviet-style communism was stitched together by nothing but violence and that it was losing its grip in Europe. Enter Castro: the charismatic bearded rebel, cigar in hand, selling the fantasy of "social justice" and "anti-imperialism."

The truth that Cuba had been prosperous, free, and thriving was buried. The myth - that communism had rescued a starving imperialist colony - was broadcast to the world, especially to American universities, where the radical "New Left" embraced Havana as an ideological Eden.

The greatest trick of Cuban communism was not only enslaving its own people; it was selling the lie to those gullible enough to listen.

Cuban citizens tried to resist. They fought in the Escambray mountains. They organized underground networks. They fought for their freedom, but at the Bay of Pigs, patriots were abandoned by halfhearted U.S. support. Castro's men crushed them. Soviet weapons, advisors, and cash poured in, keeping the regime alive. Cuba descended into tyranny on the tips of Soviet bayonets.

The cost of communism was total:

- **The economy gutted.** From industrial growth and foreign investment to ration cards and black markets. A once-booming Havana became a ruin of crumbling buildings, prostitution, and food lines.
- **Freedom erased.** No elections. No free press. No civil society. Dissent was criminalized as treason. Total control.
- **Families shattered.** Hundreds of thousands fled into exile, scattering across Miami, Madrid, and beyond. Those who stayed live under constant surveillance and fear.
- **Culture hijacked.** Art, music, education-all bent into propaganda. Creativity became service to the regime.

Cuba, once a jewel of the Caribbean, became an open-air prison.

The communist pattern is always the same: dependency replaces autonomy, fear replaces freedom, propaganda replaces truth. And once the machine is in place, it does not let go.

Cuba stands as the nearest and clearest warning to the West: communism does not "reform" nations. It devours them. It takes vibrant societies and grinds them into submission.

Dr. Gutiérrez-Boronat reminds us that the communist lie is always the same: "we will deliver justice and a much better life," but the result is always poverty, prison, and despair.

He warns that communist subversion is never homegrown. As he says,

> *The Castro Regime benefited from a steady stream of foreign advisors, weaponry, and equipment. Fifth columnists worldwide spread the doctrine of a successful socialist revolution that defeated U.S. imperialism, including within the United States. The radical American "New Left" would not have emerged without the guidance and support of the Castro Regime.*

Cuba has continued to devolve into ruin and destitution. Inflation remains in double digits. Twenty hour blackouts, water scarcity, and no trash removal are the result of an economic and energy crisis that still batters the island and that authorities no longer attempt to deny.

Yes, there are striking parallels between the collapse of free Cuba into Castro's communist dictatorship and tactics observed today, especially regarding the CCP's ambitions for America. Once in power, he consolidated control by eliminating opposition, nationalizing industries, stifling dissent, and rapidly aligning with the Soviet Bloc.

Experts like Dr. Gutiérrez-Boronat and others today warn that the CCP is advancing its interests within the United States similarly to Castro's advance in Cuba. In 1950s Cuba, Castro masked his intentions, exploiting popular frustration with corruption, manipulating the media, co-opting grassroots movements, and infiltrating institutions, all while denying outright he was a communist until the regime was secure. He built coalitions with moderates, centrists, and nationalists, then purged them violently once he took over.

Similarly, by supporting divisive "identity" movements, influencing education and media narratives, expanding control over digital/social platforms, and pressuring business and political partnerships, all without overt military confrontation, the CCP daily whittles away confidence in our institutions, mirroring how Castro undermined confidence in Cuba's government and built popular support for radical change.

The lesson: communist takeover does not require an armed invasion but advances through ideological subversion, gradual institutional co-optation, and narratives that encourage a free society to cede its freedoms. Both historical Cuba and the contemporary U.S. share the risk that a foreign-backed, anti-democratic movement can seize control by promising justice and renewal, only to deliver authoritarianism, despair, and the loss of national autonomy.

Venezuela: The Warning

To capture the significance of the fall of Venezuela, I met with Andres Guilarte, that country's noted U.S.-based freedom activist.

> *I often ask myself what Venezuela would look like today if we had maintained and protected the democracy and freedoms that Venezuelans enjoyed during the second half of the last century. The country I grew up in is nowhere near recognizable compared to the failed state it has become today. In the 1970s, we had the fourth-highest GDP per capita in Latin America. I carry a warning. The path that led Venezuela into ruin is the same path being followed in the United States, and I say this not as a theorist, but as a survivor who experienced first-hand the fall of the pearl of the Caribbean into the hands of communism.*

As recently as In the 1990s, Venezuela was Latin America's shining success story. Oil wealth fueled one of the region's highest GDPs. Public schools and universities thrived. The middle class was growing, freedoms were intact, and democratic institutions had teeth.

But socialist-inspired dependency rotted the roots. Venezuelans got used to the state handing out benefits. That dependency would become the socialist lever to enslave them.

In 1998, Hugo Chávez rode a national wave of anger at failed parties and economic stagnation. His guide? Fidel Castro's playbook, and he had Cuban intelligence and support at his back. After winning the general election, he rewrote the constitution, hollowed out democratic guardrails and sold "social justice" as a way to cement state control.

Chávez moved fast. He purged generals, installed loyalists, and fused military command with industry, subsuming oil, steel infrastructure to the armed forces. Soldiers no longer served the people; they served the regime, because their paychecks, perks, and power depended on its survival alone.

Note: that's the communist blueprint: take control of the means of coercion, then unleash them against your own people.

What happened next is no surprise. Venezuela's lifeblood - the oil industry - collapsed. Skilled employees/technocrats were fired. Stooges replaced experts. Party loyalists filled the seats.

The whole communist playbook - price controls, currency controls, and expropriations - drove nail after nail into the coffin of private enterprise and freedom. The markets died. Innovation stopped. Citizens no longer built wealth. They waited for handouts which grew more and more meager.

And, as it always happens in communist hellholes, those handouts weren't charity. They were chains. Food boxes, government stores, free clinics - each a rationed favor given by the state. Dissenters were cut off from essential supplies. Conformists were rewarded. Every bag of rice was the reward of a loyalty test. Every doctor's visit, a reminder: the Party owns you.

Then came the kill shot: the electoral system. Chávez stuffed the oversight boards with party men. He jailed the opposition, nationalized, or closed independent media.

Elections became theater: ritual affirmations of power, propaganda staged for the cameras.

The results were inevitable:

- **Hyperinflation:** Families living on flour and water. Prices doubled.

- **Infrastructure collapse:** Regular blackouts, empty water taps, hospitals without medicine.
- **Suppression:** Students jailed. Protesters beaten. Dissent labeled treason and severely punished.
- **Exodus:** Millions fleeing across Latin America and beyond.

Paramilitaries stalked neighborhoods. Death squads silenced critics. A nation of freedom and abundance was reduced to scavenging. Communism, as freedom activist Andrés Guilarte put it, "did not just bankrupt Venezuela's economy; it bankrupted our humanity."

Civil society collapsed. Neighbors became informants. Education became indoctrination. Children grew up not on freedom, but on fear and propaganda.

A once-proud, independent nation was hollowed out and enslaved.

This collapse did not happen overnight. It was step-by-step. Dependency. Centralization. Military capture. Media capture. Surveillance disguised as welfare.

By the time citizens realized what befell them, there was no return.

"America, you must listen," Guilarte warns, "Venezuela is not a tragedy on some crazy, distant shore. It is a flashing red warning light and a blaring siren. The same patterns-censorship, punishment of dissent, blind trust in centralized power-are infiltrating here and throughout the free world."

Ignore them, and our liberty will quickly vanish the same way: not with a bang, but with a series of "necessary" measures that we barely notice or simply give in to, one-by-one.

Andrés finds it hard to believe that with such catastrophic communist destruction of a once prosperous country, that support for its ideas and propaganda can find so much support inside the U.S. left. But he sees history repeating itself on American soil:

Americans see millions of Venezuelans fleeing a political system rooted in socialist policies that has transformed into a failed State, and yet, some yearn for those same policies to be implemented here… I see it happening here in America. I see how ideology has begun to replace inquiry …in places like American universities, where dissent is discouraged and conformity is rewarded. The free exchange of ideas, once the foundation of higher learning, is now often seen as a threat… I hear people speak of "equity" while punishing merit. Of "collective justice" while ignoring individual rights… "If America continues down this path, normalizing government overreach, rewarding ideological submission, punishing dissent, the destination will be the same. Maybe not tomorrow, but in a few short years. The laws of history don't bend for optimism and, as Ronald Reagan said eloquently 'freedom is never more than one generation away from extinction.'

The question is not whether America will become Venezuela, he says, "the question is whether Americans are willing to fight so they don't have to."

I couldn't agree with him more.

Hong Kong - Crushing of a Global Jewel

Hong Kong. In its glory days, it was known as the "Pearl of the Orient," "Asia's World City," "Eastern Manhattan," "Gei Wai" (奇蹟) "Miracle," "Asian Tiger."

But since the CCP took it over in 1999, the descent has been sharp, tragic, and inevitable. It's a CCP masterclass in economic self-sabotage, where authoritarian grip kills the golden goose that laid its eggs. To quote my colleague Ken Cao, Executive Director of the Center for Asian Democracy and Resilience and Chinese ex-pat, it's a "once vibrant city in handcuffs."

Cao's words consistently cut to the bone, reminding us that the CCP's "one country, two systems" was always a facade, a Trojan horse for total domination.

From Asia's Beacon to Beijing's Shadow

Remember Hong Kong before the CCP's claws fully sank in? As Cao evokes it, the city was "the freest place in Asia. Neon lights. Cantopop blaring. Global business deals sealed over dim sum and milk tea."

Under British rule and the 1997 handover's solemn "50 years unchanged" promise, Hong Kong became the world's envy: a hyper-capitalist dynamo, ranking tops in economic freedom indexes (Heritage Foundation, pre-2019). Its secret? Not just skyscrapers or low taxes, but the "predictability" or a free society that Cao champions: "Common law. Transparent media. Independent courts. The kind of rule of law you could set your watch to."

Hong Kong had been the lifeblood of a gateway economy funneling trillions in trade, finance, and talent into China. Multinationals flocked here for the stability, the IP protections, and rule of law. Freedom wasn't a "side dish," as Cao astutely notes; "it was the secret sauce." Bankers from London, filmmakers from Hollywood, and entrepreneurs from Silicon Valley built an "argumentative... and most precious, free" hub that amplified China's rise without the mainland's paranoia.

But freedom breeds jealousy, and the CCP couldn't stomach a semi-autonomous success story mocking its surveillance state. As Cao chronicles, "Beijing slowly began to move the dimmer switch."

It started subtly: "Disqualify a few lawmakers. Rewrite a few textbooks. Arrest one editor-just for 'national security.'" These weren't tweaks; they were termites gnawing at trust.

By 2019, the people, millions strong, erupted in what Cao calls a symphony of resistance: "Airports occupied. Human chains over highways. Lennon Walls blooming with sticky notes of hope."

Enter the CCP's sledgehammer - delivered under the cloud cover of draconian COVID restrictions.

The 2020 National Security Law (NSL) descended unilaterally from Beijing. No local debate, no amendments-just a "fog," as Cao brilliantly describes it, where "every word had a shadow. Every headline, a hazard."

Over 10,000 arrests followed (Amnesty International data), including pro-democracy icons like Jimmy Lai. Extradition fears turned the city into a panopticon; booksellers vanished, protests evaporated, and media outlets like Apple Daily shuttered overnight.

The Economic Reckoning: When Trust Flees, So Does the Future

The CCP's delusion? That you could "crush dissent" without "touching the money." But in the end, to borrow Cao's spoiler alert: "it touched everything."

Markets, allergic to uncertainty, recoiled. Hong Kong's Hang Seng Index plummeted 20% post-NSL (2020 data), and its status as a global financial center crumbled. FDI inflows halved by 2022 (UNCTAD reports), as "companies shifted HQs to Singapore," per Cao. Why? Because "Hong Kong's competitive moat...was trust. Kill the free press, and you don't just silence critics-you blind investors. Rewrite history, and you don't just erase the past-you scare off talent."

Even heavyweights sounded the alarm. As Cao quotes the eminent economist Stephen Roach, former Morgan Stanley Asia chair, who built his career in Hong Kong, "The party is over."

Roach's verdict in his 2022 book "Accidental Conflict" echoes the data: capital flight hit $100 billion in 2020 alone (HKMA figures), with brain drain accelerating.

"Departure gates packed. British National visas stamped. Family offices, professors, and journalists setting up shop in London, Vancouver, Taipei," Cao observes. Over 500,000 residents fled by 2023 (UK BNO visa stats), many after those midnight kitchen table conversations: Do we stay and hope, or leave and rebuild?

"When the people who love a city most decide to leave...its future leaves with them." Cao's poignant line nails the human cost, mirroring

Venezuela's elite exodus or Cuba's crisis: CCP-style oppression doesn't just jail bodies; it exiles dreams.

The Brutal Lesson: CCP Authoritarianism's Boomerang

Hong Kong's collapse is yet another case study in communist self-inflicted wounds, much like how Maduro's Venezuela nationalized oil to fund repression, only to tank GDP by 75% (IMF), or Castro's Cuba seized farms and factories, birthing a perpetual breadline. "You can't keep the money and kill the freedom that made it," Cao warns. Once China's "trusted gateway to the world," Hong Kong is now "just a gate-opened or closed at Beijing's whim."

The winners?

- **Singapore:** Now Asia's finance king, with 40% more ultra-wealthy migrants (Knight Frank 2023)
- **Tokyo:** For asset management
- **Taipei**: For tech talent

The economic cost has been dear; Hong Kong's GDP growth lagged China's by 5% annually post-NSL (World Bank). Global decoupling has accelerated, with U.S. chip bans and EU tariffs biting harder.

This is the CCP's fatal flaw: communism devours its own economic engine. Hong Kong proves it. Freedom isn't a wishy-washy political ideal, Cao reminds us, "it's the ultimate economic asset."

Ignore that, and you don't lose a city; you hemorrhage your prosperity along with everything else that we value as a free society. The truth remains unbroken: throughout history, there has never been a successful communist society. Free Hong Kong was extinguished quickly by the CCP... *without even a whimper.*

BRIEFING TEN
The Battle For Your Soul
Religious War

"When Karl Marx was asked what his objective in life was, he said, 'to dethrone God and destroy capitalism!'"
~ W. Cleon Skousen, author, The Naked Communist

"There are only two forces in the world, the sword and the spirit. In the long run, the sword will always be conquered by the spirit."
~ Napoleon Bonaparte

Eradicating God to Forge a New Tyrant

If you value God, the transcendent Source of moral order, the divine spark that endows every human with inherent dignity and divinity, as enshrined in the Western tradition from the Hebrew prophets' covenant of justice to Christ's Sermon on the Mount to the American founders' invocation of a Creator who grants inalienable rights; then you understand the extraordinary values that have flowered within this God-based society:

- **Individual Dignity:** Every person has inherent worth, not determined by state utility
- **Inalienable Rights:** Derived from Divine source, not governmental decree
- **Moral Agency:** Humans as moral beings with free will and personal responsibility

- **Ethical Universalism:** Moral standards transcend tribal, racial, or state boundaries
- **Inherent Human Equality:** All humans equal before Divine judgment
- **Consent and Covenant:** Political legitimacy requires voluntary human agreement
- **Sanctity of Conscience:** Individual belief protected from state coercion
- **Transformative Potential:** Humans can improve themselves through spiritual growth

These values are the bedrock of the West's unprecedented freedoms - speech untrammeled, worship unfettered, enterprise unleashed - and the most free, prosperous civilizations ever known upon this Earth. Upon this rock, GDP per capita has soared out of medieval and industrial subsistence to modern abundance. Literacy rates have approached universality and life expectancy has doubled. All of this because recognizing humanity's divine imprint opens up creativity, collaboration, service, and compassion in ways that no Marxist, atheistic pseudo-utopia ever could.

Western freedoms, built upon the Judeo-Christian understanding of the Divine dignity of man in all our complexity, have been a light in human history.

Karl Marx, though, in his Economic and Philosophic Manuscripts of 1844, deluded himself (and hundreds of millions of others) that he could create a "New Man" liberated from "work alienation" through a classless society. He thought he could redefine what a human being was simply by turning him into a being of unselfish labor who would create collective harmony brought about by a "dictatorship of the proletariat." In the communist Manifesto, he wrote, "Communism abolishes eternal truths, it abolishes all religion, and all morality."

In the words of W. Cleon Skousen in "The Naked Communist," Marx "...wanted a race of men who would no longer depend upon free will, ethics, morals or conscience for guidance. Perhaps, without quite realizing it, Marx was setting out to create a race of human beings conditioned to think like criminals."

What communism created was not only populations conditioned to think like criminals but totalitarian states who act like them.

Xi Jinping amplified this Marxist soul-destroying delusion of "new man," promising, for example, in his 2017 address on "Socialism with Chinese Characteristics for a New Era," a "new type of socialist person," fully molded by Party loyalty to realize the "Chinese Dream" of national rejuvenation and global domination.

Communism promises a "New Man" but has delivered everywhere a broken, atomized, spiritually crushed human being, beaten and afraid, clinging maybe to the shreds of that dream of Marxist utopia.

There's a reason for its failure.

Humans are humans: flawed yet endowed with a transcendent soul, yearning for connection with the Source of all life, and resistant to remaking God in the image of some tinpot state apparatus. We are, as Pope John Paul II said, "not merely 'a unit of labor' engaged in a perpetual class struggle," as Marx claimed, "but a creature made in the image of God, with a soul and an eternal destiny."

The Western theological tradition, rooted in the radical idea that each human bears the imago dei - the image of God - constructed a civilization unprecedented in human history: a society where individual human dignity is sacred, where rights are understood as divine endowments, not state-granted privileges.

By contrast, Marxism, like Naziism, is a "political religion" where the sacredness of human dignity is crushed under the boot of State power and loyalty. In his seminal 1938 works "The Political Religions" and "The New Science of Politics," Eric Voegelin diagnosed these two ideologies as secular cults that ape the structures of true faith by peddling utopian salvation but through human agency alone, state agency, party agency, elevating dictators, and their doctrines to divine status while scorning transcendent reality.

In his words, "The political religions imitate the form of religion in order to replace it; they promise salvation on earth but deliver only the slavery of the soul."

This perversion, he argued, arises from a spiritual vacuum in the West, where the divine order is jettisoned for "imminent eschatons" - earthly paradises engineered by elite cadres - ultimately eroding authentic human dignity and fostering totalitarian zeal in place of genuine moral and spiritual renewal.

Zohran Mamdani's 2025 victory as New York City mayor represents a dangerous flirtation with utopian communist fantasies that history has repeatedly proven unworkable, dooming the city to economic folly under the guise of equity. Mamdani peddled pie-in-the-sky promises, such as universal housing handouts, government supermarkets, a taxpayer-funded Green New Deal, and a "people's budget" - siphoning Wall Street taxes for free childcare and community utilities. He rode into power from his gilded upbringing on a wave of naive young progressives, unions, and frustrated voters. As always with socialist utopianism, his win risks ballooning deficits, stifling innovation, causing wealth flight and repeating socialism's track record of shortages and bureaucratic gridlock, turning the vibrant Big Apple into a cautionary tale of aspirational overreach where grand visions crumble into collective hardship and chaos.

The choice we face could not be more clear: we are either human beings with infinite potential, divine dignity and the freedom to pursue transcendent purposes as individuals, **or we are soulless numbers in a system dependent upon and serving the all-powerful state.**

Communism is a Religion

Xi, China, and the communist project is hell-bent on making that choice for you, destroying not only established religions across the globe, but human spirituality itself. Communism does not elevate the human soul but crushes it. It yields not prosperity but a spiritually barren empire of surveillance, cruelty, and despair, where the divine void allows only for the tyrant's iron fist.

That's why I say, "if you value God, you must know your enemy and rise to meet him."

This chapter is your primer on this battlefield.

CCP's Religious War At Home

There is no "wiggle room" allowed: communism functions as a religion that tolerates no other religions and it is working to destroy them, at home and abroad. This theologicide, the CCP's God-killing machine, honed at home, has been seeding its poison across the free world.

Marx didn't understand the human soul. When he said religion was the "opium of the people," he narrowed the spiritual impulse to those in economic despair who needed the medication of religion's hope.

But, lo and behold, with capitalism-cultivated prosperity, the human soul still aspires for connection with the Divine. The spiritual vacuum that communist atheism created, even with all its new capitalist-infused prosperity, has itself triggered new movements of religious believers in China itself. What the CCP has had to face is that spiritual yearning always lives and dies hard.

During the Cultural Revolution (1966–76), Mao banned religions. Today, the Chinese Communist Party's nearly 100 million members are required to be atheist. According to the Council on Foreign Relations report "Religion In China," the noose around religious people has been consistently tightened under Xi:

> *Under Xi, the CCP has pushed to sinicize religion, or shape all religions to conform to the doctrines of the communist Party and the customs of the majority Han Chinese population. New regulations that went into effect in early 2020 require religious groups to accept and spread CCP ideology and values. Faith organizations*

> *must now get approval from the government's religious affairs office before conducting any activities. The next year, the CCP banned unregistered domestic religious groups from sharing religious content online and prohibited overseas organizations from operating online religious services in China without a permit, particularly targeting Christianity-related content on the messaging service WeChat. (cfr.org, 2024)*

In September 2023, stricter laws required religious sites and activities to support sinicization policies which included prohibiting religious activity if it could "endanger national security, disrupt social order [or] damage national interests."

Xi has recently allowed some Chinese "home grown" religious affiliation such as Confucianism, Buddhism, and Daoism because they don't pose a challenge to the CCP's rule, they are indigenous and not "foreign invasions" like Christianity.

But all these public policies are cover for some of the most brutal, murderous religious persecution in the history of mankind. **Here is the bloody truth of the CCP's crackdown on religion in their homeland, religion by religion:**

Tibet

In 1950, the CCP brutally invaded and conquered the huge land mass of Tibet, initiating what can only be described as cultural genocide, reducing over 6,000 Tibetan Buddhist monasteries to fewer than a dozen functioning institutions.

The CCP viewed Tibetan Buddhism's spiritual authority, with the Dalai Lama as its spiritual leader, as a direct competitor to communist Party loyalty, launching campaigns that tortured and murdered an estimated 1.2 million Tibetans, nearly **one-fifth of the population.**

Monks and nuns were publicly humiliated, forced to copulate in town squares, beaten with their own prayer beads, and compelled to destroy centuries-old sacred texts and statues with their own hands.

The Panchen Lama, one of Tibetan Buddhism's highest authorities, testified in 1962 that...

> *...in some monasteries, several dozens of monks were confined in a small room and were not given food or water. They were starved to death... Some were thrown in the rivers, some were buried alive, some had their noses and ears cut off.*

Tibetan monk and torture survivor Palden Gyatso recounted in his memoir "Fire Under the Snow" (1997), based on 33 years in Chinese prisons:

> *They hung me from the ceiling by my wrists, beating me with chains until my flesh tore open and my screams echoed through the cell; they did this not just to break my body, but to shatter the faith that sustained me, leaving me a hollow shell, weeping for the gods they could never truly kill.*

Ancient scriptures were burned as fuel or pulped for fertilizer and pigsty filler while gold Buddhas were melted down and sacred frescoes dynamited. This assault was a calculated effort to erase a 1,300-year-old spiritual tradition that commanded loyalties the communist Party could not tolerate, illustrating for the world that totalitarian ideology requires the annihilation of any competing source of meaning, purpose, or transcendent authority.

The CCP considers communal devotion to the Dalai Lama as an existential threat to the absolute loyalty demanded by Marxist-Leninist ideology. Today, under Xi Jinping's "Sinicization" campaign, monks and nuns face relentless surveillance via facial-recognition tech in remaining temples, mandatory "patriotic re-education" sessions that force vows of allegiance to the Party over Buddhist precepts, and the erasure of

Tibetan-language scriptures in favor of CCP-approved propaganda, all to forge a homogenized citizenry subservient to Beijing.

A Tibetan child believed to be a reincarnated Panchen Lama disappeared and the CCP tried to replace him with a new "official Panchen Lama, though most Tibetans, of course, do not accept him as such. The original child has never since been seen.

Islam

During Mao's Cultural Revolution, Islamic sacred texts were burned and imams executed en masse, but today's horror has unfolded in something rarely seen since the Nazi Holocaust in Europe.

Since 2017, the Chinese Communist Party has waged a brutal campaign against Uyghur Muslims in the Western province of Xinjiang, imprisoning over one million people in what Beijing euphemistically calls "re-education camps" but which function as concentration camps designed to extinguish Islamic faith and replace it with worship of Xi Jinping and the Party.

The CCP calls Islam "a mental disease," and views Islam's devotion to Allah as ideological treason; loyalty must belong solely to the communist state. Because the Uyghurs are of a different, central-asian ethnic origin, this oppression also carries the whip of Han Chinese supremacy.

Survivors of the CCP onslaught describe forced consumption of pork and alcohol, systematic rape of women detainees, torture with electric batons, and psychological torment including being chained to walls for days.

Sayragul Sauytbay, a teacher forced to work in the camps, testified that detainees "were forced to renounce their faith... Those who disobeyed the rules were punished severely, they were made to sit on a chair of nails... or put in a freezing cold room."

Mosques have been demolished by the thousands (estimated at over 16,000), Qurans burned, children separated from parents and placed in state orphanages to be raised atheist, and women forcibly sterilized to prevent the next generation of believers, all corroborated by the 2022 "UN Human Rights Office Report."

The CCP has been unapologetic about this systematic murder of a people's religion because totalitarian power cannot abide any divided loyalties. And Uyghur survivor Mihrigul Tursun testified to the U.S. Congress in 2018, after enduring three years in a Xinjiang camp:

> *They electrocuted me until I lost consciousness, injected me with unknown drugs that left me vomiting blood, and separated me from my babies, whom they said had died - though I later learned they were alive and taken away; this was their way of killing our souls, forcing us to worship the Party or perish in agony, leaving scars that no prayer can heal.*

To this day, under omnipresent surveillance grids and forced "patriotic" indoctrination, Uyghurs endure torture and rape for the purpose of forging blind obedience to Beijing.

The Party's message is clear: there is no God but the State, no prophet but Xi, and submission to anything beyond communist authority will be crushed with industrial efficiency.

Falun Gong

Emerging in 1992 amid China's post-Tiananmen spiritual void, Falun Gong (aka Falun Dafa), founded by Li Hongzhi, fused traditional qigong exercises with principles of zhen-shan-ren (truthfulness-compassion-tolerance), and attracted an estimated 70-100 million practitioners by the late 1990s.

Think of that: nearly one in 10 Chinese flowed into this quiet, meditative, conservative, ethical oasis in the CCP's spiritual desert, daring to offer transcendence beyond the Party's steel-hearted dogma as balm for the soul. Through grassroots study groups and meditation parks, without a dime of state funding or hierarchical control, it literally outgrew official CCP party membership.

Yet it was this very popularity and autonomy that ignited Beijing's vicious paranoia: CCP leader Jiang Zemin viewed Falun Gong as a mortal threat to the Party's monopoly on truth, its moral code fostering loyalties that bypassed the state's surveillance web. In a 1999 speech, Jiang declared it a "serious political problem," like its "splittist" rivals (e.g. Islam, Tibetan Buddhism, Christianity) to the CCP's singular authority.

Thus began the "610 Office," a secret extralegal apparatus launched on July 20, 1999, after a silent sit-in by 10,000 practitioners outside Zhongnanhai protesting prior harassment. The 610 Office unleashed a nationwide purge of industrial-scale savagery: mass roundups of over 100,000 in the first months alone (per Amnesty International and U.S. State Department reports), torture in "black jails" involving beatings, electric shocks, sexual assault to extract "recantations" and forced psychiatric drugging to simulate madness.

And this is where we come to perhaps the most revolting fact of all, revealing the true Satanic heart of the CCP: the grotesque mass expansion of organ harvesting, with UN investigators and tribunals (2020 China Tribunal) estimating tens of thousands of Falun Gong prisoners killed annually since 2000 to fuel a $1 billion black-market transplant industry, all documented in survivor testimonies and leaked directives demanding "eradication" down to the cellular level.

Colleague Jan Jekielek, Senior Editor for The Epoch Times spent the past few years researching and writing his book, "Killed to Order" detailed for me the latest:

> *There's this massive explosion now in the forced organ harvest industry. You can see advertisements that say '2 weeks to get a new heart,' and there are phone calls where you are told, 'we can get you Falun Gong organs, whatever organs you want, just come, we'll set it up for you in a few days.'*

While Jekielek says young people are simply snatched on the street, targeting Falun Gong members - who live healthy, meditative lives - in specific has been a way to "kill two birds with one stone:"

> *There was this unwritten rule that got instituted very quickly in the early 2000s that Falun Gong deaths in the prisons and camps would be considered suicides. We're having a problem re-educating them, so if people die, well, they're not human anyway, because they're one of the five poisons, one of the things that we want to get rid of. And we the party elites, have this mandate to live forever, or at least increase longevity. These people need to be gotten rid of, there's a lot of them, they're disposable, they're dehumanized, and we can implement a whole bunch of priorities of the regime simultaneously if they become the source of healthy organs. As regions, trying to curry favor with Beijing, compete to supply the most and best organs. They're actually blood typing and tissue typing people ahead of time, they're building this giant database, and now they can kill to order.*

In the West, we have largely forgotten what diabolical, true "evil" is. But if evil thrives in our world, there are few more gut-wrenching examples today than this.

Christianity

While not as bloody as the devastation of Uyghurs, Falun Gong, or Tibetan Buddhists, the CCP's calculated crucifixion of Christianity in China, too, is soaked in blood, and amounts to a spiritual strangulation.

In 1966, Mao Zedong tried to weed out Christians and countless believers were sent off to labor camps for their "re-education." Catholic priests and nuns were coerced into marriage. In 1973, the CCP made an example of pastor Wang Zhiming by executing him in public. Mao's atheists branded Christianity a "foreign opium" of imperialism, weaponizing the Three-Self Patriotic Movement and Chinese Christian

Council to corral registered believers into state cages. House-church leaders endured arrests and torture.

With the "opening" of China in 1979 and a new public face to gain economic access to the free world, some tolerance of Christian gatherings were allowed. Then, having waged economic warfare on the West enough to gain leverage and power, Xi Jinping issued a decree in 2013 requiring "Sinicization" to bend all faiths to "socialist society," erasing the Gospel's call to higher allegiance in favor of Party worship.

Under this steel rule, pastors must swear fealty to Xi over Christ, sermons are scrubbed of biblical primacy, and Catholic bishops are Party puppets rejecting the Pope.

During the infamous 2014-2016 Henan rampage, CCP authorities toppled over 10,000 crosses from steeples with bulldozers in brutal spectacles (HRW 2023), including the widely-publicized dynamiting of the The Golden Lampstand Church in Shanxi province, a house church boasting 50,000 parishioners, built by supporters in the U.S. Mao's or Xi's portraits were plastered over the Ten Commandments in remaining churches, as documented by USCIRF's 2024 report and eyewitness accounts from ChinaAid, turning altars into propaganda shrines and forcing congregants to bow to the tyrant's gaze instead of the Lamb of God. More recently, the CCP has issued "edited Bibles for distribution in schools with notable changes, such as replacing Jesus's famous "let he who is without sin throw the first stone" in John 8 with *Jesus himself stoning the woman.*

Despite this multi-fanged campaign, it is estimated that 50-100 million underground Christians still huddle in house churches, their whispered prayers a quiet rebellion against the CCP, only to face raids that shatter families and spirits. According to the United States Commission on International Religious Freedom, Pastor Wang Yi, for example, of Early Rain Covenant Church was sentenced to nine years in 2019 for "subversion" after preaching separation of church and state, his flock beaten and dragooned into false confessions (U.S.CIRF 2022).

As I'm writing this, ChinaAid, a Texas-based human rights advocacy group, revealed that the CCP launched a "sweeping operation" across five provinces, in addition to Beijing, and Shanghai. The church said its worship venues were "raided and sealed," property was confiscated, family members of church members were harassed and more than 30 Zion Church leaders and members were detained or disappeared.

To this day, Christians endure non-stop digital surveillance: facial recognition facilitates the hauling of worshippers to "re-education" camps for forced renunciation, and entire congregations vanish into black jails (Open Doors 2024 World Watch List).

Non-Han ethnic Christian believers - including Miao hill folk or Korean migrants suffer extra lashes, including job firings, child seizures, and arrests tracked by Amnesty International. *All serve to winnow faith into submission.*

With the Christian eyes of the world on China, Xi stops short of executing yet another religious holocaust. But that doesn't mean his forces ever stop working. U.S. Congressman Representative Chris Smith and Ambassador Sam Brownback reported recently how the CCP is exporting its attempt to eradicate religion abroad as well. *"The Chinese Communist Party fears any community it cannot control. That fear is ecumenical. Christians, Muslims, Buddhists, Falun Gong practitioners, among many others in China's diverse religious landscape, face [pressure]."*

That much, anyone who reads the news can see. But, as Smith continues, the "invisible" campaign is happening right in your neighborhood:

> *The party's fears don't stop at China's borders. It exports repression: monitoring diaspora communities and congregations, silencing activism by pressuring families in China, and leaning on students and scholars to police speech on U.S. campuses. This is*

> *transnational repression. It chills speech in America, distorts what our public and policymakers hear about China, and raises risks for universities and research partners. A state willing to jail a pastor for an unapproved sermon today can coerce a supply chain, or a student or a scientist, tomorrow.*

What most observers never realize, but Smith and Brownback make clear, is that religious oppression is not to be seen as an isolated evil, but part of the CCP's ongoing hybrid warfare against each of us and our freedoms.

BRIEFING ELEVEN
The Battle For God
Spiritual War

"A society's strength or weakness depends more on the level of its spiritual life than on its level of industrialisation. If a nation's spiritual energies have been exhausted, it will not be saved from collapse by the most perfect government structure or by any industrial development. A tree with a rotten core cannot stand."
~ Aleksandr Solzhenitsyn
Russian novelist and dissident whose writings exposed the brutality of the Soviet Union's forced-labor camp system

"People without transcendent purpose are ripe for materialist seduction."
~ T. Casey Fleming

The Global Spiritual War

Let's be clear: communism is not reducible to a mere alternative economic system. *It is an anti-God machine.*

Communism abhors and rejects God and all other religions as the source of any authority. It replaces God with the state. It replaces love with fear. It replaces a truth with demonstrated lies. In fact, the truth is turned upside down. When truth is called "hate" and lies are called "love," you can be certain the fingerprints of the enemy are present.

Nearly 40% of Americans today believe we are living in the "End Times" *(Pew Research).* It's no wonder. After all, in the Book of Revelation, we are told of a world where individual autonomy is crushed, economic life is dictated by a centralized power, and people are deceived into surrendering their God-given freedom for the false promises of safety and food. And so many religious figures see the marks of the Anti-Christ in the demonstrated evils of the CCP. Clearly, Anti-God equates to Anti-Christ.

In the Book of John, Jesus warned us: "The thief does not come except to steal, and to kill, and to destroy. I have come that they may have life, and that they may have it more abundantly." (John 10:10) Indeed, in Christian theology, the mission of Satan has always been described as threefold: kill, steal, destroy. Communism, and in particular, the CCP, through its policy of unrestricted warfare, embodies these same three objectives:

- Kill faith, individuality, and moral responsibility.
- Steal private property, wealth, and the fruits of human labor.
- Destroy families, communities, culture, and the very belief in God.

It is crucial for every freedom-loving individual to understand that the CCP is not merely making war on America's economy, mind, and infrastructure, it is making war on our very soul, and the soul of the entire Judeo-Christian heritage of the West.

What we are witnessing today is, quite simply, the epic battle between good and evil, at Biblical proportions. Secular observers see the same opposition and in similar terms. Geopolitical forecaster and hedge-fund manager David Murrin, for example, recently shared with me his perspective,

Though the CCP isn't a demon with horns behind it, it's the darker aspect of human systems. Dark is the suppression of the soul. Dark is the suppression of freedom, and our ultimate potential, and our aspiration, and light is the encouragement of each individual's self-journey. This darkness would remove any light that was left in the world, without doubt.

This is rooted in the communist movement from the beginning. The communists know that if you want to conquer a nation, you must first break its spirit. Yuri Bezmenov showed us the mechanics of how communism does exactly that, decades ago, saying, "Destroy, ridicule religion, replace it with various sects and cults... as long as the accepted religious dogma is being slowly eroded and taken away from the supreme purpose of religion, which is to keep people in touch with the Supreme Being."

The strategy: leave people spiritually unmoored, because a people cut off from their highest loyalty can be made loyal to the state. Therefore, weakening Christianity in the West is meant to be a direct assault on the cultural and moral foundations that sustain liberty and bind communities in solidarity. And the CCP attack on the Christian soul is ongoing, and without pause.

This is where the "woke" infiltration and takeover of schools and universities have been so insidious. "Critical Theory" as we have seen in the chapter on Educational Warfare was imported to the West as a "long march through the institutions," in Herbert Marcuse's approving language.

After economic Marxism proved to be a failure and the "classless" society it promised in the Soviet Union led to massive and murderous purges by the ruling elite, Marxism looked for a new area where it might score a win.

The Frankfurt School's "Cultural Marxism" targeted that area as the minds and souls of the young. In true Marxist tradition, woke cultural

Marxism insists on a deliberate destruction of faith. In founding works like Dialectic of Enlightenment (1947), cultural Marxists Adorno and Horkheimer argued that religion is nothing more than a primitive tool of domination (there's that reductive, dualistic thinking of oppressor/ oppressed again). The Freudian-Marxist lens reduced spirituality to a mental disorder serving the rich: faith in God becomes nothing more than a projection of parental authority, and the idea of divine salvation into a useful illusion propping up the current wealthy-dominated order.

Post-1960s, this thinking evolved into a thorough relativism, a "hermeneutics of suspicion" that views religion through the lens of power dynamics. Everything is about oppression and victims, exactly the purist dogma that frothing mobs scream about on our campuses today.

These mobs, indoctrinated in Neo-Marxism, have co-opted admirable Judeo-Christian "social justice" traditions, such as caring for the poor and the widow and welcoming the stranger, but they've stripped away their origins in divine law, humility, personal repentance, and a life of virtue.

Reformed Soviet spy-turned-state-witness Whittaker Chambers nailed the truth decades ago, penning, "Communism is a substitute religious creed, but one which is demonic because it deliberately attempts to cut man off from his rootedness in the divine."

The result? You end up with a purist "woke progressivism" that champions equity without work or achievement, that ridicules marriage, rejects obvious biological norms and categories, and despises ecclesiastical authority, all under the guise of "resistance to power."

By retaining echoes of prophetic justice (e.g., Isaiah's call for righteousness), it masquerades as heir to the West's ethical tradition, even as it guts its core spiritual foundation. This leads to them, for example, absurdly romanticizing freedom-hating, death-cult Islamism as a counter-narrative to Western "imperialism." This topsy-turvy ideology is, in my view, the very opposite of the love of God, the opposite of the love of God in one's own soul and the soul of another. Westerners buying into the savage bile of jihadist Islam represents self-hatred, hatred of one's own culture and, in the scholar Gad Saad's words, a posturing, spiritually empty "suicidal empathy."

Our young are sacrificing our entire spiritual heritage to make way for communist and Islamic rule. And of course, the CCP plots, funds, applauds, and amplifies the cultural and religious suicide of the West at every turn.

Peter Mattisson's The Red-Green Axis (2022) along with reports from the U.S.-China Economic and Security Review Commission (2023), reveal that the CCP has invested billions in "United Front" operations: propaganda, influence campaigns, and institutional infiltration carrying this neo-Marxist, soul-denying erosion. They know that people without transcendent purpose are ripe for materialist seduction. As Aleksandr Solzhenitsyn warned in his 1978 Harvard address, when a Godless West loses its moral compass, they invite totalitarians to fill the void.

This explains the hysterical "progressive solidarity" with Hamas that have soiled our streets and campuses since the animalistic massacre of October 7, 2023. Judaism's eternal and unapologetic emphasis on divine law, communal identity, love of life, and transcendent historical purpose is antithetical to the communist mind.

By targeting Israel and Jews, neo-Marxists and their opportunistic allies (including the CCP's online and financial influence) seek to decapitate the root spiritual vitality of Western civilization, leaving a hollowed-out husk ripe for totalitarian reconfiguration. That is why CCP state media (e.g., Global Times) and influencers on Weibo/TikTok flooded narratives portraying Israel as a white "imperial proxy," to stoke anti-Western sentiment.

A 2024 report by the Foundation for Defense of Democracies reveals CCP funding to pro-Palestinian NGOs via proxies, including donations to groups like Students for Justice in Palestine that drove campus chaos. This included a calculated attempt to divide Christians from their roots and destroy the long narrative of Judeo-Christian cohesion, root and branch, the very "Tree of Life" that has bloomed freedom and resists authoritarianism throughout the West.

The Tree of Life vs. The Bringer of Death

Pastor Tommy Quick, founder of Christian Families Against Destructive Decisions, identifies the CCP and communism as "the counterfeit messiah," "an Antichrist order designed to enslave humanity under a false banner of 'peace, justice, and equality.'"

A growing, vocal subset of evangelical Christians in the West has turned to biblical prophecy to interpret the rise of China's Communist Party (CCP). For these interpreters, leaders like Mao Zedong and Xi Jinping aren't mere historical or political figures, they're harbingers of the Antichrist, fulfilling end-times warnings in Scripture. This perspective identifies communist authoritarianism as the fulfillment of biblical warnings about global deception and persecution.

In the pantheon of murderous 20th-century villains, Mao Zedong looms large for many Christian commentators as embodying the exact qualities of the biblical Antichrist: a deceptive leader who exalts the state above God and demands worship through ideology.

One prominent voice is David Wilkerson, the late Assemblies of God pastor and author of the prophetic bestseller The Vision (1973). Wilkerson described communism under Mao as a "satanic system" that "prepares the soil for the Antichrist."

In a 1974 sermon transcribed in his book "America's Last Call," he linked Mao's cult of personality to the "man of lawlessness" described in the New King James version:

> *Let no one deceive you by any means; for that Day will not come unless the falling away comes first, and the man of sin is revealed, the son of perdition, who opposes and exalts himself above all that is called God or that is worshiped, so that he sits as God in the temple of God, showing himself that he is God.*

For Wilkerson, Mao's elevation of the CCP as the one infallible authority, erasing religion and enforcing Maoist thought as gospel, embodied this exact foretold self-deification, turning the state into an idol.

Similarly, Hal Lindsey, author of "The Late Great Planet Earth" (1970), which sold over 35 million copies, portrayed Mao-era China as part of the "kings of the East" in Revelation 16:12 ("The sixth angel poured out his bowl on the great river Euphrates, and its water was dried up, to prepare the way for the kings from the east").

Lindsey argued in a 1980s update to his book that Mao's atheistic regime, with its mass mobilization and anti-Christian campaigns (destroying churches and Bibles), was "training grounds for the beast's army," preparing a deceived populace for the ultimate Antichrist. Lindsey's influence persists in prophecy circles, where Mao is seen not necessarily as the Antichrist but as a prototype, embodying the erasure of God in favor of state worship.

Fast-forward to today, and Xi Jinping has become the focal point for those extending Mao's legacy into contemporary end-times narratives. Xi's consolidation of power, via the 2018 abolition of term limits, the social credit system, and bloody suppression of religious freedoms, has drawn parallels to a rising global satanic deceiver.

Franklin Graham, son of Billy Graham and CEO of Samaritan's Purse, has been among the most outspoken on this. In a 2020 interview with Decision Magazine (Billy Graham Evangelistic Association), Graham called Xi's regime "a modern-day Roman Empire" that "demands worship of the state, much like the beast in Revelation 13." He referenced verses 1–4, connecting them to Xi's "quasi-religious" authoritarian doctrines and expanding power grabs around the world:

> *Then I stood on the sand of the sea. And I saw a beast rising up out of the sea, having seven heads and ten horns, and on his horns ten crowns, and on his heads a blasphemous name. Now the beast which I saw was like a leopard, his feet were like the feet of a bear, and his mouth like the mouth of a lion. The dragon gave him his*

power, his throne, and great authority. And I saw one of his heads as if it had been mortally wounded, and his deadly wound was healed. And all the world marveled and followed the beast. So they worshiped the dragon who gave authority to the beast; and they worshiped the beast, saying, "Who is like the beast? Who is able to make war with him?" (NKJV)

More explicitly prophetic is Perry Stone, a charismatic televangelist and founder of Voice of Evangelism, who in his 2022 book Decoding the Prophets' Mysteries and a YouTube sermon series ("China and the End Times," viewed over 500,000 times), labels Xi directly as a potential "forerunner to the Antichrist." Stone argues that the CCP's fusion of surveillance tech (e.g., facial recognition enforcing loyalty) with atheistic ideology fulfills the "mark of the beast" in Revelation 13:16–17:

He causes all, both small and great, rich and poor, free and slave, to receive a mark on their right hand or on their foreheads, and that no one may buy or sell except one who has the mark or the name of the beast, or the number of his name. (NKJV)

He cites Xi's 2013 speech proclaiming "the Chinese Dream" as a call for total allegiance, mirroring the Antichrist's demand for absolute worship. Stone weaves this into broader geopolitics, warning that U.S. alliances with China could invite the "Great Tribulation."

Lance Wallnau, a New Apostolic Reformation leader and author of "God's Chaos Candidate" (2016), goes further in his podcast. Wallnau portrays Xi as the "dragon" of Revelation 12:3 (a red dragon with seven heads), embodying satanic opposition to God's people. In a March 2024 episode titled "China's Role in Bible Prophecy," he claims the CCP's Uyghur camps and Christian crackdowns signal the prelude to global persecution, urging believers to pray against "antichrist spirits" in Beijing.

For interpreters like Stone and Wallnau, communist systems, in their pure form, prepare the way for this kind of figure: erasing God, rewriting morality, and demanding total allegiance to the State. Xi's portrait in every government building and the CCP's cult-like indoctrination are seen as obvious rehearsals for the beast's throne.

Whether Mao or Xi is literally the anti-Christ, they and the entire CCP apparatus is clearly, viciously and unalterably anti-Christ and anti-Christianity. As it says in Ephesians 6:12, "we do not wrestle against flesh and blood, but against... spiritual hosts of wickedness." The satanic forces they have unleashed on their own people, especially people of faith, can only be viewed as a forerunner of what they intend to impose on the rest of us, should they get the chance.

If you and I have anything to do about it, they never will get that chance.

BRIEFING TWELVE
You Are Already A Soldier In World War III

"There are real actions that you can take that are constructive, and we can win.
*If we actually get our s*** together, we can and will win!*
For all our flaws... our civilization is incredibly strong and powerful.
With the pillars of Western civilization - science, democracy, the rule of law, creativity, freedom of speech, capitalism - if all of these pillars work, thrive and flourish, nothing can stop us. Islamism and the CCP?
These are just like cancers that are infecting a diseased body because the immune system has been compromised.
If we are strong in ourselves, those will just die,
because they're fundamentally weak.
They're like cancer cells. Cancer cells are weak.
They can only take over if they get a foothold.
We just need to stop them. Now."
~ Senior Advisor, Royal College of Defence Studies, London (on condition of anonymity)

"A whole of society attack from the CCP requires a whole of society response from the U.S. and its allies."
~ T. Casey Fleming

As you now know, this is not a guide about the future. It is a survival guide for WWIII which has been occurring now, globally: in your world, your country, your family, in your devices, your body, your mind - *while everyday life continues to appear normal.*

It is a war unlike any we have fought in the past. This time, citizens, you and I, not the military, are attacked everyday, by an integrated web of methods that go unnoticed or are tolerated "noise" just under the threshold that requires taking military action. Today's Unrestricted War prosecuted by the China Axis of Russia, Iran, N. Korea, Pakistan, terrorist groups and drug cartels must not be confused with the Cold War of the 20th Century. Unrestricted War is many levels more sophisticated in complexity, stealth, speed, and lethality. Let this sink in: this is Total "Whole of Society" War. ***It is the Final War.***

These pages say the quiet part out loud, detailing that sense almost everybody feels today that something is very wrong on the world stage. That our systems are not working as they should. That our electronics, our information, our social and legacy media, our critical infrastructure - water, power grids, food supply - are all compromised and threatened..

A deeper cut is that most people in the West feel we have lost our moral center, our connection to our fundamental Judeo-Chrisitan and enlightenment values, fading under the flood of Marxist ideology that has been injected into our daily lives, education and information feeds, creating chaos and demoralization. The exact result that the CCP and its minions have worked so hard to create.

Many experts concur that we are running out of time. Several, including my colleague and former Deputy Assistant Secretary of Defense, Frank Gaffney, fear it may be too late. I say that we have **less than 10 years** to win this Gray Zone war, or we will be lost forever.

The previous chapters gave you a thorough reconnaissance of our enemy at work on the battlefield. This briefing brings it all together to help assure that your commitment to rejecting and reversing these attacks will be at least equally strong.

The next briefing offers you the first level of action steps you should be taking - as an individual, family member, as a consumer, as a citizen of a democratic state, and as a human being with a divine soul.

This is not a job for our politicians alone, or our business leaders. Our elite classes are economically compromised. Our military and security apparatus, by its own admission, operates in silos and the left hand does not often know what the right hand is doing. It's so bad, Edward Haugland, leading expert in Cognitive War and retired intelligence community executive, author of "*The Cognitive War*" calls it a situation of "titanium siloes of sub-excellence."

In this war, no battlefront can be viewed on its own. Peter Schweitzer correctly lays out some of the interlocking pieces and how they work together:

> *Economic warfare gave China the leverage to build and control the very tech supply chains that power apps like TikTok. Legal warfare shields them under U.S. corporate lobbying and lawyers who bend Congress away from real restrictions. Media warfare launders CCP narratives through influencers and friendly journalists. And cultural warfare pumps corrosive messages-nihilism, addiction, self-hatred-straight into our kids' veins. All while the CCP censors its own population from those very same toxins.*

Grant Newsham adds how COVID-19 revealed this coordinated aggression in new ways:

> *COVID-19 also was potent as financial warfare. It led to massive U.S. government spending to counter the effects of the economic downturn. This further debased the U.S. dollar and ultimately led to the highest inflation in forty years-making life difficult for all citizens. It also threatens the dollar's role as the world's reserve currency, something China has been angling to overcome for many years. So you see how it works: biological warfare ties into other warfares-such as financial warfare, economic warfare, psychological*

warfare, international organization warfare, media warfare, etc., and all are mutually reinforcing. The cumulative effect wears down the opponent and creates entropy, affecting their ability to resist or to conduct kinetic operations.

David Murrin, the brilliant Global Forecaster, ran down the depth of the entire CCP plan in a recent conversation with our team:

The CCP plans to dominate the world. It's built a system to do exactly that. It considers independence and individual thought and democracy to be a virus. They see individuality and decision-making as a threat. They use social engineering to ensure that the system obeys them. It's an exacerbation of a hierarchical system, which China has always been, and it ensures the people at the top control everyone else. And if you dissent: you are removed.

Their software picks up the few individuals, like ourselves, who would speak out against them. It removes them and their genes, so that the pool will obey them. And we can see how effective that process is, because they applied it to a hostile society in the form of the Uyghurs. They tortured them, they conditioned them, they made them sterile, they did things which, honestly, everyone should be jumping up and down about in woke camp, but no one seems to take any notice, and they subdued them. And then they took that technology, and they went to Hong Kong with the Chinese, six generations of democracy and capitalism, and in three months, bang, the whole system obeyed them. That is terrifying, because that gives them the engineering to go to any country in the world and subjugate it.

Murrin went on to warn how this time is different both in sophistication and scale…

No one's ever had this ability. Yes, you could be Germany or the Soviet Union, and you do it crudely. This is a clinical subjugation of a

> *system by removing individuals. They are late in their expansionary process because they have been delayed by American power. Ideally, in their expansionary curve, they should have done it from 1975 onwards, but America imposed a glass ceiling on them, and the only way they got through the ceiling was a covert plan that goes back to 1996 and the third Taiwan Strait crisis, where they covertly induced us to invest in them to get cheap manufacturing and keep our inflation down. They then nicked everything we had, whether it was in the manufacturing bases or through their extraction process with 200,000 hackers with IQs over 150, stripping everything that moved. They used a manufacturing base to take the IP, and they created an arms race.*

Then he tied in exactly what we have been driving home in this guide: unrestricted warfare is integrated across every part of our lives:

> *And just when the arms race really accelerated, they released a pandemic to destroy our debt dynamics. And at the same time, they kept in reserve the rare earth methodology, where just when we wanted to rearm, just when we woke up, the very things we needed to rearm were taken from us. That is a strategic plan of depth and complexity that no one in the world has ever created. That's thirty years of planning. So we are facing something that's overwhelmed us. And at the same time, not only is it overwhelming us from the outside, it's overwhelming us from the inside. It's infiltrated every single aspect of our society.*

You can never again unsee the fact that you are standing right smack in the middle of an active Whole of Society and Whole of World theater of war.

Which brings us to my whole purpose of writing this guide - to wake you up to take action:

BASED ON CURRENT INTELLIGENCE

CHINA'S UNRESTRICTED WAR AGAINST YOU

THE BATTLEFIELD IS EVERYWHERE FOR COMMUNIST TAKEOVER

POLITICAL WAR
ECONOMIC WAR
TRADE WAR

DRUG WAR
BIOLOGICAL WAR

CYBER WAR
TECHNOLOGY WAR
ALGORITHMIC WAR
DATA & IP THEFT
ESPIONAGE

GLOBAL ELITES
CAPTURED CORPORATE ELITES
CAPTURED POLITICIANS
WEF, WHO, UN

CCP TOTALITARIAN CHINESE COMMUNIST PARTY

CCP AXIS
RUSSIA, IRAN, N KOREA, PAKISTAN, CARTELS
TERRORISTS | RADICAL ISLAM
HACKERS, TRAFFICKERS, SURVEILLANCE

COGNITIVE WAR
EDUCATION WAR
CULTURE WAR
SPIRITUAL WAR
RELIGIOUS WAR

HUMAN ATROCITIES
FORCED ORGAN HARVESTING
ENSLAVED WORK CAMPS
EXTREME PERSECUTION

A Whole of Society Attack Requires a Whole of Society Response

You, the reader, have a crucial role to play. How you can take action now will be addressed in the next chapter, and that is the work of FreedomForever.Global, a movement based on this survival guide and the Constitution that gives "Voice to the Voiceless," which I invite you to join.

Bottom line: You can't successfully fight the enemy if you don't know their history, goals, and their strategy.

Now you know it. Let's debrief and deepen the truths that you have been learning in the previous pages.

Truth One: The CCP's China is Your Enemy

We are at war.

You are in World War III.

Not a hot "kinetic" war - at least not yet.

And not a "cold" war, as we had with a much weaker, poorer, disorganized, and frankly, drunk Soviet Union.

We are in a hot, hybrid inferno. An unrestricted war. An active war.

We are at war with the CCP's China - not the oppressed people of China, but their overlord, the totalitarian communist Party.

And our enemy is the most capable, sadistic, tech-advanced, well-funded, formidable, and determined enemy in history. One that we have built by doing nonstop business deals, allowing our IP to be stolen and buying their products. The CCP will never compromise. They see 100% global communist domination as their sole destiny. They are faking they support a 'multipolar world' but the end game is total domination. The choice is freedom or communism, freedom or tyranny.

At the heart of the CCP's aggressive expansionism lies a pernicious, increasingly articulated Han supremacism, rooted in China's ancient self-conception as the "Middle Kingdom," the eternal center of the world, with all other nations relegated to vassal status, compelled to serve and enable Beijing's economic and military dominance.

This worldview, steeped in centuries of imperial entitlement and racial hierarchy, fosters a deep-seated suspicion and contempt for all outsiders, viewing non-Han peoples as subjects to be reengineered, humiliated, or eradicated if they resist assimilation into a Han-defined "Chinese identity."

Under Xi Jinping, this ideology shows itself in brutal "normalization" and "racial fusion" policies across Xinjiang, Tibet, and Inner Mongolia, where mass Han migration overwhelms indigenous populations, religious practices are demolished, "reeducation" camps detain millions in forced indoctrination, and histories glorifying Han hegemony erase the cultures of Uyghurs, Tibetans, and Mongols - culminating in genocides that sterilize, enslave, and slaughter to forge a monolithic "civilizational state."

Xi's doctrine projects China as a singular nation of a singular culture, promoting a Han master race presiding over the so-called "Community of the Common Destiny of Mankind," where dissenters are crushed and global rivals are stepping stones. All nations must be profoundly alarmed: to dismiss the CCP as anything less than an existential adversary is to court the same fate as its internal victims: subjugation or annihilation.

If you still cling to the delusion that the Chinese Communist Party's (CCP) is merely a "competitor" or economic partner, a narrative peddled by globalist elites to print money for themselves and soothe uneasy consciences, you are now waking up to the reality: China under the CCP is not our ally, nor our rival in a fair game of markets, but a predatory, supremacist juggernaut hell-bent on our subjugation through a shadow war that corrodes our soul and weakens our ability to defend ourselves.

Truth Two: The CCP's Unrestricted War Against You is Operating at Full Speed

Official Doctrine: CCP publicly embraces "unrestricted warfare" leveraging every means possible (drugs, legal, criminal, cyber, economic, technological, psychological, biological) for dominance, bypassing - or preparing for - conventional military conflict. They are:

- **Atheist Totalitarians:** The CCP functions as militant atheist rulers, crushing faith communities, banning religious practice, and persecuting spiritual leaders to eradicate independent sources of moral authority so all are loyal to the Party.
- **Familial Destroyers:** Decades of enforced one-child horrors shattered Chinese family structure, drained population vigor, and substituted state control over private life - now promoted as "social harmony."
- **Genocidal Aggressors:** In Xinjiang and Tibet, the CCP commits mass internments, forced sterilizations, mass organ harvesting, and cultural erasure - clear acts of genocide against ethnic and religious minorities.
- **Biological Warriors:** The CCP aggressively generates bio-weapons and disseminates biowarfare disinformation (see: COVID-19) - obscuring origins, stalling global response, and undermining cognitive trust in Western institutions.
- **Drug Dealers:** Multiple CCP state-linked companies churn out fentanyl and other powerful drug precursors, driving a nationwide overdose epidemic in America and the world; CCP partnerships with transnational criminal groups weaponize drug flows as acts of economic and social sabotage, a soft-kill strategy to demoralize and depopulate the West without invasion.
- **Infrastructure Saboteurs:** CCP firms embed "kill switches" in undersea cables (Huawei's 5G dominance, per 2023 FCC bans), power grids (smart meters from state grid proxies), IoT

devices (webcams, EVs, routers like TP-Link), and solar panels (80% U.S. market share), vulnerable to remote shutdowns, (ASPI 2022 report)-priming the West for blackouts that would paralyze wartime response.

- **Economic Vampires:** The CCP drains American innovation through relentless intellectual property theft (hundreds of billions annually), manipulates trade, and weaponizes global supply chains, rare earths, and currency creating strategic dependence and vulnerability.
- **Institutional Infectors:** Infiltration campaigns target Wall Street, Washington, state capitals, school boards, and universities - recruiting influencers, funding proxies, and exerting systemic covert leverage over U.S. decision-making.
- **Cyber Predators:** China executes daily attacks on U.S. government, business, and infrastructure, exploiting system weaknesses; responsible for record-breaking breaches, endangering critical national security assets.
- **Mass Infiltrators:** The Chinese Communist Party orchestrates the covert movement of 200,000 military-age males into the United States equal to the population of Akron, Ohio - exploiting immigration vulnerabilities; a strategic demographic incursion with potential to destabilize security in sleeper cells, overwhelm infrastructure, and compromise national defense readiness.
- **Cognitive and Information Warriors:** CCP operatives push divisive propaganda, disinformation, and psychological operations across social media, academia, and think tanks. Their aim: divide Americans, undermine institutions, fund and support street mobs, and achieve "mind dominance" as a weapon of war.
- **Forward-Staging Military Logisticians:** The Chinese Communist Party sent over 200,000 military age men into the United States, has acquired land and warehouse properties

proximate to U.S. military installations, and embedded a flood of mysterious Chinese-national truck drivers who hold newly obtained commercial licenses. In short, they have created a forward-operational capability able to immediately deploy against critical domestic defense targets.

- **Educational Subvertors:** CCP-backed Confucius Institutes, curriculum projects, and research partnerships steer American students toward self-censorship, CCP legitimacy, and Marxist ideological realignment-doubling as intelligence gathering and espionage recruitment platforms.
- **Political and Institutional Infiltrators:** Mass-scale influence ops seek to co-opt U.S. politicians, media figures, scholars, and business elites; diaspora communities face pressure and surveillance, while dark money finances proxies to silence critics.
- **Propagandists:** CCP media and agents twist global debate, spreading lies about origins of pandemics, ethnic repression, U.S. history, and democracy - eroding factual discourse and manipulating world opinion.
- **Alliance-Breakers:** The CCP relentlessly exploits fractures in NATO and allied coalitions, targeting weak links via economic offers and disinformation to undermine collective defense and political unity.
- **Ideological Colonizers:** They repackage Marxist doctrine as "common prosperity" - seducing Western scholars, activists, and organizations into supporting policies that ultimately serve CCP centrism and global influence.
- **Spiritual and Cultural Warriors:** In America, the CCP attacks faith institutions, family networks, and moral values. By promoting collectivism and neo-Marxist ideology, they seek to dissolve spiritual anchors and weaken civic resilience.

- **Drone and Proxy Warfighters:** They flood the Taiwan Strait with CCP-built swarms - masking PLA power in exercise form - while grooming proxies across Africa and Latin America, binding nations in Belt and Road debt that buys basing rights and dependency primed for hybrid strikes against U.S. allies.

In short: every single sector of our individual and social sovereignty is under maximum malicious, hybrid, multidimensional attack. That is why former FBI Director Christopher Wray warned that the CCP is "the adversary of our time," and FBI head Kash Patel has highlighted Beijing's "malign foreign influence" as the greatest threat to U.S. sovereignty.

We are witnessing Sun Tzu's patient "win the war without fighting" incarnate, but twisted by Xi Jinping into an almost psychopathic winner-take-all blitzkrieg against faith, family, institutions, freedom, and Western alliances. A total-war where the CCP has pulled out all the stops in pulverizing America into a fractured husk, ripe for complete takeover and domination.

Their "Unrestricted Warfare" doctrine - codified in the 1999 PLA manual - treats economics, tech, elites, and all of culture as active battlegrounds, mobilizing a whole-of-society spy network under Article 7 of China's National Intelligence Law, compelling citizens, firms, and proxies to collect intel, as seen in the 2022 arrests of 2,000+ CCP-linked agents in the U.S. alone. Under a communist regime, all citizens have a national duty to spy when commanded.

Truth Three: We Are Now In "The Perfect Storm"

We are living through a convergence of threats unlike any in modern history, together forming a perfect storm that puts our existence as a free society at immediate risk.

Decades of permissive policy, economic dependence, intellectual weakness, cultural generosity, greed, gullibility, leftist subversion, and willful blindness have allowed infiltration of our federal, state, and local governments, corporate boardrooms, universities, media networks, and even religious institutions.

Many of the leaders we should be counting on to guard our political union and our way of life are compromised by financial ties, ideological alignment, or sheer fear of confronting the CCP. As retired General Michael Flynn warned, this is a fight for our lives, our families, and our liberties, and our government cannot be relied upon to shield us.

The CCP has made their move, and are ever more aggressive about it, but hardly anybody is listening. Partly because people in the West don't want to believe it and partly because this war is invisible to most eyes or operating in the shadows. But the storm is breaking over us now. Denial is no longer an option, The only way forward is a citizen-led response that understands the scope of the threat, refuses compromise, and mobilizes every resource to resist.

Truth Four: The 45 Goals of Communism Have Been Achieved In Front of Your Eyes

On January 10, 1963, Representative Albert S. Herlong Jr., a Democrat from Florida, stepped to the microphone in the U.S. House of Representatives and dropped something so explosive it should have sent shockwaves across every corner of the Republic: an enemy's war plan already in motion.

Herlong, a WWII U.S. Navy veteran and staunch anti-communist had, in 1959, introduced a bill to establish a federally funded Freedom Academy that would counteract foreign countries' communist propaganda. He had been witnessing the creeping ideological rot in schools, media, and government and wanted this particular information - this "list" exposed to the largest possible audience. So he read it into the official Congressional Record where it couldn't be buried.

The document that Herlong read was the "45 Goals of International Communism," the cold, methodical Marxist objectives aimed at dismantling America from within. This list came from the 1958 book "The Naked Communist," written by former FBI agent, W. Cleon Skousen, who had seen firsthand how Moscow and its ideological agents operated. His career connected him with classified cases, surveillance operations, and reports that mapped the communist playbook. He knew the goal wasn't physical military invasion, it was **infiltration without resistance.** His book stripped the ideological skin off Marxism and revealed the muscle and bone beneath: media capture, cultural disarmament, moral breakdown, and political subversion. Skousen documented what he saw: the phony "peace" campaigns that masked societal corrosion, the courtroom battles twisting justice into surrender, the academic inversions designed to destroy patriotism and Western values in younger generations.

Skousen understood something most Americans, and far too many members of Congress didn't - and still don't - or want to face: communism will present itself as progress, as compassion, as social justice. It will wear the language of civil rights while poisoning the very liberties it claims to defend. He wrote the book to wake up the public before the inversion became irreversible. When Herlong read the list of 45 Goals, the battle plans of the enemy were laid out for everyone to see.

On that January day, Herlong revealed the Marxist gameplan: eliminate prayer in schools, undermine religion, infiltrate the media, control artistic expression, promote obscenity under the banner of freedom, discredit the U.S. Constitution, push global unelected governance under the UN, weaken defense by promoting universal disarmament, and normalize Marxist principles in education and culture. The desired result: a decayed America unable and unwilling to fight back. You have been witnessing exactly the execution of that plan in these pages.

Washington's political class has mostly met the publicizing of this list with avoidance. To acknowledge the danger meant admitting massive infiltration had already happened: inside schools and universities, Congress, Wall Street, newspapers, and even church pulpits. For many, silence was safer - and more lucrative in the short term. It meant admitting that the resurgent, Post WWII optimistic America was not as safe as it seemed. The media? Largely indifferent, or hostile. Network editors brushed it aside, treating it as fringe or conspiratorial. Ironically, that dismissiveness proved one of Skousen's list of communist goals: the infiltration of mass communications to shape perception and dictate what was "serious" news.

As you have been reading in these pages, the "45 Goals" Skousen identified were anything but a conspiracy. They were a step-by-step "destruction manual" that, over the decades, has sunk its tendrils ever deeper into our freedom. We can track every single goal against the real-world erosion of American resilience: faith replaced by state ideology, patriotism replaced by globalism, Western values of economic and speech freedom fractured by a steady feed of Marxist indoctrination.

Danger in Kennedy's bright 1963 felt theoretical to most Americans and far from our shores. But today it feels so much closer, not merely near us, but within us. Beijing's CCP, tech-perfecting Soviet dark arts of ideological warfare, has been implementing an updated version of the "45" blueprint, only this time with mind-bogglingly advanced digital tools, systemic economic leverage, endless funding, and viralized cultural division tactics. All of them, far more powerful and prolific than anything Skousen could have imagined. "The Red Tsunami," he warned, was already rising in 1963 - is now crashing across our entire homeland in the U.S. and around the world.

The Lethal 45: Communist Goals for Takeover of America

Here are the exact 45 Goals compiled by Skousen, adapted to the CCP and today, with my updates on their execution and advancement. As you read them, recall the details you have read in the previous chapters, and you will be connecting the dots - as I and the other experts in counterintelligence have been doing our very best to make public in recent years.

1. U.S. acceptance of coexistence as the only alternative to atomic war.

The CCP has been successful in promoting this through decades of U.S.-China "cooperative engagement" policies, framing economic interdependence as a bulwark against opposing the rise of China. The CCP is leveraging nuclear and other arsenals to deter escalation. Success: Near-complete in shaping U.S. policy.

2. U.S. willingness to capitulate in preference to engaging in atomic war.

CCP efforts have succeeded via asymmetric warfare doctrines and gray-zone tactics making full conflict appear catastrophic. U.S. restraint in responses to CCP aggression reflects this mindset. Success: Influential in risk-averse U.S. strategies.

3. Develop the illusion that total disarmament by the United States would be a demonstration of moral strength.

The CCP has advanced this indirectly through UN disarmament forums and propaganda portraying U.S. arms reductions as ethical leadership, while rapidly modernizing its own nuclear forces. Success: Moderate, as CCP hypocrisy undermines full illusion but sows Western self-doubt.

4. Permit free trade between all nations regardless of communist affiliation and regardless of whether or not items could be used for war.

The CCP's integration into global trade via WTO accession in 2001 has been a massive triumph, with unrestricted U.S. exports of dual-use tech (e.g., semiconductors) and biotech enabling military advancements like hypersonic weapons and bioweapons. Success: Highly successful, fueling CCP's economic and military rise.

5. Extension of long-term loans to Russia and Soviet Satellites.

While direct U.S. loans to Russia ended post-Cold War, U.S. capital and IP has flooded China. U.S. indirect facilitation via global finance persists. Success: Total.

6. Provide American aid to all nations regardless of communist domination.

U.S. aid continues to flow to CCP-influenced regimes, directly or indirectly through China, often enriching CCP-aligned tyrants while bypassing people. CCP mirrors this with "no-strings" aid to Africa and Latin America, subverting U.S. influence. Success: Strong for CCP, as it exploits U.S. aid gaps to expand soft power.

7. Grant Recognition of Red China. Admission of Red China to the U.N.

Fully accomplished: U.S. recognized PRC in 1979, and CCP joined UN Security Council in 1971 with veto power, blocking resolutions on

Uyghurs and Taiwan. CCP uses this to shield allies like North Korea. Success: Complete and leveraged for global veto dominance.

8. Set up East and West Germany as separate states in spite of Khrushchev's promise in 1955 to settle the Germany question by free elections under supervision of the U.N.

The CCP supported the Soviet division of Germany, and today benefits from a unified but economically intertwined Europe vulnerable to its influence (e.g., via German trade reliance). No direct U.S. reversal. Success: Achieved historically; CCP exploits lingering divisions in EU politics.

9. Prolong the conferences to ban atomic tests because the United States has agreed to suspend tests as long as negotiations are in progress.

The CCP adheres loosely to the 1996 CTBT (unsigned by U.S./China), conducting subcritical tests while pushing endless UN talks that constrain U.S. programs. U.S. moratorium since 1992 aligns with this. Success: High, as CCP advances arsenal (e.g., 2020s silo expansions) amid stalled global bans. Trump directs nuclear weapons testing to resume for the first time in over 30 years.

10. Allow all Soviet satellites individual representation in the U.N.

Like the Soviets, the CCP champions this for its allies and client states, expanding anti-Western voting blocs in the UN General Assembly. Over 50 such states now align with CCP on key votes. Success: Very successful, amplifying CCP's multilateral influence.

11. Promote the U.N. as the only hope for mankind.

If its charter is rewritten, demand that it be set up as a one-world government with its own independent armed forces. CCP promotes the UN as a multipolar tool, vetoing reforms that threaten its power while pushing Sustainable Development Goals to erode sovereignty. No full one-world shift, but CCP's peacekeeping contributions (2nd largest) build influence. Success: Partial, using the UN to normalize authoritarian norms.

12. Resist any attempt to outlaw the communist Party.

The CCP has evaded global bans, thriving as the world's largest party (98 million members) and influencing U.S. academia/labor to resist domestic anti-CCP laws (e.g., via Confucius Institutes). U.S. FARA registrations target CCP fronts. Success: Highly resilient, with minimal legal threats.

13. Do away with all loyalty oaths.

U.S. oaths persist (e.g., for officials, military), but CCP-influenced DEI initiatives in education soften patriotism. The CCP itself demands absolute loyalty via oaths in China. Success: Limited in U.S., but CCP erodes Western equivalents through cultural infiltration.

14. Continue giving Russia access to the U.S. Patent office.

The CCP has massively exploited U.S. patents, stealing IP worth $600B annually (per IP Commission), far surpassing Russia. U.S.-China tech transfers continue despite CFIU.S. reviews. Success: Overwhelming for CCP, fueling innovation theft.

15. Capture one or both of the political parties in the United States.

The CCP influences both U.S. parties via lobbying (e.g., Biden-era trade deals, Trump tariffs softened by business ties), but no full capture. United Front Work Department targets elites. Success: Partial penetration, via donations and elite capture.

16. Use technical decisions of the courts to weaken basic American institutions by claiming their activities violate civil rights.

The CCP amplifies this through propaganda and U.S. allies pushing "human rights" lawsuits against institutions (e.g., election integrity cases framed as suppression). Supreme Court shifts aid CCP narratives on free speech. Success: Moderate, exploiting judicial activism.

17. Get control of the schools.

Use them as transmission belts for socialism and current communist propaganda. Soften the curriculum. Get control of teachers' associations. Put the party line in textbooks. The CCP funds U.S. K-12/college programs via Confucius Institutes (banned but rebranded), promoting pro-CCP curricula; heavily subsidizes U.S. Universities; CRT/DEI echo socialist equity. Teacher unions lean left. Success: Significant in higher ed, growing in K-12.

18. Gain control of all student newspapers.

The CCP influences campus media through funding and self-censorship on China issues (e.g., 2020s protests); U.S. student papers often avoid criticizing CCP due to donor pressure. Success: Partial, via indirect control in elite universities.

19. Use student riots to foment public protests against programs or organizations which are under communist attack.

CCP-backed groups (e.g., pro-Hamas protests with anti-U.S. elements) sow chaos and division, disrupting campuses against Israel/U.S. policies. 2024 riots upgraded 1960s tactics. Success: Effective in mobilizing unrest against Western institutions and dividing the public.

20. Infiltrate the press.

Get control of book-review assignments, editorial writing, and policy-making positions. The CCP owns stakes in Western media (e.g., via proxies in Hollywood, news outlets) and censors criticism through economic leverage; U.S. press soft on CCP trade/human rights. Success: Substantial, with self-censorship prevalent.

21. Gain control of key positions in radio, TV, and motion pictures.

The CCP dominates global media via CGTN, TikTok (ByteDance), and Hollywood co-productions avoiding anti-CCP content (e.g., no Taiwan in films). U.S. outlets like NPR echo CCP lines on climate. Success: High in digital/streaming, growing in traditional.

22. Continue discrediting American culture by degrading all forms of artistic expression.

The CCP promotes "ugly" modernism in U.S. art scenes via grants, while censoring its own; Western postmodernism aligns with degrading patriotism. Success: Indirectly advanced, as CCP exploits cultural relativism.

23. Control art critics and directions of art museums. "Our plan is to promote ugliness, repulsive meaningless art."

The CCP influences U.S. museums through donations (e.g., Beijing-backed exhibits); critics often laud CCP-state art as "innovative." Success: Moderate, via financial leverage in cultural institutions.

24. Eliminate all laws governing obscenity by calling them "censorship" and a violation of free speech and free press.

U.S. obscenity laws weakened post-1960s; the CCP uses "free speech" rhetoric abroad while enforcing strict domestic censorship. This duality aids global narrative control. Success: Aligned with Western liberalization, benefiting CCP hypocrisy.

25. Break down cultural standards of morality by promoting pornography and obscenity in books, magazines, motion pictures, radio, and TV.

The CCP floods global markets with state-tolerated porn via apps like WeChat, while domestically censoring; U.S. moral decline (e.g., OnlyFans boom) erodes family structures CCP seeks to exploit. Success: Contributory, amplifying chaos.

26. Present homosexuality, degeneracy, and promiscuity as "normal, natural, healthy."

The CCP suppresses LGBTQ+ domestically but promotes it abroad to fracture Western morals (e.g., via media exports); U.S. shifts weakening traditional masculine roles including protectiveness. Success: Effective in sowing division, instilling confusion, breaking family authority over Trans issues and children.

27. Infiltrate the churches and replace revealed religion with "socialist" religion. Discredit the Bible and emphasize the need for intellectual maturity which does not need a "religious crutch."

CCP's Three-Self Church in China exemplifies this; in the U.S., "progressive" theology echoes marxist language and "social justice" over classic religious doctrine. Success: Growing in Western seminaries.

28. Eliminate prayer or any phase of religious expression in the schools on the grounds that it violates the principle of "separation of church and state."

U.S. school prayer banned since 1962; Weekly church attendance down from 70% (1963) to 20% (2025) according to Pew Research. CCP atheism reinforces global secularism pushes. Success: Fully realized in the U.S., mirroring CCP's anti-religion stance.

29. Discredit the American Constitution by calling it inadequate, old-fashioned, out of step with modern needs, a hindrance to cooperation between nations on a world-wide basis.

CCP propaganda (e.g., via CGTN) portrays the Constitution as racist, classist, and outdated; U.S. debates on "living document" echo this. Success: Influential in academic and leftist circles.

30. Discredit the American founding fathers. Present them as selfish aristocrats who had no concern for the "common man."

CCP-backed curricula (e.g., in U.S. schools) emphasize 1619 Project-like views; founders vilified as slaveholders. Success: Widespread in education, eroding national pride.

31. Belittle all forms of American culture and discourage the teaching of American history on the ground that it was only a minor part of "the big picture." Give more emphasis to Russian history since the communists took over.

CCP promotes "global history" in U.S. texts minimizing America; 1619/CRT curricula downplay founding, though Russian focus waned post-USSR. Slavery presented as uniquely American. Success: Strong in belittling U.S. exceptionalism.

32. Support any social movement to give centralized control over any part of the culture.

The CCP exploits U.S. movements and global bodies to consolidate control over education, healthcare, welfare, mental health, and policing. This includes national curricula, single-payer healthcare, centralized welfare programs, and federalized safety reforms, often reinforced by non-elected organizations like the WHO, which expand authority beyond elected oversight. These shifts weaken local autonomy, embed dependency, and open channels for ideological influence, surveillance, and strategic leverage over American cultural and social systems.

33. Eliminate laws or procedures which interfere with the operation of the communist apparatus.

Statutes like FARA and anti-espionage laws still exist but enforcement against CCP networks is weak. Foreign-influence probes are slow, prosecutions rare, and security reviews of CCP-linked academic, tech, and agricultural acquisitions are often diluted or blocked politically. Visa vetting lapses allow operatives into research labs; export-control loopholes let sensitive tech transfer abroad. In China, the CCP abolishes internal restraints, tightening one-party control. In the West, legal erosion enables strategic penetration with minimal resistance.

34. Eliminate the House Committee on Un-American Activities.

HUAC dissolved in 1975; CCP benefits from lack of similar probes into its influence ops. Success: Achieved, reducing oversight.

35. Discredit and eventually dismantle the FBI.

The CCP exploits cyber intrusions, insider recruitment, and disinformation to erode trust in the Bureau's integrity. Breaches of FBI systems and theft of investigative data undermine operational confidence. Concurrently, politicized domestic controversies - such as disputed handling of 2016 election probes, high-profile whistleblower claims, and selective leak campaigns - amplify public distrust. While the FBI remains intact, sustained reputational damage hampers its counterintelligence effectiveness, creating openings for CCP operations and reducing deterrence capacity.

36. Infiltrate and gain control of more unions.

The CCP leverages ties with groups like the International Longshore and Warehouse Union (ILWU) and global labor fronts aligned with Chinese state interests to influence U.S. labor policy. Collaboration occurs through exchange programs, funding channels, and solidarity campaigns shaped by CCP narratives. The AFL-CIO's ideological shift toward left-leaning global causes creates openings for policy synergy. Influence is most effective in key sectors tied to trade, shipping, and manufacturing, yielding moderate but strategic penetration.

37. Infiltrate and gain control of big business.

The CCP systematically embeds influence within U.S. big business through dependency on Chinese manufacturing, rare-earth resources, and market access. Tech giants like Apple, Qualcomm, and Tesla rely heavily on Chinese supply chains and labor, ceding the CCP economic leverage over pricing, operations, and compliance. "Elite capture" occurs via the China Council for the Promotion of International Trade (CCPIC) and other state-linked bodies, compromising business leaders with incentives, preferential contracts, and the promise of access to Chinese markets in exchange for policy alignment. Joint ventures in China require Party cell integration, giving CCP operatives insight and potential veto power over U.S. corporate strategies. Success: broad, entrenched, and difficult to reverse.

38. Transfer some of the powers of arrest from the police to social agencies. Treat all behavioral problems as psychiatric disorders which no one but psychiatrists can understand or treat.

"Defund-the-police" initiatives and legislative reforms divert certain arrest and intervention duties to social workers, mental-health teams, and community programs. Some jurisdictions classify behavioral issues as psychiatric matters, limiting police authority. The CCP employs a similar framework in Xinjiang by labeling dissent and non-conformity as psychological or ideological disorders, enforced through "re-education" centers. Such policies reduce traditional law-enforcement reach, expand bureaucratic control over behavior, and mirror CCP social-management tactics. Success: Advancing within progressive municipalities.

39. Dominate the psychiatric profession and use mental health laws as a means of gaining coercive control over those who oppose communist goals.

CCP labels dissenters "mentally ill" for detention; U.S. therapy mandates for "extremism" echo. Success: Strong domestically for CCP.

40. Discredit the family as an institution. Encourage promiscuity and easy divorce.

The CCP's one-child policy (1979-2015) deliberately weakened multi-generational family structures, fracturing family and kin networks, and state dependence. CCP social campaigns continue to promote state loyalty over familial bonds. In the U.S., no-fault divorce laws, normalized casual relationships, and gender-ideology movements erode traditional marriage stability, trends all amplified through CCP-linked cultural exports, entertainment partnerships, and academic influence. By reshaping values around family and sexuality, the CCP advances a model where the state, rather than the family, is central. Success: culturally well-embedded.

41. Emphasize the need to raise children away from the negative influence of parents. Attribute prejudices, mental blocks and retarding of children to suppressive influence of parents.

CCP youth indoctrination mirrors U.S. school-parent conflicts (e.g., CRT and gender-change privacy fights). Success: Increasing in education systems.

42. Create the impression that violence and insurrection are legitimate aspects of the American tradition; that students and special-interest groups should rise up and use "united force" to solve economic, political, or social problems.

The CCP amplifies U.S. riots (e.g., 2020) as "legitimate protest" via media; Antifa/BLM narratives fit. Success: Highly effective in destabilization.

43. Overthrow all colonial governments before native populations are ready for self-government.

The CCP backs revolutionary movements and coups across Africa, Asia, and the Pacific, supplying arms, ideological training, and diplomatic recognition to anti-colonial factions. They create political vacuums, fostering instability, authoritarianism, and economic dependency, conditions Beijing can exploit. Today, the Belt and Road Initiative (BRI) functions as a neo-colonial apparatus, extending Chinese control through debt-trap infrastructure deals, elite capture, and strategic port acquisitions. By filling governance gaps with CCP-friendly regimes and economic reliance, China sustains influence over critical resources and geopolitical choke points. Success: historically transformative, with ongoing leverage in multiple regions.

44. Internationalize the Panama Canal.

Handover to Panama in 1999; CCP now controls key ports via Hutchison, militarizing access. Success: Achieved, with CCP dominance.

45. Repeal the Connally Reservation so the U.S. cannot prevent the World Court from seizing jurisdiction over domestic problems. Give the World Court jurisdiction over nations and individuals alike.

The Connally Reservation restricts the International Court of Justice (ICJ) from ruling on U.S. domestic matters without consent. The CCP promotes universal jurisdiction within UN legal bodies, seeking to override such protections and subject both nations and individuals to external adjudication. Through diplomatic lobbying and alignment with Global South blocs, Beijing advances frameworks eroding U.S. legal sovereignty. Success: partial, with growing pressure in international forums to dilute reservation authority.

As you can see, the assault is systematic, focused, and relentless and the public - those who have not read these pages - is still asleep. As Haugland says:

> *"The reality is that Americans live in a make-believe sanctuary, a blissful bubble, that no longer exists. Our enemies understand and have exploited that blissful ignorance to advance their subversion from within. They have studied our government, military, laws, and governance and know how and where to unstitch the seams to exploit our vulnerabilities."*

The time to break that ignorance and reverse that subversion is now.

The biggest fear of our enemy is that you and the public will become informed of their strategy and take action. You now have the power. The next brief is the "next-steps outline" of your survival guide.

The Call to Consciousness

Thinking in first principles is hard.
Global systems are complex.
And when something affects us negatively,
our cognitive biases scream for simple answers.

But simple answers don't solve systemic problems.
Curiosity does.
Awareness does.
Critical thinking does.
Staying emotionally astute and intellectually open does.

You're going to need that level of consciousness to navigate what's coming next.

Before I close, I want to alert you to a danger - related - but coming from another direction. A senior UK Military advisor who asked to remain anonymous correctly observed:

The predators from above are as bad as external threats like the CCP. The oligarchs, who rule the world through their foundations, their money and usury, and the control of the financial system have their tentacles into pretty much every aspect of life. WHO, WEF, the UN, they also can impose what I consider the CCP model of total control through digital ID, currencies, surveillance, lockdown protocols and we are on our way to a restrictive social credit system ourselves. Eyes on everything you do, say, view online, post, or spend. Technology is now super-enabling them, allowing their evil tentacles to get much deeper. We're in real danger.

For example, in China now, under digital ID, digital currency, and extreme surveillance with AI, every move is tracked and controlled. As an example, you must spend your wages and savings within a fixed period (60 days at present) to save the economy or you simply lose that money. That's how the totalitarian CCP keeps "consumer spending" unnaturally high.

In the West, the CCP can only accomplish this once we've lost our mental and spiritual vitality to fight back against control for the top.

This truth has never been more true, as Thomas Jefferson eloquently stated: "the price of liberty is eternal vigilance." Therefore, know this and emblazon it on your heart:

Our freedoms cannot be taken from us. *We surrender them.*

Or, as Abraham Lincoln said, "If we falter and lose our freedoms, it will be because we destroyed ourselves."

Freedom is never free. We cannot surrender our freedom to those who promise "free" healthcare, college education, blanket debt forgiveness, or equality of results rather than opportunity, where resources and outcomes are forcibly equalized. Those pushing these goals are deceptive, trying to ensnare you with dazzling promises that can never be delivered but will deliver them to power - as history has proven 100%.

The enemy is inside our gates. They have been perfecting their destruction of America and the free world for decades. Infiltrating, subverting, stealing IP, brainwashing our citizens into "useful idiots" to cement their failed and diabolical ideology of socialism and communism towards complete takeover of the U.S. and free world. Every American and free world citizen must accept the mission to root out all anti-freedom enemies and their programs and deny them funding and an audience. Anti-freedom ideologies and movements must be banned with severe consequences in all free world societies. In fact, free speech must have underlying laws to guarantee free speech with the strong exception and ban of providing a platform for anti-freedom movements to destroy itself.

The day we understand and agree the right wing and the left wing are part of the same bird - one that wants to diminish or eliminate our freedoms - only then can America continue to soar.

We must come together as all freedom-loving humans with respect and dialogue against the existential enemies of our time. However difficult, we must prevail. We will prevail.

Freedom or totalitarian communism. It's your choice.
You are now informed. Choose a side now.

BRIEFING THIRTEEN
The Final Battle For The World

Your Citizen Survival Guide

"America is the final battlefield and you are a soldier."
~ T. Casey Fleming

The Path Forward

You are now awake in a sleeping world.

> *The dark factories of China, just like the Orcs and Trolls in Lord of the Rings, are working away with their forges and hammers, and they are doing it now as we sleepwalk into WWIII. The difference is that In previous wars, there were places in the world that could be safe havens. Lots of people ask me today, 'where should I go?' And I say, 'you don't get it. There will be nowhere to go. You either fight, or you're f****d. If we fall under what is truly the Dark Emperor, there will be nowhere to hide. We're looking at whether individuality and democracy are extinguished for hundreds or thousands of years. We're looking at the future of mankind, our souls, our beings, our beliefs. We are looking at a wave of darkness, and I think it is a terrible darkness we face.*
>
> *~ David Murrin*

As you have learned, the battle is not coming. The battle is already here. You didn't ask for this war. You didn't provoke it. You may not have even known it was happening. But the Chinese Communist Party has been waging unrestricted warfare against you, your family, your community, your economy, your freedom - for decades.

And here's the hardest truth you have to face, now that you are informed:

Your Government Isn't Going to Save You

Not because they don't want to. Not because they're incapable. But because they are significantly compromised, siloed and bureaucratic, financially motivated and willfully and often unknowingly blind - the U.S., Canada, UK, EU, Australia, right down the line.

The CCP's target isn't the White House or 10 Downing. They are targeting you.

The CCP isn't trying to conquer the Pentagon - yet. They're working to conquer your health, your wallet, your job, your mind, your children's education, your faith, your very will to value and stand up for your freedoms. They want to conquer us, but avoid a shooting war if they can.

Cognitive war. Economic war. Biological war. Drug war. Political war. Spiritual war: the artillery isn't landing in some distant battlefield. It is decimating your home, your financial future, your child's mind, your soul.

You.

Thomas Paine wrote in 1776, "These are the times that try men's souls. The summer soldier and the sunshine patriot will, in this crisis, shrink from the service of their country; but he that stands by it now, deserves the love and thanks of man and woman."

We are exactly in such a time now.

The difference is this: In 1776, you could see the redcoats coming. Muskets firing. Flags high. Drums beating. You could spot the enemy on the horizon.

Today, the enemy is largely invisible. The warfare is mostly silent. The invasion has arrived not with soldiers, but through cyber hacks, illicit drugs, supply chains, TikTok algorithms, bribes, pharmaceutical dependencies, and financial leverage. The CCP doesn't want to occupy all of American soil - yet. They want to own American minds, bodies, and futures.

The soil will follow.

And they're winning.

"It is now time to change those things we cannot accept."
~ T. Casey Fleming

Why This Section Exists

You've read the evidence. You've seen the strategy. You know the threat.

The question is no longer: "Is this happening?"

The question is: "What are YOU going to do about it?"

The power to stop this doesn't rest in Congress. It rests in you.

It rests in all of us, each citizen, and we must, as an American and global society, come together against our common enemy, overcome our differences, and bond together so we can fight as one. One team. One Fight.

It's time to take stock and unite. All Americans, and all free citizens, regardless of political beliefs:

1) have much more in common with each other than our enemy, and
2) share a common existential enemy.

As you will see below, your counter-offensive begins with how you vote with your wallet, your clicks, your choices, your voice.

The CCP has spent forty years waging unrestricted warfare against us using our own rules, our own freedoms and frankly, our own greed and open society as weapons. Now it's time to turn that asymmetry around.

"The path forward must be the pursuit of knowledge - reclaiming personal education, agency, critical thinking, and the power to own our minds and futures."
~ T. Casey Fleming

Courage to Face What's Coming

This brief is going to ask something difficult of you.

It's going to ask you, now that you've woken up, to stop living in denial. And to stop pretending that someone else, the government, the military, "the experts," is going to fix this for you. To lead.

It will take courage.

Courage to look at the world as it is, not as you wish it to be. Courage to admit we've been asleep while the enemy continues to advance.

Courage to change your habits, your purchases, your information sources, your routines. Courage to speak up when your friends, your family, your neighbors would rather stay comfortable and accuse you of "paranoia" or "conspiracy theory" or - worst of all - "racist China-phobia."

Thomas Paine didn't mince words in "Common Sense," saying, "The laying a country desolate with fire and sword, declaring war against the natural rights of all mankind... is the concern of every man to whom nature hath given the power of feeling."

The CCP has already laid waste to our industrial base, our pharmaceutical independence, our economic security, and the lives of hundreds of thousands of Americans through fentanyl and COVID-19.

If you have "the power of feeling," if you care about your family, your country, your freedom-then this is your fight.

What This Briefing Gives You

This is a *briefing of action.* You will find here:

- ☑ Economic survival steps - How to protect your Þnances, diversify away from CCP dependencies, and vote with your wallet.
- ☑ Supply chain independence - How to source American-made (or ally-made) products for everything from food to technology.
- ☑ Cognitive defense - How to protect your children from TikTok, your family from propaganda, and your mind from manipulation.
- ☑ Biological resilience - How to prepare for supply chain disruptions, pandemics, and stock up in case of infrastructure attacks like Volt Typhoon.
- ☑ Political engagement - How to pressure your elected ofÞcials, expose CCP inßuence, and demand accountability.
- ☑ Spiritual fortitude - How to resist demoralization, strengthen your faith, and rebuild the values that make us strong.
- ☑ Community action - How to organize locally, create resilience networks, and build a grassroots counter-offensive from the ground up.

This chapter is no longer in my hands: it's your field manual.

It's your checklist. Your playbook. Your personal call to arms - not with bullets, but with informed, coordinated, relentless citizen action.

The Choice Is Yours

In 1776, Thomas Paine wrote, "Tyranny, like hell, is not easily conquered; yet we have this consolation with us, that the harder the conflict, the more glorious the triumph."

The CCP blusters, but it is not invincible. They have vulnerabilities. They depend on our money, our technology, our markets, our compliance. Their population is significantly overstated and largely miserable and enslaved.

The moment we-you-stop feeding the monster, the balance shifts.

But it requires commitment and action. Not tomorrow. Not "when things get bad enough." Now.

The only question is: Will you stand and fight-or shrink from the service your family and country needs?

Consider this chapter as a brief introduction to the first stages of your role as a citizen in this "Whole of Society" fight.

Let's begin.

The Top 20 Basics for All American and Allied Citizens

1. **Get this survival guide and personal action plan in the hands of everyone you know** so they can be informed and on the same page. Stand behind it. Use it as a peace offering and tool for positive discussion with others who may see the world differently. Come together. Show compassion, grace, and kindness. After all, our enemy is committed to dividing us - *don't let yourself be played any longer.* We are all brothers and sisters *united in the same fight and share a common enemy who is set to destroy us.* Get this survival guide as mandatory reading in your family, extended family, colleagues, public and private schools, universities, and churches in the U.S. and worldwide. *A Rasmussen Reports and the Heartland Institute poll found 51% of young voters prefer democratic socialist [communist] in the 2028 White House.
2. **Display the American flag and allied flags at every opportunity:** your home (inside and out), business, apparel, car, backpack, luggage, websites - everywhere. Make it a proud, cultural icon again **- America 2.0.** This powerful symbol

not only unites us, it communicates our commitment to freedom, each other, and our allies.

3. **It begins in your house - not the White House. Champion a powerful renewal of America's moral, cultural, and spiritual values.** Regularly declare your family values, rights, faith, and freedom to your family and extended family - yes, the same ones grandma drove home. Document them in writing. Strongly place faith and God back into the center of yourself and your family. Lead by example.
4. **Important: Regularly write and demand state and federal lawmakers:**
    1) **Ban all foreign influence in the US and our allies:** All investments, purchases of companies and real estate, investments in technology and innovation, lobbying, media, protest and riot funding, campaign donations, non-profit donations, think tank funding, school and university donations, and more. *None of this is allowed in China. Why do we allow it here?*
    2) **Demand the country of manufacture and assembly to be displayed** on all products and product descriptions online.
    3) **Demand our representatives immediately begin decoupling our supply chain** from our enemy and replace it with staunch allies (the CCP has been decoupling from the US for the past 5 years to place China under "war footing")
    4) **Quadruple espionage and treason laws.** Include banning the use of all 'honeypots' (blackmail and control) by anyone on U.S. soil.
    5) **Ban Chinese students** (spies via required CCP loyalty pledge) from U.S. schools and universities.

6) **Demand an Electronic Bill of Rights (EBOR)** *led by an unbiased entity.* Note: This is only the beginning of what is required to unwind decades of vulnerability by tracking and exploiting citizens and their personal data by technology companies and the CCP. AI will accelerate these vulnerabilities.

5. **You are in ultimate control - not the government or business CEO's.**

   1) **You vote every day with your wallet and credit card.** If it plugs in, or an app, never trust it or buy any technology from China or Hong Kong. If you have a Chinese app, delete it. Yes, it also means TikTok - *regardless of who owns it.* Remember, you and your children survived without it before it hit the market. With respect to Chinese products, expect the CCP to claim other countries as the country of manufacture - since the CCP are masters at the shell game and plausible deniability. *U.S. internet and foreign apps are banned in China for a reason, why do we allow them here?*

   2) **Dutifully and regularly use your new knowledge and your right to vote to replace all those state, local, and federal representatives who act against protecting our freedom granted by our forefathers.**

6. ***Don't buy anything from China or Hong Kong*** **-** top of the list are all consumables, food, cosmetics, vape products, synthetic drugs, or clothing from China. That cute top, knockoff purse, cheap tool, or gadget is not worth directly funding your own destruction.

7. **Review all of your investments, pensions, and 401K's -** ensure they are not invested in China or Hong Kong. Check stocks, bonds, mutual funds, ETFs, and all investments.

8. **Regularly screen your media to include tested, trusted sources.** Many legacy media and social media are heavily

compromised with censorship, enemy misinformation, AI driven propaganda, and nefarious narrative. The news isn't about news anymore - instead of objectively reporting to all people - it's about protecting some people while destroying others. *If your media sources have not regularly discussed the content of this guide - ask yourself why - and find a new trusted sources.*

9. **Implement a dopamine reduction and anti-cognitive war campaign with your family. Do not allow the enemy to rob your child's mind and identity.** Each week, reduce today's current 7-9 hour screen time by an hour with the goal of no more than an hour each day reviewing content online. Replace screen time with social in-person activities, sports, outdoors, games, projects, and volunteering. Technology has been allowed to run rampant with no oversight for far too long. Again, exercise critical thinking. Stay vigilant, think critically, seek suppressed truth, and prepare in all areas for a world that may become increasingly hostile to dissent.
10. **Organize your community, serve on your school boards and local/state government. Continuously mentor our youth on our values and their importance.**
11. **Replace TP-Link routers, Kasa products, and other existing technology from China.** (See appendix)
12. **Harden your devices** (MFA, updates, backups, never use public Wi-Fi without a trusted VPN. Usually, free VPNs are disguised malware. *Nothing is free.*)
13. **Assume your smartphones, smart televisions, and cameras and mics are *always on sending your personal data to the CCP.*** This includes security cameras, baby monitors, and doorbell cameras. They can be turned on remotely, not showing they are on - even speakers can be reversed as mics. If it is connected to the internet or wi-fi, it is a vulnerability and can be easily hacked.

14. **Teach family members manipulation-recognition techniques** and regularly practice family critical-thinking skills.
15. **Be a citizen servant leader to ensure freedom. Train our youth to be citizen servant leaders. It matters now more than ever.**
16. **Advocate school, local, and national officials** for transparency in foreign funding and program disclosures.
17. **Volunteer time and donate** to local health, civic, or education resilience programs.
18. **Keep calm and verify with critical thinking** before amplifying crises or sensational claims - online or in person. If you feel rage, you're likely being manipulated.
19. **Stay alert and keep learning.** Build your own trusted network.
20. **Join FreedomForever.Global** - Keep ***The Red Tsunami*** active in your life with fellow Americans and our free allies in a shared community, with truth, updates, and actions for defending yourself and your family against your enemy. FreedomForever. Global gives a voice to the voiceless. Led by faith and freedom under the U.S. Constitution - America 2.0. Know the truth on top issues, where to vote during elections, and just as important - where to vote everyday with your wallet - so you don't continue to feed your enemy. A 501c3 tax deductible and non-profit membership organization for truth and protecting freedom. *(Note: in development at the time of printing).*

www.FreedomForever.Global

As President Ronald Reagan reminded us:

> *"Freedom is a fragile thing and it's never more than one generation away from extinction. It is not ours by way of inheritance; it must be fought for and defended constantly by each generation, for it comes only once to a people. And those in world history who have known freedom and then lost it have never known it again."*

And President John F. Kennedy's words have never rung more true:

> *"And so, my fellow Americans: Ask not what your country can do for you - ask what you can do for your country.*
>
> *"My fellow citizens of the world: Ask not what America will do for you - but what together we can do for the freedom of man."*

Whole of Society Response

To Counter CCP Drug War

A few of these actions that may have been mentioned previously are instrumental in a whole of society response.

1. Stay informed about local drug trends via public-health alerts and community coalitions.
2. Support and volunteer with local addiction-treatment and harm-reduction programs.
3. Carry and learn to use Narcan (naloxone) if you live or work in a community with opioid risk (follow local laws and training).
4. Safely dispose of unused prescription drugs at take-back events or secure drop boxes.
5. Teach youth and family members about the risks of illicit drugs and how to refuse offers. "One pill can kill."
6. Report suspicious trafficking activity to local law enforcement or anonymous tip lines.

7. Advocate for well-funded border and customs inspection resources and intelligence sharing.
8. Back community policing and cross-agency task forces focused on organized trafficking networks.
9. Support drug testing and toxicology capacity at local health departments and hospitals.
10. Promote treatment-first policies (expand access to care) - less demand reduces market leverage.
11. Push for transparent reporting on seizure data, source attribution, and public alerts.
12. If you encounter suspected contaminated drugs, avoid sharing sensational unverified claims - instead notify public-health authorities.

To Counter CCP Biological War

1. Keep record of vaccinations and/or routine public-health precautions current for you and your dependents.
2. Support funding and staffing for local public-health labs, surveillance, and rapid diagnostic capacity.
3. Report unusual clusters of illness to public-health authorities promptly.
4. Avoid spreading unverified disease rumors; share official updates and reputable sources.
5. Advocate for strict biosafety and biosecurity oversight of local research institutions and community labs.
6. Do not participate in or disseminate DIY biology experiments outside regulated environments; report suspicious biological activity.
7. Back policies that strengthen pathogen-research transparency, export controls, and international norms on biological weapons.
8. Keep a basic household emergency kit and family plan for natural or intentional public-health incidents.

9. Volunteer or support community resilience initiatives (senior outreach, care networks) that lessen vulnerability during health crises.
10. Support local training for healthcare workers in outbreak detection and PPE use.
11. Push elected officials to fund cross-jurisdictional incident response planning and public-health communications.

To Counter CCP Cyber War

1. **Fight for your Electronic Bill of Rights (EBOR)** managed by an *unbiased third party.* Every free person must protect their privacy and data (Data War). FreedomForever.Global will pursue and plan to lead EBOR.
   According to Rex M. Lee, technology executive and security advisor: "The Electronic Bill of Rights (EBOR) is a nonprofit cyber, civil, and human rights initiative grounded in a simple truth: human beings are moral agents endowed with freedom, free will, inherent dignity, and fundamental rights.

   History shows that when power concentrates - through religion, government, or markets - it tends toward coercion and abuse. To counter this, humanity created safeguards like the Magna Carta, constitutional governance, and the Bill of Rights. Written nearly 250 years ago, our original Bill of Rights could not anticipate the power and risk of modern technology. It must evolve.

   Today, unprecedented power is concentrated in data, AI, superintelligence, quantum computing, and global digital surveillance systems capable of shaping behavior, access, opportunity, and even truth at planetary scale.

   EBOR is *not anti-technology.* It is *pro-human.*

EBOR affirms human primacy by promoting AI, quantum, and digital systems that respect privacy, security, safety, consumer choice, civil liberties, and human rights. It calls on Big Tech and government to treat people as citizens with constitutional rights - not as products exploited through surveillance capitalism, monopolistic practices, and manipulative algorithms.

Without enforceable protections, these systems risk repeating history's worst abuses - this time encoded in software and scaled globally. Already, AI-driven platforms contribute to addictive, harmful, and sometimes deadly outcomes, with quantum computing poised to amplify these risks.

EBOR exists to ensure advanced digital systems:

- Align with human values
- Serve human well-being
- *Enhance freedom rather than replace it*
- Protect national security from foreign influence, surveillance, and data exploitation

EBOR establishes modern safeguards so technology remains a tool for human creativity, dignity, and freedom - never an instrument of control.

This is about:

- The future of freedom in the digital age
- Ensuring technology serves humanity - not the other way around

Demand *third-party managed* EBOR with your congressional representatives and technology providers."

2. Whenever you, your children, your grandchildren put a smartphone up to their face, *think of it as a loaded gun.*

Technology, apps, and algorithms have that level of permanent power against the brain.

3. Use your phone predominantly as a communication device and much less for content and news.
4. Always assume your smartphone, computer, and TV cameras and mic are on - even when the device is off. Smartphone signals can be blocked from espionage and surveillance via Faraday pouches.
5. Use strong, unique passwords and a reputable password manager.
6. Enable multi-factor authentication (MFA) on all accounts that offer it.
7. Keep devices, operating systems, and apps up to date with automatic security patches.
8. Back up important data offline or to an encrypted cloud backup.
9. Be skeptical of unsolicited emails, texts, or social-media messages - verify before clicking links or opening attachments.
10. Use privacy settings on social networks and limit oversharing of personal details.
11. Avoid conducting sensitive business on public Wi-Fi (including airports and hotels); use a trusted VPN at all times.
12. Avoid using charging kiosks at airports
13. Install and maintain reputable anti-malware/endpoint protections on personal devices.
14. Learn basic phishing indicators and run tabletop phishing exercises at work or with family.
15. Check app permissions periodically and uninstall unused or suspicious apps.
16. Prefer vetted, widely used hardware/software vendors for critical devices; avoid unknown, unsupported tech for sensitive tasks.

17. Support stronger national cyber-hygiene education programs and funding for local CERTs.
18. If you run an organization, require vendor security reviews and contract clauses for supply-chain integrity.

To Counter Cognitive War

1. Reduce screen time. The goal is to use your device for primarily communication. Be overly selective on your news. Don't let yourself or your family get caught up in disinformation or propaganda.
2. Follow multiple reputable news outlets across the political spectrum for corroboration.
3. Learn common manipulation techniques (emotional framing, false dichotomies, impersonation, bots) and teach them to family.
4. Use pre-bunking tools and short media-literacy games; run a short "manipulation of the week" at work or school.
5. Flag and report coordinated bot or troll activity to platform moderation teams.
6. Support local journalism and fact-checking organizations with subscriptions or donations.
7. Keep a browser extension or checklist for rapid source verification (reverse image search, URL checks).
8. Run group debriefs after encountering viral claims to decompress and verify collectively.
9. Teach kids and students critical thinking habits and how to evaluate social feeds.
10. Avoid amplifying unverified claims even when condemning them - link to official verification if available.
11. Advocate for platform transparency on political/ad targeting and for labelling state-linked media.

12. Participate in community resilience programs that teach recognition of influence operations.
13. Support public funding for inoculation/media-literacy programs in schools and libraries.
14. If you suspect targeted CCP influence in your community (e.g., espionage, repeated false narratives), report to civil-society watchdogs or appropriate government channels. Remember, when it comes to Chinese nationals who are often blackmailed and controlled by the CCP, as Xi Van Fleet says, altering Reagan's famous dictum "Trust, but verify." She adds, "I hate to say it but I don't trust Chinese people who I haven't known."

To Counter CCP Education War

1. Teach and demand critical thinking, source evaluation, and research literacy in local schools.
2. Support transparency around foreign funding and partnerships at local universities and K–12 programs.
3. Ask school boards and universities about disclosures for foreign gifts, Confucius-type programs, and research partnerships.
4. Encourage robust academic-freedom protections and open debate on campus.
5. Promote STEM and bioethics education that emphasizes safe, regulated research practices.
6. Volunteer as a guest lecturer or mentor to bring civic-minded perspectives into classrooms.
7. Push for clear policies on international student and researcher vetting tied to sensitive technologies.
8. Advocate for balanced exchange programs that include reciprocity, oversight, and cultural orientation.
9. Support open repositories and peer review to reduce stealth influence in scholarship.

10. Encourage libraries to curate reliable information resources and media-literacy workshops.
11. Back teacher training on spotting and countering foreign propaganda influences in curricula.
12. Demand public reporting of foreign program activities in K–12 and higher education.
13. Foster community science programs with strict safety norms and reporting lines.
14. Insist on ethical review boards for partnerships that could transfer sensitive capabilities.

To Counter CCP Economic War

1. Stop buying products made in China. End stop.
2. Buy local when feasible to reduce reliance on opaque foreign supply chains.
3. Diversify suppliers for small businesses; avoid single-source dependence on high-risk vendors.
4. Vet products for provenance and consider lifecycle/supply-chain transparency when purchasing.
5. Support policies that screen foreign investment in critical infrastructure and technologies.
6. Advocate for resilient stockpiles for key medical and industrial supplies at local and national levels.
7. Pressure elected officials for stronger export controls and enforcement on sensitive tech.
8. Encourage businesses to conduct due diligence on foreign ownership and funding sources.
9. Use market influence: favor companies with transparent supply chains and responsible sourcing.
10. Support workforce retraining programs to reduce economic leverage from foreign manufacturing shifts.

11. Report suspicious acquisition attempts in your community (land, ports, data centers) to local authorities.
12. Back cooperative regional purchasing and mutual aid agreements for critical goods.
13. Protect personal financial data: monitor accounts, freeze credit if targeted, and report scams.
14. Vote and lobby for trade policies that balance openness with strategic resilience. No China or Hong Kong.
15. If you run a business, require contractual security and audit clauses for foreign subcontractors.

To Counter Cultural War

First and foremost, I want to give a nod to my colleague, David Murrin, the Global Futurist with a message from London. Americans need to align efforts in a whole of nation response:

> *"Your civil war is actually making America weaker. Whatever differences you Americans have, you are going to get wiped out unless you bond and face this overwhelming enemy which will swamp every single choice we have. I urge a Reaganesque uniting America and every single ally into a tight framework that can compete with Chinese scale. So, first magnitude effect: stop fighting between yourself."*

1. *Participate in civic life: vote, attend town halls, and hold officials accountable* on foreign-influence issues.
2. Support community arts and cultural programs that celebrate local diversity and civic values.
3. Be skeptical of foreign-funded cultural initiatives; ask for transparent funding disclosures.
4. Report coordinated influence campaigns that appear to target local politics, civic institutions, and American values.

5. Promote open debate and pluralism - resist polarization that foreign actors exploit.
6. Encourage local media to investigate and report on foreign influence with evidence and transparency.
7. Back laws and policies requiring disclosure of foreign funding for political advertising and advocacy.
8. Teach and model respectful civic discourse to reduce polarization and exploitation.
9. Vet groups before donating to ensure they're locally accountable and transparent about funding.
10. Support watchdog NGOs monitoring foreign political influence and campaign finance.
11. If approached by a foreign interest with offers that could affect local politics, notify elections officials or ethics boards.
12. Push for school and library programs that contextualize foreign cultural content rather than uncritically accept it.
13. Encourage platforms and broadcasters to label state-sponsored or state-linked content.

To Counter CCP Religious and Spiritual War

1. Encourage houses of worship to require transparency on foreign donations and visiting speakers. No China, Russia, Iran, N. Korea. Pakistan.
2. Support interfaith networks that strengthen community cohesion and reduce exploitation risk.
3. Be alert to radical Islam (violent Islamist extremism) in local, state, and federal elections and vote those candidates out. It is their 'religious' duty to replace U.S. and allied government and law and replace it with Sharia Law. Radical Islam is not to be confused with peaceful Islam. (This is not racism, it's radical Islam's war against America and our allies.)
4. Teach congregations how to identify manipulation disguised as spiritual counsel or political messaging.

5. Audit and publicly list foreign funding for major religious or cultural projects where appropriate.
6. Promote community-based social services that reduce vulnerability to outside coercion.
7. Train faith leaders in basic digital hygiene and how to spot online influence targeting their communities.
8. Build partnerships between faith groups and local civic leaders to share alerts about manipulative campaigns.
9. Resist politicization of religion by external actors; prioritize pastoral care and community stability.
10. Offer workshops on media literacy and critical thinking for congregants.
11. Encourage reporting of coercive or deceptive recruitment tactics to law enforcement or community mediators.
12. Create emergency support networks within congregations for members targeted by outside pressure.
13. Advocate for legal transparency measures on foreign funding that respect religious freedom.
14. Ensure youth programs include curricula on consent, coercion, and influence recognition.

60-Day Plan to Counter the Red Tsunami: Phase 1

Here's a quick 60-Day "Cleanse" to begin doing your part.

This 60-day checklist distills the essentials into actionable steps to build personal, family, and community resilience against CCP influence across multiple fronts.

Phase 1 focuses on foundational habits and quick wins: securing your home and mindset, reducing economic dependencies, and fostering awareness without overwhelm. Aim to complete 1-2 items per week, tracking progress in a journal.

These basics lay the groundwork for deeper phases (e.g., Phase 2: Community Engagement and Phase 3: Advocacy and Innovation). Remember: Start small, stay consistent, and verify everything.

Core Daily/Weekly Habits (Days 1-15: Build Your Foundation)

- Display the American flag prominently at home, work, or in your community to symbolize unity and vigilance (e.g., on porches, desks, or social media profiles).
- Review and harden primary devices: Enable MFA on all accounts, install automatic updates, and create offline backups for photos/documents.
- Teach family members (or hold a 30-minute session with household/kids) basic manipulation-recognition techniques: Spot emotional framing, false dichotomies, or bots in news/ social media.
- Replace media input with trusted sources: Subscribe to 3-5 trusted sources across the spectrum (e.g., AP, Reuters, local outlets) and use a fact-check tool like Snopes or FactCheck. org daily.
- Sign up for local community emergency alerts (e.g., via FEMA app or city websites) and review/create a simple household emergency plan (e.g., evacuation routes, supplies for 72 hours).
- Get rid of TP-Link routers and replace them with U.S./allied brands; scan for other Chinese-made IoT devices (cameras, smart plugs) and unplug/uninstall.
- Keep calm and verify: Practice pausing 24 hours before sharing any crisis/sensational claim-cross-check with 2+ sources before amplifying.
- Share this guide (The Red Tsunami) with at least 20 people in your circle (family, friends, colleagues) and discuss one key takeaway together.
- Join "FreedomForever.Global" for community, ongoing support, and resources.

Economic and Supply Chain Essentials (Days 16-30: Cut Dependencies)

- Audit purchases: Commit to no new Chinese-made products-if it plugs in, is an app, or is consumable (food, clothing, that $17 top), avoid China/HK origins; opt for U.S., EU, or allied alternatives.
- Buy local or diversified: Shop at farmers' markets/small businesses for food/goods; use apps like Buycott to scan barcodes for supply chain origins.
- Protect financial data: Monitor bank/credit accounts weekly, freeze credit if concerned, and use strong/unique passwords with a manager (e.g., LastPass).
- Support resilient habits: Stock basic non-Chinese household essentials (e.g., 1-month supply of meds/tools from trusted sources) and encourage neighbors to do the same.
- For businesses/households: Review vendors for foreign risks; diversify suppliers and require transparency on sourcing.

Personal Security and Health Basics (Days 31-45: Safeguard Body and Mind)

- Counter Drug-Warfare: Stay informed via local public-health alerts; learn naloxone use (if in opioid-risk area) through free training; safely dispose of unused meds at take-back events.
- Counter Biological-Warfare: Update vaccinations for yourself/family; build a basic emergency kit (water, non-perishables, masks); report unusual illness clusters to health authorities.
- Counter Cyber-Warfare: Install reputable anti-malware (e.g., Malwarebytes); avoid public Wi-Fi for sensitive tasks-use a VPN (e.g., ExpressVPN); run a family phishing awareness drill.
- Counter Cognitive-Warfare: Pause before sharing provocative content; install a browser extension (e.g., NewsGuard) for

source verification; teach kids one critical-thinking habit (e.g., "Who's behind this?").

- Counter Education Warfare: Discuss foreign influence in schools with your kids/teachers; demand transparency on funding (e.g., Confucius Institutes) via emails to school boards.
- Counter Religious/Spiritual Warfare: If in a faith community, encourage transparency on foreign donations; join or support interfaith networks for cohesion.

Civic and Community Actions (Days 46-60: Engage Locally)

- Get involved locally: Attend a school board or town hall meeting; volunteer/donate to a health, civic, or education program (e.g., literacy workshops, addiction support).
- Advocate for transparency: Contact school/local/national officials about foreign funding disclosures (e.g., in education, research, or cultural events).
- Counter Cultural Warfare: Participate in local civic events (vote, town halls); support arts/programs celebrating American values; report suspicious foreign-funded initiatives to watchdogs.
- To All Fronts: Report any suspicious activity (trafficking, hacks, influence ops) to authorities (local police, FBI tip line, CISA); back policies for border inspections, media literacy in schools, and supply-chain resilience.
- Reflect and unite: As David Murrin urges from London, bond with allies-host a discussion on reducing internal divisions to face external threats; promote respectful discourse to avoid exploitation.
- Measure progress: At day 60, review your checklist, share successes with your network, and plan Phase 2 (e.g., deeper advocacy like pushing for export controls or community training).

This Phase 1 checklist empowers you to reclaim control in 60 days, turning awareness into action. This is the foundation of your freedom. For Phase 2 and beyond, join FreedomForever.Global.

We need you. We need each other.

BRIEFING FOURTEEN

A New Vocabulary For A New World

"You've got two options. You can keep living in your little pink rose cloud, and believe me, the thing in your darkest mind you know is going to come true will come true - and eat you alive. Or you can face your fears, you can face this enemy, you can join together, and have a chance. Which option do you choose?"
~ David Murrin

The world has changed.
The old Cold War with the Soviet Union has given way to the new, "all aspect" Unrestricted War of the CCP. There existed an old vocabulary that every informed citizen needed to know in order to understand the geopolitics of the day. But to truly understand the seismic shift where we are now confronting China's strategy of Unrestricted Warfare, where war is not declared, and every domain of life is weaponized, every free citizen needs to understand the new vocabulary of the new world.

1. **Anarcho-tyranny**: A system in which the state wields harsh power against the innocent while failing or refusing to use that power to perform basic duties like maintaining safety. In anarcho-tyranny, authorities neglect to punish real criminals yet criminalize the law-abiding, producing a mix of near-anarchy and selective tyranny. The result is a regime that violates the rights of ordinary citizens while using punishment of the

non-compliant as its central aim with the goal of to enforce conformity and obedience among the innocent (control), not to stop crime or uphold justice.

2. **Anarchy**: A state of disorder due to absence or nonrecognition of authority or other controlling systems.
3. **Anomie**: A state of social instability resulting from the erosion or breakdown of societal norms, values, and cohesion, often exploited by adversaries to create division. Unlike the Cold War's ideological battles that reinforced binary loyalties (e.g., democracy vs. communism), today's anomie is amplified by disinformation and cultural fragmentation, making societies more vulnerable to external manipulation without overt conflict.
4. **Assassin's Mace (Shashoujian):** Originating from ancient Chinese military lore in texts like the "Unorthodox Strategies" (ca. 2nd century BCE), the term refers to a hidden weapon, symbolizing a surprise, lethal strike from an underdog. In modern People's Liberation Army (PLA) doctrine, it refers to asymmetric warfare tools: secret, high-tech capabilities designed to exploit vulnerabilities in a superior enemy's forces, such as cyber warfare. The strategy emphasizes rapid, paralyzing effects to "cripple" overmatch (e.g., U.S. military superiority) without direct confrontation, reflecting Sun Tzu's principles of indirect victory.
5. **Belt and Road Initiative (BRI):** China's global infrastructure investment program, launched in 2013, which expands economic influence through loans and projects in over 150 countries. Unlike Cold War aid programs (e.g., Marshall Plan), it often creates debt dependencies, enabling strategic leverage without military occupation.
6. **Cognitive Warfare:** The use of information and psychological operations to shape perceptions, beliefs, and decision-making at a societal level. This evolves beyond Cold War propaganda

(e.g., Radio Free Europe) into AI-driven, targeted manipulation via social media, making "hearts and minds" battles more pervasive and subtle.

7. **Liminal:** Relating to a sensory threshold: barely perceptible or capable of eliciting a response. (Eg. Unrestricted War).
8. **Cloward-Piven Strategy:** A 1966 political theory by sociologists Richard Cloward and Frances Fox Piven, proposing mass overload of welfare systems to create a fiscal crisis and force implementation of guaranteed income programs. In modern geopolitical contexts, it's invoked as a blueprint for internal destabilization through policy-induced chaos, contrasting with Cold War external subversion tactics by emphasizing domestic economic saturation to erode self-reliance and institutional trust.
9. **Colonization of the Mind:** A strategy to infiltrate and reshape cultural, educational, and intellectual spaces to align foreign narratives with local populations. Distinct from Cold War ideological exports (e.g., communism vs. capitalism), it focuses on long-term memetic (idea-based) domination through media, academia, and tech platforms, psychologically manipulating beliefs and perceptions.
10. **Comprehensive National Power (CNP):** A Chinese strategic framework that quantifies a nation's total strength by measuring all sources of power-military, economic, technological, political, diplomatic, cultural, and informational-rather than focusing solely on defense capabilities. China uses CNP as an analytical tool to assess both its own position and its competitors' weaknesses across every dimension of national capability. This holistic approach allows China to identify non-military vulnerabilities in adversaries and systematically actively exploit them through coordinated campaigns that integrate economic warfare, technology dominance, information operations, and

political influence, all while staying below the threshold of traditional armed conflict.

11. **Cultural Marxism:** The strategic infiltration of cultural institutions-such as education, media, and arts-to transform societal values toward collectivism and away from traditional individualism. This differs from Cold War cultural diplomacy (e.g., U.S. exports of Hollywood films), as it operates covertly within domestic spheres to undermine from within, blending ideological subversion with modern influence operations.
12. **Debt-Trap Diplomacy:** A tactic where loans for infrastructure lead to economic dependency, allowing creditors (e.g., China) to gain control over assets or policy. This contrasts with Cold War economic aid, which was often grants or low-interest loans without such coercive strings attached.
13. **Deep State:** Entrenched networks of bureaucrats, intelligence officials, and political elites operating beyond democratic oversight to influence policy. In the post-Cold War era, this concept highlights how internal U.S. structures can be perceived as complicit in or resistant to addressing hybrid threats, unlike the era's more transparent containment bureaucracies focused on external enemies.
14. **Democratic Socialism:** A new name to soften socialism and communism so that it can be more easily absorbed by the public.
15. **Digital Pearl Harbor:** Metaphor from 1990s U.S. security warnings, coined by Richard Clarke and the 1998 President's Commission on Critical Infrastructure Protection, likening cyber surprises to the 1941 Pearl Harbor attack. It envisions a massive, state-sponsored cyber assault crippling infrastructure-like power grids and finance-without physical violence, causing economic ruin and chaos. Emphasizes digital vulnerabilities

as asymmetric weapons, urging cyber defenses to avert "bloodless" devastation and global fallout.

16. **Elite Capture:** Buying, bribing, or compromising Western elites, executives, and politicians.
17. **Gaslighting:** Psychological manipulation tactics designed to make individuals or groups doubt their own memories, perceptions, or sanity, often through repeated denial or misdirection. Building on Cold War-era disinformation, it now thrives in digital spaces (e.g., state-sponsored bots), eroding trust in institutions and facts on a personal and societal scale.
18. **Gray Zone Warfare:** Conflict strategies operating in the ambiguous space between peace and open war, employing non-traditional methods like cyber intrusions, economic coercion, and proxy actions to achieve objectives without triggering full-scale response. This expands beyond Cold War proxy wars (e.g., Vietnam), allowing sustained pressure through deniable means in multi-domain environments.
19. **Hybrid Warfare:** The integration of conventional military, irregular tactics, cyber attacks, disinformation, and economic pressure in a seamless campaign. Unlike the Cold War's clear distinction between hot wars and espionage, hybrid approaches (e.g., Russia's in Ukraine) blur lines to avoid escalation into kinetic war while achieving strategic goals.
20. **Information Warfare:** The strategic use of information and communication technologies to disrupt, deceive, or dominate adversaries, encompassing cyber attacks, propaganda, and data manipulation. This surpasses Cold War information efforts (e.g., jamming broadcasts) by weaponizing the internet for real-time, global-scale operations that target both military and civilian domains.
21. **Inversion Matrix:** A conceptual framework in modern information warfare where adversaries flip narratives to portray

themselves as victims and the opponent as aggressors (e.g., inverting "democracy promotion" into "imperialism"). This builds on Cold War psychological ops but leverages digital echo chambers for rapid, global-scale inversion.

22. **Invisible Invasion:** Demographic, cultural, personnel, infrastructure, and economic penetration replacing tanks and infantry.
23. **Little Green Men:** Soldiers who show up without flags, patches, or names. They stir chaos, grab land, and intimidate locals while their government denies they even exist. It's an invasion on the sly.
24. **Lawfare:** The weaponization of legal systems, international courts, and regulatory proceedings to constrain adversaries, harass opponents, or advance strategic goals. Contrasting with Cold War legal diplomacy (e.g., treaty negotiations), it now includes adversarial use of U.S. courts or global bodies to tie down resources without kinetic action.
25. **Mass Formation Psychosis:** A collective psychological phenomenon where large populations enter a trance-like state of heightened suggestibility, becoming susceptible to manipulative narratives amid anxiety or isolation. In today's context, it differs from Cold War mass mobilization (e.g., anti-communist campaigns) by exploiting social media echo chambers for rapid, organic spread of adversarial influence.
26. **Memetic Warfare:** The deployment of internet memes, viral content, and cultural symbols as tools for psychological and ideological influence, spreading ideas like viruses to shape opinions. This is a digital evolution from Cold War leaflets and posters, enabling low-cost, decentralized attacks that bypass traditional media gatekeepers.
27. **Narrative Control:** The coordinated management of public discourse through media, influencers, and algorithms to

dominate perceptions and suppress counter-narratives. Unlike Cold War state media battles (e.g., Voice of America vs. Pravda), it involves state and non-state actors vying for control in fragmented, user-driven online ecosystems.

28. **Progressive / Progressivism:** Communism
29. **Psychological Operations (PsyOps):** Planned operations to influence target audiences' emotions, motives, and behaviors through selected information and actions. While rooted in Cold War tactics (e.g., leaflet drops in Korea), modern PsyOps integrate AI and social engineering for precision targeting, extending beyond battlefields to everyday civilian life.
30. **Salami-slicing:** Tactics that are the death by a thousand cuts. One small slice of land here, one tiny "policy change" there. Each step looks too minor to risk a fight - but stack them together and you wake up one morning and realize half your house is gone.
31. **Sharp Power:** Coercive influence operations that manipulate information ecosystems and civil society abroad, often through state-backed media or proxies. It differs from Cold War "soft power" (e.g., cultural diplomacy like jazz tours) by being more authoritarian and disruptive, aiming to undermine rather than attract.
32. **Soft Power:** The ability to shape preferences and behaviors through attraction, culture, and values rather than coercion or payment. Coined post-Cold War, it contrasts with the era's hard power focus (e.g., military alliances) by emphasizing appeal in today's interconnected world, though adversaries often mimic it for deceptive ends.
33. **Strategic Corruption:** The deliberate and systematic undermining of institutions through corrupt practices to weaken governance and sow discord. This goes beyond Cold War espionage (e.g., bribery of officials) into orchestrated campaigns

that exploit economic ties, eroding trust in democracies from within.

34. **Three Warfares:** A unified doctrine taught by China's People's Liberation Army (PLA) since 2003, integrating psychological warfare (to shape perceptions and morale), public-opinion warfare (to influence media narratives and societal views), and legal warfare (to leverage laws and international norms for advantage), all designed to bend an adversary's will without firing a shot. This non-kinetic strategy contrasts with Cold War's emphasis on military deterrence and propaganda, by enabling peacetime dominance through tools like global platforms (e.g., youth-dominated video apps with opaque algorithms, such as TikTok), which amplify subtle influence on a massive scale.
35. **Tyranny:** Cruel and oppressive government or rule.
36. **United Front:** The Chinese Communist Party's strategy to co-opt and mobilize overseas allies, diaspora communities, and organizations for influence without direct confrontation. In contrast to Cold War front organizations (e.g., communist parties), it emphasizes infiltration of elites, businesses, and institutions for subtle alignment, achieving political or ideological objectives across multiple domains.
37. **Unrestricted Warfare:** A 1999 Chinese military doctrine (from the book by Qiao Liang and Wang Xiangsui) advocating conflict across all domains-economic, cyber, legal, and cultural-without traditional battlefield limits. This marks a shift from the Cold War's focus on symmetric military parity to asymmetric, "non-war" disruptions involving non-traditional, multi-dimensional conflict methods.
38. **Useful Idiot:** A person who believes they are fighting for a cause without fully comprehending the consequences of their actions, and who does not realize they are being manipulated by the cause's leaders. The term was often used during the

Cold War to describe non-communists regarded as susceptible to communist propaganda and psychological manipulation.

39. **Weaponization of Everything:** Xi Jinping's phrase from 2013 speeches on "civil-military fusion," expanding warfare to encompass all societal domains-supply chains, apps, universities, media, AI-as integrated tools for national security and geopolitical dominance. China's holistic strategy, blurring civilian-military lines to weaponize economic interdependence, information flows, and innovation against rivals, seeks to weaponize everyday elements into asymmetric advantages in hybrid conflicts.
40. **Whole-of-Society Warfare:** A comprehensive mobilization of government, private sector, civil society, and individuals to counter threats, often used by adversaries like China to integrate economic and social levers. This expands beyond the Cold War's "whole-of-government" military focus (e.g., containment policy) into a total societal competition.

This list provides a framework for understanding complex modern strategies of cultural and political influence that differ significantly from Cold War-era tactics.

Appendix I
Top Methods of Unrestricted War

No	Method
1	Biological War
2	Drug War
3	Cognitive War
4	Cyber War
5	Education War
6	Economic War
7	Political War
8	Culture War
9	Religious War
10	Spiritual War
11	Technology War
12	Data War
13	Algorithmic War / AI, Quantum, Digital Superintelligence *(exponential threat that multiples all other methods)*
14	Social Media War
15	Psychological War
16	Propaganda War
17	Narrative War
18	Subversion War

No	Method
19	Legal War / Lawfare
20	Trade War
21	Supply Chain War
22	Rare Earth Mineral War
23	Financial War
24	Resource War
25	Ideological War
26	Espionage / Intelligence War
27	Critical Infrastructure War
28	Telecommunications War
29	Agriculture War
30	Food War
31	DarkNet War
32	Terrorist War
33	Space War | EMP War / Direct Energy War
34	Drone War
35	Kinetic / Conventional War *(final stage, if required)*
36	Nuclear War
37	Anything / Everything War

THEREDTSUNAMI.COM

Appendix II
Top CCP Brands To Avoid

THE RED TSUNAMI

TOP CCP BRANDS TO AVOID

EVERY DOLLAR, EURO, OR POUND SPENT ON CCP BRANDS IS FUNDING YOUR ENEMY'S PLAN TO DESTROY YOU. ALWAYS CHECK WHERE THE PRODUCT IS MANUFACTURED. CHINESE APPS ARE SENDING YOUR DETAILED PERSONAL DATA TO THE CCP. REMEMBER: FOUR OUT OF FIVE OF THE MOST DOWNLOADED APPS ARE CCP ORIGINATED.

No	Brand	Notes
1	TikTok	Regardless of ownership, these five apps have China/CCP coding, servers, and encryption keys. Watch: "Temu & SHEIN Just Got Destroyed..." http://www.youtube.com/watch?v=vHOicQFITG0
2	Zoom	
3	SHEIN	
4	Temu	
5	CapCut	
6	DH Gate	
7	Alibaba	
8	JD.com	
9	TP-Link / Kasa	
10	Huawei	
11	Xiaomi	
12	ZTE	
13	Goertek	
14	Oppo	
15	Tencent	
16	DeepSeek AI	
17	WeChat	
18	QQ.com	
19	Baidu	
20	TCL	*TVs, Monitors*
21	Lenovo	*Computers, laptops*
22	Haier	*Appliances*
23	Hisense	*Appliances*
24	Hikvision	*Surveillance cameras*
25	DJI	*Drones*

THEREDTSUNAMI.COM

THE RED TSUNAMI

TOP CCP BRANDS TO AVOID

No	Brand	Notes
26	Sheglam	*Cosmetics*
27	Luckin Coffee	Coffee shops, coffee
28	Lilith Games	*Video Games*
29	Genshin Impact	*Video Games*
30	Black Myth	*Video Games*
31	PUBG Mobile	*Video Games*
32	Call of Duty: Mobile	*Video Games*
33	Honkai: Star Rail	*Video Games*
34	BYD	*Automobiles*
35	Nio	*Automobiles*
36	Insta 360	*Cameras*
37	Pop Mart	Blind Boxes
38	Bluetti	
39	Anker	*Chargers, electronics*
40	CASETiFY	*Phone Cases*
41	Creality	*3D Printers*
42	NetEase	*Media & Entertainment*
42	EcoFlow	*Portable Power Stations, solar panels*
43	Florasis	*Cosmetics*
44	SmallRig	*Video and photo accessories*
45	FlowerKnows	*Cosmetics*
46	Zeelool	*Eyewear*
47	Lilysilk	*Bedding, silk pillowcases, sleep masks*
48	Rolife, ROKR, MewooFun	*Toys*
49	Coofandy, Ekouaer, Avidlove, Ancheer	*Apparel*
50	UGREEN	*Data Cables, chargers, adapters*

THEREDTSUNAMI.COM

TOP CCP BRANDS TO AVOID

No	Brand	Notes
51	AnyCubic	*3D Printers, Filament*
52	Ecovacs, Foodom	*Robot Vacuum Cleaners*
53	Elegoo	*3D Printers*
54	Commense	*Apparel, dresses, tops, bottoms*
55	Cupshe	*Apparel, swimwear*
56	ChicMe	*Apparel, women's*
57	Halara	*Apparel, women's*
58	VIVAIA	*Shoes*
59	Midea	*Appliances, HVAC systems, robots*
60	Momcozy, Babycozy	*Maternity products, diapers, wipes*
61	CFMOTO, ZEEHO	*EV Motorcycles, ATVs*
62	CHiQ	*Electronics, TVs, Refrigerators, A/C*
63	JAC Motors, Refine, Heyue	*Trucks, buses, cars, EVs*
64	Jeulia	*Jewelry*
65	Shokz	*Bone headphones, earbuds*
66	Alper	*Robotic pool cleaners*
67	Unice	*Hair Extensions*
68	Govee	*LED, Smart lighting*
69	Qihoo 360	*360 Security Software, Antivirus,* ***Malicious***
70	Ohuhu	*Marker Pens*
71	PatPat	*Maternity & Child products*
72	Cider	*Clothing*
73	VeSync	*Smart appliances, Smart home*
74	Deerma	*Small appliances*
75	Telegram	*CCP Axis: Russian Messaging App*

Source: https://pandayoo.com/top-50-companies-brands-from-china-you-need-to-know/
Infographic: Kantar Brands, Londonhttps://www.kantar.com/campaigns/brandz/china

THEREDTSUNAMI.COM

Appendix III
Global Brands Made or Assembled in China

Item	Company
Smartphones, Tablets	*Apple, Samsung, Google Pixel*
Laptops, PCs	*Lonovo, Dell, HP, Apple MacBooks*
Smart TVs	*Samsung, Sony, TCL, Hisense*
Smart Home Devices	*Amazon Echo, Google Nest, Apple HomePod, Kasa, Xiaomi smart speakers, smart lights, IoT appliances*
Security Cameras & Video doorbells	*Ring (Amazon), Arlo, Hikvision, Dahua*
Network Equipment	*Cisco, Netgear, TP-Link, Huawei Routers, Switches*
Wearables	*Apple Watch, Fitbit, Xiaomi Mi Band, Samsung Glaxy Watch, Goertek, OEM Devices*
Audio Devices	*Bose, JBL, Sony headphones, speakers, Anker Audio*
Gaming Consoles & Accessories	*Sony PlayStation, Microsoft Xbox, Lenovo Legion gaming laptops, peripherals*
Chargers, Accessories	*Anker, Belkin, Apple chargers, cables*
Drones, Imaging Devices	*DJI, GoPro*
Robotic Vacuum Cleaners	*iRobot, Roborock, Ecovacs*
Smart appliances	*Samsung & LG refrigerators, washing machines, ovens (with smart connectivity)*
Monitors, Displays	*Dell, HP, Lenovo*
Storage Devices	*Western Digital, Seagate external drives*
Autos	*Buick Envision, Lincoln Nautilus, Volvo EX30 and S90, Polestar 2 and 3*

SOURCE: Janie Sun Research

THEREDTSUNAMI.COM

Appendix IV
Major U.S. Companies with Chinese Ownership

Company
Smithfield foods
GE Appliances / Haier
Motorola Mobility
AMC Theatres
Nexteer Augomotive
Waldorf Astoria - NYC
Legendary Entertainment / Wanda Group
Strategic Hotels & Resorts
Cirrus Aircraft
Ingram Micro
Henneges Automotive
245 Park Avenue - NYC
Hytera Communications
Inspur Group
Riot Games
Karma Automotive
Terrafugia
Milwaukee Tools
Rockwell Tools
Work Tools

SOURCE:
https://businessday.ng/world/article/here-are-13-major-u-s-companies-under-chinese-ownership/
https://bigedition.com/msn/us-companies-china-owned
https://www.slashgear.com/1896136/tools-brands-owned-chinese-companies/

THEREDTSUNAMI.COM

Appendix V
Espionage and Blackmail (Exercise Extreme Caution)

ANYTHING AND EVERYTHING CAN BE WEAPONIZED.
FOR INSTANCE, WE OFTEN FOCUS ON NEW TECHNOLOGIES BEFORE REALIZING HOW THEY CAN AND OFTEN ARE **WEAPONIZED AGAINST US.**

EVERY TECHNOLOGY IS A DOUBLE-EDGED SWORD:
EACH HAS A POSITIVE SIDE FOR WHICH IT WAS DESIGNED, BUT ALSO A POTENTIAL DARK SIDE IN THE ENEMY'S HANDS.
THE FOLLOWING SITES AND LOCATIONS REQUIRE ADDITIONAL CAUTION BASED ON REPORTS OF ESPIONAGE AND BLACKMAIL.

Location
LinkedIn
Facebook
Jobs / Employment Boards
Gaming Apps and their chatrooms
Dating Apps
Conferences
Public Wi-Fi - Including malls, coffee shops, restaurants, bars, hotels & airports
University Events
Restaurants and Bars

THEREDTSUNAMI.COM

Appendix VI
How to Review the News Like a Strategist

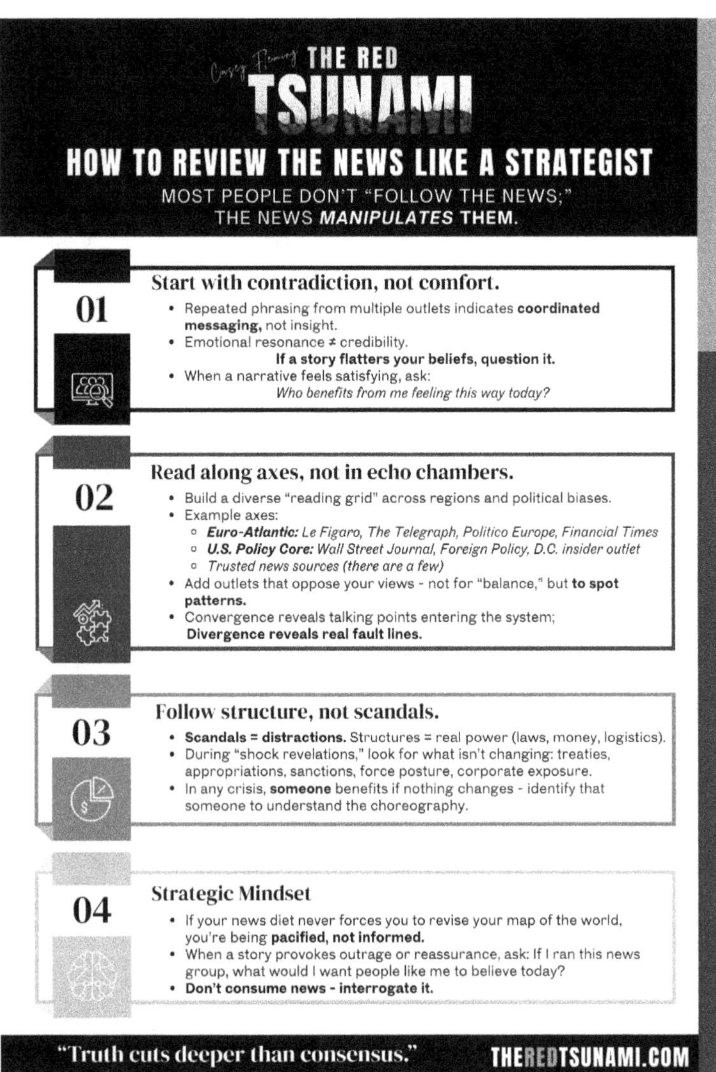

Appendix VII
The Ultimate Cheatsheet for Critical Thinking

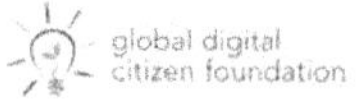

The Ultimate Cheatsheet for Critical Thinking

Want to exercise critical thinking skills? Ask these questions whenever you discover or discuss new information. These are broad and versatile questions that have limitless applications!

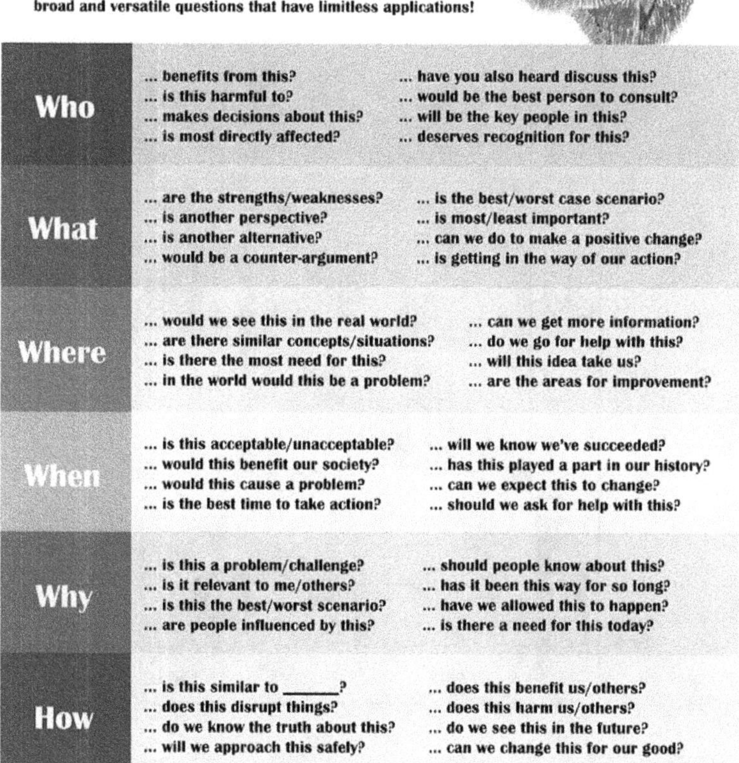

Who	... benefits from this? ... is this harmful to? ... makes decisions about this? ... is most directly affected?	... have you also heard discuss this? ... would be the best person to consult? ... will be the key people in this? ... deserves recognition for this?
What	... are the strengths/weaknesses? ... is another perspective? ... is another alternative? ... would be a counter-argument?	... is the best/worst case scenario? ... is most/least important? ... can we do to make a positive change? ... is getting in the way of our action?
Where	... would we see this in the real world? ... are there similar concepts/situations? ... is there the most need for this? ... in the world would this be a problem?	... can we get more information? ... do we go for help with this? ... will this idea take us? ... are the areas for improvement?
When	... is this acceptable/unacceptable? ... would this benefit our society? ... would this cause a problem? ... is the best time to take action?	... will we know we've succeeded? ... has this played a part in our history? ... can we expect this to change? ... should we ask for help with this?
Why	... is this a problem/challenge? ... is it relevant to me/others? ... is this the best/worst scenario? ... are people influenced by this?	... should people know about this? ... has it been this way for so long? ... have we allowed this to happen? ... is there a need for this today?
How	... is this similar to ______? ... does this disrupt things? ... do we know the truth about this? ... will we approach this safely?	... does this benefit us/others? ... does this harm us/others? ... do we see this in the future? ... can we change this for our good?

globaldigitalcitizen.org

Appendix VIII
Roadmap to Final Totalitarian State

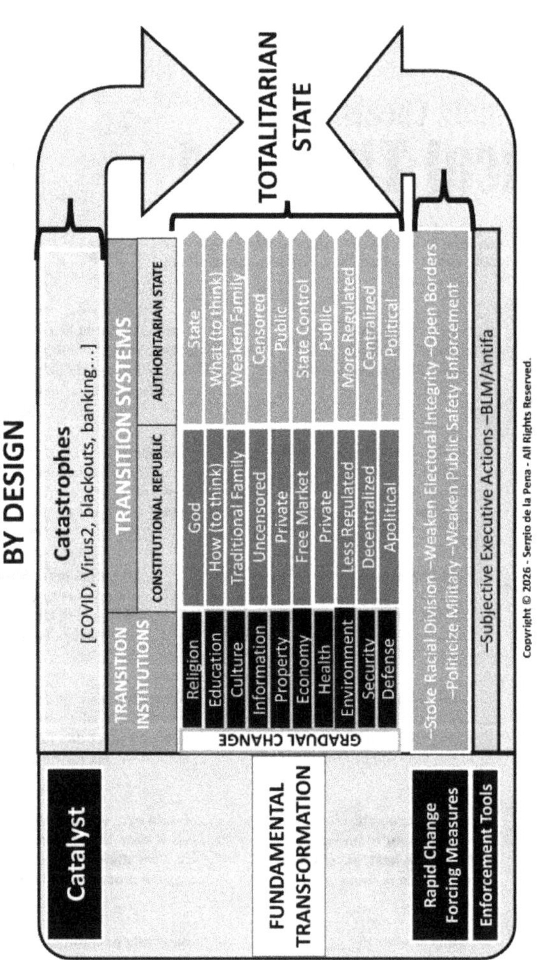

Source: Sergio de la Pena, COL., United States Army (ret.), Former Deputy Assistant Secretary of Defense for Western Hemisphere Affairs (2026).

Further Reading

1. Blackwill, Robert D., and Ashley J. Tellis. Revising U.S. Grand Strategy Toward China. New York: Council on Foreign Relations Press, 2015.
2. Bloom, Allan. The Closing of the American Mind. New York: Simon & Schuster, 1987.
3. Brady, Anne-Marie. Magic Weapons: China's Political Influence Activities under Xi Jinping. New York: Routledge, 2023.
4. D'Souza, Dinesh. The Roots of Obama's Rage. Washington, D.C.: Regnery Publishing, 2010.
5. Easton, Ian. The Chinese Invasion Threat: Taiwan's Defense and American Strategy in Asia. Arlington, VA: Project 2049 Institute, 2018.
6. Economy, Elizabeth C. The Third Revolution: Xi Jinping and the New Chinese State. Oxford: Oxford University Press, 2018.
7. Economy, Elizabeth C. The World According to China: How China Sees the World and How It's Changing It. Cambridge, UK: Polity Press, 2022.
8. Economy, Elizabeth C., and Michael Levi. By All Means Necessary: How China's Resource Quest Is Changing the World. New York: Oxford University Press, 2014.
9. Fanell, James E., and Bradley A. Thayer. *Embracing Communist China: America's Greatest Strategic Failure.* Washington, D.C.: Encounter Books, 2024.
10. Freire, Paulo. Pedagogy of the Oppressed. New York: Bloomsbury, 1970.
11. Gertz, Bill. Deceiving the Sky: Inside Communist China's Drive for Global Supremacy. New York: Encounter Books, 2021.

12. Gill, Bates. Daring to Struggle: China's Global Ambitions under Xi Jinping. Oxford: Oxford University Press, 2021.
13. Gottfried, Paul. After Liberalism: Mass Democracy in the Managerial State. Princeton, NJ: Princeton University Press, 1999.
14. Halper, Stefan. The Beijing Consensus: How China's Authoritarian Model Will Dominate the Twenty-First Century. New York: Basic Books, 2019.
15. Haugland, Edward. The Cognitive War: Why We Are Losing and How We Can Win. (Independently Published). 2023.
16. Horowitz, David. The Professors: The 101 Most Dangerous Academics in America. Washington, D.C.: Regnery Publishing, 2006.
17. Hung, Ho-Fung. China and the Transformation of Global Capitalism. Baltimore: Johns Hopkins University Press, 2016.
18. Jekielek, Jan, Killed to Order: China's Organ Harvesting Industry and the True Nature of America's Biggest Adversary. New York: Skyhorse Publishing, 2026.
19. Kissinger, Henry. On China. New York: Penguin Press, 2011.
20. Kurtz, Stanley. Radical-in-Chief: Barack Obama and the Untold Story of American Socialism. New York: Threshold Editions, 2010.
21. Nathan, Andrew J., and Andrew Scobell. China's Search for Security. New York: Columbia University Press, 2012.
22. Navarro, Peter, and Greg Autry. Death by China: Confronting the Dragon—A Global Call to Action. Upper Saddle River, NJ: Pearson Education, 2011.
23. Pei, Minxin. China's Crony Capitalism: The Dynamics of Regime Decay. Cambridge, MA: Harvard University Press, 2016.
24. Pipes, Richard. Communism: A History. New York: Modern Library, 2001.
25. Radosh, Ronald, and Joyce Milton. The Rosenberg File: A Search for the Truth. New Haven, CT: Yale University Press, 1997.

26. Schell, Orville, and John Delury. Wealth and Power: China's Long March to the Twenty-first Century. New York: Random House, 2013.
27. Schell, Orville, and John Delury. Wealth and Power: China's Long March to the Twenty-first Century. New York: Random House, 2013.
28. Shambaugh, David. China Goes Global: The Partial Power. Oxford: Oxford University Press, 2013.
29. Shirk, Susan L. China: Fragile Superpower. New York: Oxford University Press, 2007.
30. Ward, Jonathan D. T. China's Vision of Victory. Durham, NC: Atlas Publishing and Media Company, 2019.
31. Wurmbrand, Richard. Karl Marx and the Satanic Roots of Communism. Bartlesville, OK: Living Sacrifice Book Company, 1976.
32. Xi Van Fleet. Mao's America: A Survivor's Warning. New York: Center Street, 2024.

Recommended Documentaries, Podcasts, TV Series and Films

1. Barnwell, Robin, director. China Undercover. London: PBS Frontline / Channel 4, 2020. Television documentary.
2. Bognar, Steven, and Julia Reichert, directors. American Factory. Yellow Springs, OH: Higher Ground Productions, 2019. Documentary.
3. Chai, Jing, director. Under the Dome. Beijing: Chai Jing Studio, 2015. Documentary.
4. Chan, Liang, director. The Great Hack: China's Social Credit System. Hong Kong: Insight Films, 2023. Documentary.
5. Chey, Tim, director. The Firing Squad. Nashville: Epoch Studios, 2024. Feature film.
6. Fowle, Ali, director. China's Digital Dictatorship. Doha: Al Jazeera English, 2023. Television documentary.
7. Hu, Katherine, director. The Final War: The 100 Year Plot to Defeat America. Washington, D.C.: The Epoch Times, 2022. Documentary.
8. Jones, James, director. China's Vanishing Muslims. Boston: PBS Frontline, 2019. Television documentary.
9. Jones, James, director. The Battle for Hong Kong. Boston: PBS Frontline, 2020. Television documentary.
10. Klayman, Alison, director. Ai Weiwei: Never Sorry. New York: IFC Films, 2012. Documentary.
11. Lee, Brandon, director. The Cobra Fang. Los Angeles: Dragon Studios, 2023. Film.
12. Ma, Yan, director. Unrestricted War: Report on Inside the CCP's Biological War against the Free World. 2025. Documentary.
13. Orlowski, Jeff, director. The Social Dilemma. 2020. Documentary.

14. Ross, Warwick, and David Roach, directors. Red Obsession. Sydney: Lion Rock Films, 2013. Documentary.
15. Schachtel, Jordan, director. Hollywood Takeover: China's Control in the Film Industry. Washington, D.C.: The Epoch Times, 2024. Documentary.
16. Stirzaker, Tim, director. China: The New Empire. London: BBC, 2020. Television documentary series.
17. Trey, Torsten, director. State Organs. Washington, D.C.: Doctors Against Forced Organ Harvesting, 2020. Documentary.
18. Yin, Grace, director. Medical Genocide: Hidden Mass Murder in China's Organ Transplant Industry. 2023. Documentary.

Articles of Note

1. Asia Times Analysts. "China's Drone Swarms and Unmanned Warfare Capabilities." *Asia Times,* August 2025. https://asiatimes.com/2025/08/chinas-drone-swarms-just-got-smarter-faster-and-harder-to-kill/.

2. Bebber, Jake R. *Cognitive Competition: Conflict and War from an Ontological Perspective.* Washington, D.C.: Hudson Institute, 2024. https://www.hudson.org/defense-strategy/cognitive-competition-conflict-war-ontological-approach-robert-jake-bebber.

3. Bebber, Jake. "Unasked Question: Will the Chinese Communist Party Endure?" *Hudson Institute,* n.d. https://www.hudson.org/defense-strategy/cognitive-competition-conflict-war-ontological-approach-robert-jake-bebberhe.

4. Brown, Kerry. "AI Governance in China: Ethics, Domestic Policy, and Global Implications." *Technology and Society* (2024).

5. Center for Strategic and International Studies (CSIS). "Interpret: China Analysis Archive." Washington, D.C.: Center for Strategic and International Studies (CSIS), 2023. https://interpret.csis.org/analysis/.

6. Chen, Dora. Economic Coercion and China's Trade Diplomacy. Sydney: Lowy Institute, 2025.

7. China Power Team. "What Does China Really Spend on Its Military?" *China Power* (Center for Strategic and International Studies), originally published December 28, 2015; last updated September 24, 2025. Accessed December 16, 2025. https://chinapower.csis.org/military-spending/.

8. CSIS Experts. "On China: Monitoring CCP's Global Reach." Washington, D.C.: Center for Strategic and International Studies (CSIS), 2025. https://www.csis.org/special-initiatives/on-china.

9. Fleming, C., E. Qualkenbush, and A. Chapa. "The Secret War Against the United States: The Top Threat to National Security and the American Dream, Cyber and Asymmetrical Hybrid Warfare — An Urgent Call to Action." *Cyber Defense Review.* West Point, NY: U.S. Army Cyber Institute, 2017. https://cyberdefensereview.army.mil/Portals/6/Documents/CDR%20Journal%20Articles/The%20Secret%20War%20Against%20the%20United%20States_Fleming_Qualkenbush_Chapa.pdf?ver=2018-07-31-093713-297.

10. Fleming, Casey. "BlackOps Partners' Strategic View on CCP Influence and Unrestricted Warfare." Webinar presented at the Consilium Institute, 2025.

11. Fravel, M. Taylor. "Strategic Disruption Can Thwart Invasion of Taiwan." *U.S. Naval Institute Proceedings,* December 2024. https://www.usni.org/magazines/proceedings/2024/december/strategic-disruption-can-thwart-invasion-taiwan.

12. Fravel, M. Taylor, George J. Gilboy, and Eric Heginbotham. "Estimating China's Defense Spending: How to Get It Wrong (And Right)." *Texas National Security Review* 7, no. 3 (2024). https://tnsr.org/wp-content/uploads/2024/06/TNSR-Journal-Vol-7-Issue-3-FRAVEL-2.pdf.

13. Freedberg, Sydney J. Jr. "Generals Worry U.S. May Lose in Start of Next War: Is Multi-Domain the Answer?" *Breaking Defense,* May 14, 2018.

https://breakingdefense.com/2018/05/generals-worry-us-may-lose-in-start-of-nextwar-is-multi-domain-the-answer/.

14. Freedom House. "China: Freedom in the World 2025 Country Report." Freedom in the World 2025. Washington, D.C.: Freedom House, 2025. https://freedomhouse.org/country/china/freedom-world/2025.

15. Henderson, Robert. "China's Military Modernization and Regional Security." *International Security Journal* (2025).

16. Heritage Foundation. *Winning the New Cold War: A Plan for Countering China.* Washington, D.C.: The Heritage Foundation, 2023. https://www.heritage.org/china/report/winning-the-new-cold-war-plan-countering-china.

17. Hoover Institution Researchers. "Chinese Hedge Fund and CCP Control in Strategic Sectors." Stanford, CA: Hoover Institution, 2024.

18. Johnston, Ian M., and Michael Gallagher. *Political Warfare and Disinformation in the Indo-Pacific.* Canberra: Australian Strategic Policy Institute (ASPI), 2025.

19. Kardon, Isaac, Anthony Saich, and Alice Miller. *The CCP at 101: Essays on Its History and Future.* Newport, RI: U.S. Naval War College and Salve Regina University, 2025. https://carnegieendowment.org/research/2025/06/the-life-of-the-party-past-and-present-constraints-on-the-future-of-the-chinese-communist-party?lang=en.

20. Kardon, Isaac, Yu-Hsuan Chiu, and James Kelly. *The Life of the Party: Past and Present Constraints on the Future of the Chinese*

Communist Party. Washington, D.C.: Carnegie Endowment for International Peace, 2025. https://carnegieendowment.org/research/2025/06/the-life-of-the-party-past-and-present-constraints-on-the-future-of-the-chinese-communist-party?lang=en.

21. Lin, S. (2025). CCP in crisis & post-Xi/CCP era. Consilium Institute.

22. Ludwig, Jake. *China's Hybrid Warfare against the West.* Washington, D.C.: Center for Strategic and International Studies (CSIS), 2024.

23. Mastro, Oriana Skylar. *The Geopolitics of China's Expansion: An Analysis of Influence Operations.* Washington, D.C.: Center for a New American Security (CNAS), 2025.

24. MERICS (Mercator Institute for China Studies). "Whispering Advice, Roaring Praises: The Role of Chinese Think Tanks under Xi Jinping." Berlin: MERICS, 2024. https://merics.org/en/report/whispering-advice-roaring-praises-role-chinese-think-tanks-under-xi-jinping.

25. Nye, Joseph S. Jr. "Soft Power in Chinese Foreign Policy." *Harvard International Review* (2024).

26. Ohlberg, Mareike, and Lucrezia Shao. *China's Global Influence Networks in Europe.* Berlin: Mercator Institute for China Studies (MERICS), 2023. https://merics.org/en/report/chinas-global-influence-networks-europe.

27. Ohlberg, Mareike. "Mareike Ohlberg | German Marshall Fund of the United States." Berlin: German Marshall Fund of the United States (GMF), 2025. https://www.gmfus.org/find-experts/mareike-ohlberg.

28. Pillsbury, Michael. "How China's Long March Strategy Shapes Its Global Ambitions." *Brookings Institution,* 2021.

https://www.brookings.edu/articles/the-long-game-chinas-grand-strategy-to-displace-american-order/.

29. Saich, Anthony. "Serving the People by Controlling Them: How the Party Is Reinserting Itself into Daily Life." Berlin: MERICS (Mercator Institute for China Studies), 2025. https://merics.org/en/report/serving-people-controlling-them-how-party-reinserting-itself-daily-life.

30. Shambaugh, David. "China's Domestic Politics and Global Influence." *Journal of Contemporary China* (2024).

31. Sino Insider Contributors. "Analyzing CCP's Strategy for Modernizing Chinese Enterprises." *SinoInsider,* May 29, 2025. https://sinoinsider.com/2025/05/ccp-strategy-goals-behind-modernizing-chinese-enterprises/.

32. Spalding, Robert. "Defending America from the CCP's Political Warfare." Congressional hearing testimony, U.S. House Committee on Oversight and Accountability, 2024. https://oversight.house.gov/wp-content/uploads/2024/10/CCP-Report-10.24.24.pdf.

33. Stanford Review. "Investigation: Uncovering Chinese Academic Espionage at Stanford." *Stanford Review,* 2025. https://stanfordreview.org/investigation-uncovering-chinese-academic-espionage-at-stanford/.

34. Tatlow, DiDi Kirsten. "Exclusive: 600 U.S. Groups Linked to Chinese Communist Party Influence Effort with Ambition Beyond Election." *Newsweek,* October 26, 2020. https://www.newsweek.com/2020/11/13/exclusive-600-us-groups-linked-chinesecommunist-party-influence-effort-ambition-beyond-1541624.html.

35. The Asia Group. "2024 Legislative Landscape on China." Washington, D.C.: The Asia Group, 2024. https://theasiagroup.com/wp-content/uploads/2024/02/China-and-the-U.S.-Congress-2024-.pdf.

36. The Diplomat Contributors. "Inside China's Military-Civil Fusion Program." *The Diplomat,* April 2024. https://thediplomat.com/2024/04/chinas-military-civil-fusion-space-program/.

37. UNESCO. Clearinghouse on Global Citizenship Education – Critical Thinking Tools. Paris: UNESCO, n.d. https://gcedclearinghouse.org/resources/.

38. Van Oudenaren, John S., and Peter W. Singer. "China's Burgeoning Drone Arsenal Shows Power of Civil-Military Fusion." *Defense One,* June 2025. Accessed December 16, 2025. https://www.defenseone.com/ideas/2025/06/chinas-drone-arsenal-shows-power-civil-military-fusion/406118/.

39. Xue, Lan, and Zeng Yi. "How Some of China's Top AI Thinkers Built Their Own AI Safety Institute." Washington, D.C.: Carnegie Endowment for International Peace, 2025. https://carnegieendowment.org/research/2025/06/how-some-of-chinas-top-ai-thinkers-built-their-own-ai-safety-institute?lang=en.

Works Cited

1. American Society of Anesthesiologists. "Adults 65 Years and Older Not Immune to the Opioid Epidemic, New Study Finds." News Release, October 2025. https://www.asahq.org/about-asa/newsroom/news-releases/2025/10/adults-65-years-and-older-not-immune-to-the-opioid-epidemic.
2. Angela Y. Davis, Gina Dent, Erica R. Meiners, and Beth E. Richie. "Abolition. Feminism. Now." Haymarket Books, 2022. https://amzn.to/44yV9No
3. BBC News. "Trump Directs Nuclear Weapons Testing to Resume for First Time in Over 30 Years." BBC News, December 10, 2025. https://www.bbc.com/news/articles/c4gzq2p0yk4o.
4. Borger, Julian. "China 'More Brazen and Damaging Than Ever,' Says FBI Director." The Guardian, February 1, 2022. https://www.theguardian.com/world/2022/feb/01/china-more-brazen-and-damaging-than-ever-says-fbi-director.
5. Breitbart News. "Breitbart Business Digest: What Trump Knows About China That the Media Won't Tell You." Breitbart News, April 16, 2025. https://www.breitbart.com/economy/2025/04/16/breitbart-business-digest-what-trump-knows-about-china-that-the-media-wont-tell-you/.
6. Brownback, Sam. "China's War on Religion Matters to the U.S." The Washington Times, October 27, 2025. https://www.washingtontimes.com/news/2025/oct/27/chinas-war-religion-matters-us/.
7. Burke, Garance, Dake Kang, and Byron Tau. "U.S. Tech Sales Help Build China's Surveillance State Despite Repeated Warnings." Associated Press, October 29, 2025. https://apnews.com/article/

chinese-surveillance-silicon-valley-trump-administration-congress-21c5f961b1fd22f9a9e563ebe64e5582.

8. Bushwick, Sophie J. "On Children as Cognitive War Casualties." JAMA 332, no. 14 (December 10, 2024): 1359–1360. https://doi.org/10.1001/jama.2024.16803.
9. Business Insider. "FBI Head Calls China 'the Greatest Long-Term Threat' to the U.S. and Alleges Chinese Plots to Steal U.S. Data and Forcibly Repatriate Its Citizens." Business Insider, July 7, 2020. https://www.businessinsider.com/fbi-christopher-wray-china-tries-to-force-citizens-back-home-2020-7.
10. Canadian Broadcasting Corporation. "Nortel Collapse Linked to Chinese Hackers." CBC News, February 25, 2012. https://www.cbc.ca/news/business/nortel-collapse-linked-to-chinese-hackers-1.1260591.
11. Chambers, Whitaker. Witness. New York: Random House, 1952.
12. Council on Foreign Relations. "Religion in China." Council on Foreign Relations, April 2024. https://www.cfr.org/backgrounder/religion-china.
13. Doran, Michael. "Foreign Communists Are Funding and Training Violent Leftist Radicals in U.S." MSN News, August 2, 2024. https://www.msn.com/en-us/news/world/foreign-communists-are-funding-and-training-violent-leftist-radicals-in-us/ar-AA1NEGZy.
14. Federal Bureau of Investigation. FBI Guidance on Counterintelligence and Academic Security. Federal Bureau of Investigation, 2023. https://www.linkedin.com/d5x88uJ.
15. Feinberg, Susan Edelman. "Andrew Cuomo Campaign Aide Worked for Companies Tied to Chinese Communist Party." New York Post, June 14, 2025. https://nypost.com/2025/06/14/us-news/andrew-cuomo-campaign-aide-worked-for-companies-tied-to-ccp/.
16. Fife, Robert. "Did Huawei Bring Down Nortel? Corporate Espionage, Theft, and the Parallel Rise and Fall of Two Telecom Giants." National Post, February 22, 2020. https://nationalpost.com/news/

exclusive-did-huawei-bring-down-nortel-corporate-espionage-theft-and-the-parallel-rise-and-fall-of-two-telecom-giants.

17. Global Times Editorial. “Western Societies Have Become Laboratories of Social Experiment—Gender Confusion, Family Dissolution, and Moral Chaos. China Offers Stability While the West Descends into Ideological Madness.” Global Times, 2023.
18. Greene, Robert. The 33 Strategies of War. New York: Viking Penguin, 2006.https://amzn.to/4aoBLXg
19. Harry Fisher & Stephanie Pierucci. “Safe and Effective, For Profit: A Paramedic’s Story Exposing American Genocide.” Pierucci Publishing, 2024. https://amzn.to/4pc7aRf
20. Haugland, Edward W. The Cognitive War: Why We Are Losing and How We Can Win. Murfreesboro, TN: Cognitive War Press, 2022.
21. Heeb, Gina. “FBI Says It Opens New Espionage Investigation into China Every 10 Hours.” Forbes, April 14, 2021. https://www.forbes.com/sites/ginaheeb/2021/04/14/fbi-says-it-opens-new-espionage-investigation-into-china-every-10-hours/.
22. Jason M. Nagata, Jennifer H. Wong, and Kristen E. Kim, “Social Media Use Trajectories and Cognitive Performance in Adolescents,” JAMA Network Open 7, no. 2 (2024): e2350350, https://doi.org/10.1001/jamanetworkopen.2023.50350.
23. Jin, Canrong. “Remarks at the Beijing Foreign Policy Forum.” Beijing, June 2022. School of International Studies, Renmin University of China. https://en.ruc.edu.cn.
24. Kerry K. Gershaneck, “Strategies for Combating China’s Plan to“Win without Fighting” : Marine Corps University Press, 2020
25. Lindsey, Hal, with C. C. Carlson. The Late Great Planet Earth. Grand Rapids, MI: Zondervan, 1970.
26. Lutz, Jessie G. “The People’s Republic of China and Christianity: A Brief Introduction.” Education About Asia 20, no. 2 (2015). https://www.asianstudies.org/publications/eaa/archives/the-peoples-republic-of-china-and-christianity-a-brief-introduction/.

27. Mozur, Paul, and Chris Buckley. "How China's Secretive Spy Agency Became a Cyber Powerhouse." The New York Times, September 28, 2025. https://www.nytimes.com/2025/09/28/world/asia/how-chinas-secretive-spy-agency-became-a-cyber-powerhouse.html
28. MyWifeQuitHerJob Ecommerce Channel. " YouTube Video, 12:37. Posted December 9, 2025. https://www.youtube.com/watch?v=vHOicQF1TG0.
29. Nagata, Jason M., Jennifer H. Wong, and Kristen E. Kim. "Social Media Use Trajectories and Cognitive Performance in Adolescents." JAMA Network Open 7, no. 2 (2024): e2350350. https://doi.org/10.1001/jamanetworkopen.2023.50350.
30. Newsham, Grant. When China Attacks: A Warning to America. Washington, D.C.: Regnery Publishing, 2023.
31. Noble, Philip Lenczycki, and James Lynch. "Exclusive: Karen Bass Raked In Cash from Chinese Intel-Tied Bankers before Hiring Them." Daily Caller News Foundation, July 25, 2025. https://dailycallernewsfoundation.org/2025/07/25/exclusive-karen-bass-raked-in-cash-from-chinese-intel-tied-bankers-before-hiring-them/.
32. Paine, Thomas. Common Sense. Philadelphia: W. and T. Bradford, 1776.
33. Parents Defending Education. Little Red Classrooms: China's Infiltration of American K–12 Schools. Washington, D.C.: Parents Defending Education, 2022. https://defendinged.org/investigations/little-red-classrooms-china-infiltration-of-american-k-12-schools/.
34. People's Liberation Army Strategic Assessment. "Western Military Recruitment Faces a Crisis Due to Declining Physical Fitness, Mental Health Issues, and Lack of Patriotic Motivation among Youth. This Represents Strategic Vulnerability." 2021.
35. Robin DiAngelo. "White Fragility: Why It's So Hard for White People to Talk About Racism." Beacon Press, 2018. https://amzn.to/48HOIPT

36. Sasa, Makoto, director. Fire Under the Snow. Tokyo: Skyfish Films, 2008. Documentary.
37. Sawchuk, Stephen. "Why GOP Politicians Are Talking About K–12 Chinese Language and Culture Classes." Education Week, October 2023. https://www.edweek.org/policy-politics/why-gop-politicians-are-talking-about-k-12-chinese-language-and-culture-classes/2023/10.
38. Schweizer, Peter. "How China Weaponizes the Capitalist System Against Us." The Hill, July 7, 2023. https://thehill.com/opinion/national-security/4139278-how-china-weaponizes-the-capitalist-system-against-us/.
39. Skousen, W. Cleon. The Naked Communist. Salt Lake City: Ensign Publishing Company, 1958.
40. Sophie J. Bushwick, "On Children as Cognitive War Casualties," JAMA 332, no. 14 (December 10, 2024): 1359–1360, https://doi.org/10.1001/jama.2024.16803.
41. Sun Tzu. The Art of War. Translated by Lionel Giles. New York: Dover Publications, 2002. https://amzn.to/4s263W4
42. Texas A&M University. "FBI Director Christopher Wray on China, Cybersecurity, and Greatest Threats to U.S." Texas A&M Today, April 10, 2023. https://stories.tamu.edu/news/2023/04/10/fbi-director-on-china-cybersecurity-and-greatest-threats-to-us/.
43. The Daily Caller. "U.S. News Section." The Daily Caller, 2025. https://dailycaller.com/section/us/.
44. The Locke Society. "What If China Owned Your Private School?" Locke Society, 2023. https://lockesociety.org/what-if-china-owned-your-private-school/.
45. The Washington Post. "Chinese Espionage at Stanford University." The Washington Post, June 5, 2025. https://www.washingtonpost.com/opinions/2025/06/05/chinese-espionage-stanford-university/.
46. The Washington Times. "Chinese Spies, Harassers Target American Universities, Security Center Warns." The Washington

Times, September 1, 2025. https://www.washingtontimes.com/news/2025/sep/1/chinese-spies-harassers-target-american-universities-security-center/.

47. U.S. Army University Press. “China’s Impact on American Education.” Military Review, September–October 2019. https://www.armyupress.army.mil/Journals/Military-Review/English-Edition-Archives/September-October-2019/China-Impact-on-Ed-extract/.
48. U.S. Department of Defense. PAWS: Gen. Flynn Book V3.1. Washington, D.C.: Department of Defense, September 3, 2024. https://media.defense.gov/2024/Sep/03/2003536122/-1/-1/0/PAWS_GEN%20FLYNN%20BOOK%20V3.1%201.PDF.
49. U.S. Department of State. “Confucius Institutes Advance Chinese Propaganda on Campuses.” U.S. Embassy in Georgia, August 13, 2020. https://ge.usembassy.gov/confucius-institutes-advance-chinese-propaganda-on-campuses/.
50. U.S. House of Representatives, Select Committee on the Strategic Competition Between the United States and the Chinese Communist Party, “Investigation Findings: CCP’s Role in the Fentanyl Crisis,” Washington, D.C., 2024, https://chinaselectcommittee.house.gov/media/investigations/investigation-findings-ccps-role-fentanyl-crisis.
51. U.S. House of Representatives. “Confucius Classrooms.” Committee on Education and the Workforce (Republicans), 2025. https://edworkforce.house.gov/news/documentsingle.aspx?DocumentID=409584.
52. U.S. House of Representatives. Hearing on Confucius Classrooms and Chinese Influence in American Education. Committee on Education and the Workforce (Republicans), 2025. https://edworkforce.house.gov/calendar/eventsingle.aspx?EventID=409522.

53. U.S. House of Representatives. Letter to Futurewei Technologies Regarding CCP Technology Influence and Cyber Operations. Select Committee on the Strategic Competition between the United States and the Chinese Communist Party, September 24, 2025. https://selectcommitteeontheccp.house.gov/sites/evo-subsites/selectcommitteeontheccp.house.gov/files/evo-media-document/2025-09-24-letter-to-futurewei.pdf.
54. U.S. House of Representatives. Select Committee on the Strategic Competition Between the United States and the Chinese Communist Party. "Investigation Findings: CCP's Role in the Fentanyl Crisis." Washington, D.C.: U.S. House of Representatives, 2024. https://chinaselectcommittee.house.gov/media/investigations/investigation-findings-ccps-role-fentanyl-crisis.
55. Van Fleet, Xi. Mao's America: A Survivor's Warning. Function, 2023.
56. Voegelin, Eric. The Political Religions. Translated by Matthias F. Kaiser and Jürgen Gebhardt. Columbia, MO: University of Missouri Press, 1986. Originally published 1938.
57. Wallnau, Lance. God's Chaos Candidate: Donald J. Trump and the American Unraveling. Dallas, TX: Gateway Publishing, 2016.
58. Wang, Huning. "Western Culture Has Become a Culture of Death—Abortion, Euthanasia, Declining Births, and Spiritual Emptiness. Socialist Culture Promotes Life, Family, and Collective Purpose." Party Theory Journal, 2019.
59. Wang, Yi. "Remarks at the Munich Security Conference." Speech, Munich, Germany, February 19, 2022. Ministry of Foreign Affairs of the People's Republic of China. https://www.fmprc.gov.cn/mfa_eng/zxxx_662805/202202/t20220220_10644631.html.
60. Wei Fenghe. "Speech at the 18th Shangri-La Dialogue." Singapore, June 2, 2019. Ministry of National Defense of the People's Republic of China. https://www.mod.gov.cn/en/news/2019-06/02/content_4842814.htm.

61. Wilkerson, David. America's Last Call: On the Brink of a Financial Holocaust. Lindale, TX: World Challenge Publications, 1998.
62. Xi Jinping, Secure a Decisive Victory in Building a Moderately Prosperous Society in All Respects... (Report to the 19th National Congress of the Communist Party of China, October 18, 2017), Foreign Languages Press, 2017.
63. Xi, Jinping. Secure a Decisive Victory in Building a Moderately Prosperous Society in All Respects and Strive for the Great Success of Socialism with Chinese Characteristics for a New Era: Delivered at the 19th National Congress of the Communist Party of China, October 18, 2017. Beijing: Foreign Languages Press, 2017.
64. Xi, Jinping. Xi Jinping: The Governance of China, Volume IV. Beijing: Foreign Languages Press, 2022.
65. Xi, Jinping. Xi Jinping: The Governance of China, Volume IV. Beijing: Foreign Languages Press, 2022.
66. Yan, Xuetong. "American Decline Is Fundamentally a Moral Decline. A Society That Cannot Distinguish Between Right and Wrong, Male and Female, Citizen and Non-Citizen, Cannot Maintain Global Leadership." Foreign Affairs Analysis, 2020.
67. Yu, Miles. "Understanding China's Antisemitism." Hudson Institute, Religious Freedom Initiative, 2024. https://www.hudson.org/religious-freedom/understanding-china-antisemitism-miles-yu.
68. Zhang, Weiwei. The China Wave. 2012. Updated lectures, 2022.
69. Zhao, Lijian. "Regular Press Conference of the Ministry of Foreign Affairs of the People's Republic of China." Beijing, March 24, 2021. Ministry of Foreign Affairs of the People's Republic of China. https://www.fmprc.gov.cn/mfa_eng/xwfw_665399/s2510_665401/202103/t20210324_9172355.html.

Index

C

D

E

I

J

K

L

M

N

V

W

X

Y

Z

Publisher's Note

Share this guide as if your life depends on it.

Order copies as thoughtful gifts for family, friends, neighbors, colleagues, churches, schools, universities, and those across the aisle. Every young adult turning sixteen, and again at age twenty, should receive this guide as a gift.

Pay it forward.

Visit https://theredtsunami.com/products-list where you can invest in discounted copies of this guide for designated beneficiaries at a discount off retail.

Please identify a beneficiary to whom you can send copies of this urgent survival guide. We suggest a local:

University
Library Network
Hospital or Healthcare Facility
Community Center
Gym or Wellness Studio
Church or Synagogue
High School or Middle School

About The Author

Top in-demand keynote, two-time TEDx speaker, frequent media contributor, government agency advisor, and author of *"The Red Tsunami: The Silent Storm Killing Your Freedom."*

T. Casey Fleming's expertise spans counterintelligence, national security strategy, and unrestricted war, placing him as a trusted source for intelligence-based insight in today's global chaotic environment. Fleming is founding Director of IBM's early Cybersecurity Division and former Director of Deloitte Consulting's Global Risk and Strategy group. He later completed several technology turnarounds that were successfully acquired. Fleming also advises senior leadership of the Fortune 500 and Global 1000. Top government agencies he advises include: the U.S. Congress, Pentagon, DOJ, FBI, NCSC, SEC, U.S.-China Economic & Security Review Commission, Select Committee on the CCP, The White House, and others.

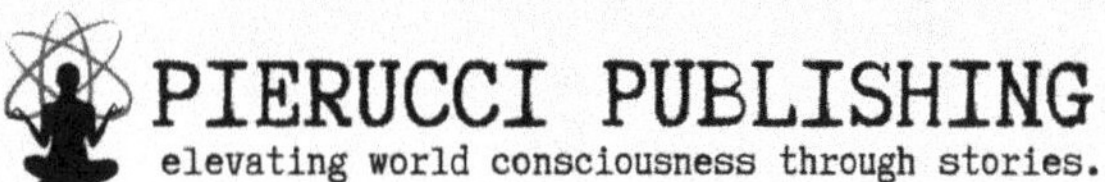

WARNING

Due to the content in this guide, the war against free speech, as well as the ongoing cyberwar being waged by our adversaries, it is highly likely that this title will be censored.

Please purchase a hardcover copy and keep it in a safe place.

We also recommend that you advise everyone you care about to obtain a copy.

Discounted bulk purchases will be accepted at www.theredtsunami.com while supplies last.

PIERUCCIPUBLISHING.COM

THEREDTSUNAMI.COM

www.ingramcontent.com/pod-product-compliance
Lightning Source LLC
Chambersburg PA
CBHW070151310326
41914CB00089B/854
9781962578844